THE Data Warehouse Toolkit

The Data Warehouse Toolkit

PRACTICAL TECHNIQUES FOR BUILDING DIMENSIONAL DATA WAREHOUSES

Ralph Kimball

 JOHN WILEY & SONS, INC.
New York   Chichester   Brisbane   Toronto   Singapore

Publisher: Katherine Schowalter
Editor: Robert Elliott
Managing Editor: Susan Curtin
Text Design & Composition: Pagesetters Incorporated

Designations used by companies to distinguish their products are often claimed as trademarks. In all instances where John Wiley & Sons, Inc. is aware of a claim, the product names appear in initial capital or all capital letters. Readers, however, should contact the appropriate companies for more complete information regarding trademarks and registration.

This text is printed on acid-free paper.

This publication is designed to provide accurate and authoritative information in regard to the subject matter covered. It is sold with the understanding that the publisher is not engaged in rendering legal, accounting, or other professional service. If legal advice or other expert assistance is required, the services of a competent professional person should be sought.

Library of Congress Cataloging-in-Publication Data:
Kimball, Ralph
    The data warehouse toolkit / Ralph Kimball
    p.   cm.
    Includes index.
    ISBN 0-471-15337-0

Printed in the United States of America
10   9   8   7

FOREWORD

Several years ago, when I first heard Ralph Kimball speak on DSS and data warehouse, my thoughts were that here was a body of work that surely deserved to be compiled in a book. In fact, I believe I asked Ralph when he was going to write a book after I introduced myself to him at the conclusion of his talk. But at that time there were only seminars and articles.

Since that day, the world of DSS and data warehouse has grown enormously and has been legitimatized in the marketplace. End users were the first to get the message as to the potency of DSS and data warehouse. Upon discovering data warehouse, end users wondered why the world of database and information systems had taken so long to understand what their real issues and concerns were. Once end users supported the DSS, and data warehouse movement and tangible results began to be apparent, it was a predictably short time until the hardware vendors, software vendors, and consultants all got the message as well.

Today there is an entire subindustry that is devoted to data warehouse and DSS. The world of information systems has matured to the point where much more than OLTP is recognized as valid and useful.

And throughout the growth and maturation of the DSS industry—standing attentively like a midwife—has been Ralph Kimball with his stark cognizance of reality and his revolutionary approaches to DSS systems and data warehouse design. But Ralph does not just have good ideas. Unlike theoreticians, who push their unproved theories into the world as gospel before anyone has successfully made them work, Ralph has always tested his ideas in the unforgiving crucible of reality. Only after an idea has been forged from white-hot elements and beaten into gleaming, mirrorlike razor-sharp steel does it pass the test of readiness for public consumption. It is then that Ralph speaks out.

The other day I got a phone call from Ralph. He said the book was ready. (I must tell you that was exceedingly good news.) I got an early copy of the book. I have read the text in its nascent form and I believe it to be one of the definitive books of our industry. If you take the time to read only one professional book, make it this one. Information systems professionals (and no small number of businesspeople) are going to find that they cannot successfully and profitably conduct their businesses without this book and the concepts found within it. For one thing, the competition will be using it, so just to maintain parity, Ralph's book will be mandatory reading.

There is wisdom contained within these pages. Ralph has done all of us a favor by doing the hard work of sitting down and writing. (And in case you haven't done it, sitting down and writing a book is indeed hard work.) I sincerely hope you will find the wisdom of Ralph Kimball to be as valuable as I know it to be.

W. H. Inmon
Prism Solutions
Aug. 27, 1995

ACKNOWLEDGMENTS

I would like to thank my wife Julie and my children Sara and Brian for their consistent and unflagging support throughout my twenty years of learning and working in the decision support marketplace. Julie has been my business partner and advisor, and many times her instincts about the business world have proved to be uncannily accurate.

It also gives me pleasure to thank David Liddle and Don Massaro for giving me the opportunity to help them build Metaphor Computer Systems in 1982. At Metaphor I was profoundly influenced by Charles Irby, Yogen Dalal, and especially the irrepressible K.C. Branscomb. K.C. later encouraged me to start my own company, which, after a few twists and turns, led to Red Brick Systems in 1989.

Thank you, Chris Erickson, for doing such a capable job with Red Brick. It gives me great pride to see the company in such good hands. Thank you, Rich Merz, for helping me with Star Tracker.

I would like to thank the hardworking reviewers of this book for many helpful suggestions. The book has been tightened up and, I hope, presented much more clearly as a result of their suggestions. The reviewers included Bill Inmon of Prism Solutions, Simon Griffiths of Discovery Solutions in Johannesburg, Roger Eberlin of Hewlett-Packard, Margy Ross of Decision Works in Minneapolis, Leo Gelman of Red Brick Systems, Annemarie Cronje of HiPerformance Systems in Johannesburg, Glen Kalina of Hewlett-Packard, Vic Andrade of Hewlett-Packard, and Cecelia Bellomo of Hewlett-Packard.

Finally, I would like to thank Bob Elliott and his colleagues at Wiley Computer Books for being as excited about this book as I am.

CONTENTS

INTRODUCTION

This is a book for you, the owners, managers, and implementers of a data warehouse. It is a toolkit of design principles and techniques that when applied to specific end user needs and specific legacy databases will allow you to plan and build an enterprise-level data warehouse. This book is much more specific than most books on this subject. We will take you all the way down to the bedrock of how to organize the data for legibility, and how to organize the data to answer important kinds of business questions. Once this bedrock is established, you will be able to build a major, enterprise-level data warehouse that will grow with your organization's changes and with your capacity to source more data for the warehouse itself.

This book is intended for the technical business analyst who works in the Information Systems (IS) department of a large organization and who either manages or is directly responsible for building the enterprise data warehouse. If you are a technical business analyst then you have a multidisciplinary job with skills and responsibilities both for the business information in your organization and for the appropriate use of computer technology to deliver this information to workers throughout your organization. Ideally, you have one or more of the following responsibilities:

- Manager of corporate data warehouse development
- Data Architect for the data warehouse
- End User Applications Development Manager for the data warehouse
- Data Extract Programmer between a legacy system and the data warehouse
- Database Administrator for the data warehouse
- End User Applications Programmer/Business Analyst for the data warehouse

Conversely, if you have one of the following roles, you will find this book very useful as background information in order to understand what the people listed above need in their jobs:

- Vice President, Information Systems
- Chief Information Officer (CIO)
- System Administrator, UNIX Server Operations
- Network System Administrator
- End User Department Manager (the primary client of the data warehouse)

This book is aimed at the serious professional who has some understanding of his or her own IS department and some understanding of how computer technology is deployed in a typical large organization. The book is mildly technical, and definitely assumes that you can provide a one-sentence definition of a number of the major operational computers and applications in your environment, and that you can provide a one-sentence definition of terms like *transaction processing*, *decision support*, *legacy system*, *mainframe*, *network*, *personal computer*, *relational database*, and *graphical user interface*.

This book develops the techniques of data warehouse design *by example*. In Chapters 2 through 11 we systematically develop all of the major examples that are needed to design any data warehouse. These chapters are not discrete handbooks for each industry type. *These chapters are meant to be read by every reader, in order*. For example, the chapter on insurance will be incomprehensible unless you have read the preceding chapters on grocery stores, manufacturing shipments, and big dimensions. In the author's experience, it is often easier to grasp the main elements of a design technique by stepping away temporarily from the all too familiar complexities of one's own applications in order to think about "another business." This approach also has the benefit that you will broaden your business exposure by thinking about other businesses.

In order to bridge the gap between your detailed understanding of your own business and the examples from other businesses, some care has been taken to provide an unusually complete **glossary**. Whenever a word is used in a narrow business context for the first time (like *glossary*), it is set in bold type and expanded in Appendix C. We hope you will find this breadth of industry examples and terminology understandable and interesting.

If you read this book, you will learn how to design the data warehouse for both end user legibility and the capacity to address the key business issues in your organization (Chapters 2 through 11). You will learn how to assess the needs of your organization and how to match these needs to the available data (Chapter 12). You will learn the classic design techniques for data warehousing including handling slowly changing dimensions, heterogeneous products, and accumulating snapshots (Chapters 2 through 6). You will learn the main administrative responsibilities of running a data warehouse (Chapters 12 through 16). You will learn how to plan for the crucial step of adding prestored summaries or aggregates to your data warehouse (Chapter 13). You will learn what the back room and front room administrative and development responsibilities are (Chapters 14 and 15). You will learn in detail what the application and reporting challenges are in transferring data from the database management system (DBMS) onto the user's desktop in usable formats (Chapter 16). And finally, you will learn about some of the new areas of research and development in data warehousing from which you can expect significant new product development from data warehouse vendors in the next two to three years (Chapter 17).

This book comes with a CD-ROM that contains data and software. Please refer to the read.me.TXT on the CD-ROM for any last minute changes and updates. Each database example in this book is provided on the CD-ROM as a Microsoft Access database in exactly the form shown in the book. Although each database is artificially generated, some care has been taken to make the examples realistic and big enough to be interesting. Many of the central fact tables have up to 10,000 records. The enclosed software is a Visual Basic reporting application called Star Tracker™. There is an enclosed license agreement that you will have to read and agree to in order to use Star Tracker and in order to keep me from being liable for your data warehouse. End user and administrative manuals for using Star Tracker are included in this book as Appendices D and E. Star Tracker is all you need to use the CD-ROM and the enclosed databases in Microsoft Windows environments. You can also take Star Tracker and point it at any other appropriately structured dimensional database that presents an ODBC interface to your PC, including Red Brick, Oracle, Sybase, and Informix. Software updates for Star Tracker are continuously available for free on the author's web home page at http://www.rkimball.com.

DIMENSIONAL MODELING

Fundamentally, this is a book about dimensional modeling and how to build a dimensional data warehouse and keep it running. Dimensional modeling is a new name for an old technique for making databases simple and understandable. When a database can be visualized as a "cube" of three, four, or even five or more dimensions, people can imagine slicing and dicing that cube along each of its dimensions. This book shows how to build dimensional models of businesses that are easily understood and navigated by end users. Perhaps just as important, these models can be understood and navigated by software so that user interfaces can be made simple and the performance of the queries can be made acceptable. Finally, this book is about applying the techniques of dimensional modeling specifically to relational databases.

WHY MODEL?

Dimensional modeling gives us the ability to visualize data. The ability to visualize something as abstract as a set of data in a concrete and tangible way is the secret of understandability. Let's try a simple example. Imagine a business where the CEO describes what the company does as follows:

"We sell products in various markets, and we measure our performance over time."

As data warehouse designers, we listen carefully to these words and we add our own special emphasis:

"We sell *Products* in various *Markets*, and we measure our performance over *Time*."

Most people find it easy to think of this business as a **cube** of data, with labels on each of the edges of the cube, such as shown in Figure I.1. Any point inside the cube is at the intersection of the coordinates defined by the edges of the cube. For the business described above, we label the edges of the cube as *Product*, *Market*, and *Time*. Most people can imagine that the points inside

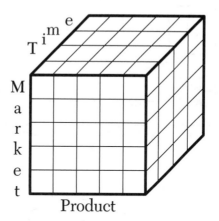

FIGURE I.1

The dimensional model of a business: Each point in the cube contains measurements for a particular combination of Product, Market, and Time.

the cube are where the measurements of the business for that combination of Product, Market, and Time are stored. This is the dimensional model.

If this perspective seems too simple, then good! A model of data that starts by being simple has a chance of remaining simple at the end of the design. A model of a business that starts by being complicated will surely be complicated at the end. In Chapter 1 we will show how this simple "cubist" approach is implemented in a relational database.

Now compare the dimensional model of the business with a **data dependencies model** of the business as shown in Figure I.2. Here we have taken the same business, but instead of talking to the CEO we have dug up the detailed data entity charts of the business that describe how every item on a sales invoice relates to every other item and what all of the many-to-many and many-to-one relationships between data elements are. This picture certainly reveals more detail about the data relationships than the dimensional picture does. But does it contribute to understanding the business? Unfortunately, most people cannot hold a diagram like this in their minds and cannot understand how to navigate it usefully.

There is a false sense of security in the diagram detail. "If it's detailed, it must

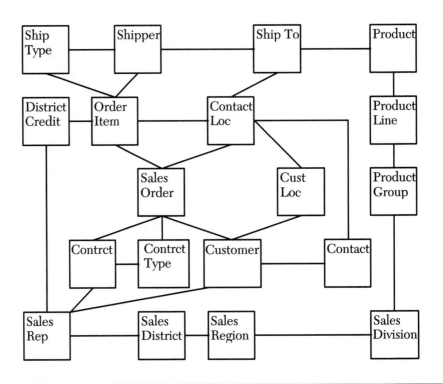

FIGURE I.2

The data dependencies model of a business.

be good." The truth is that relationships among data are best viewed dynamically on a screen, not by static road maps that the users try to hold in their minds. Both the dimensional model of a business and the data dependencies model of a business are capable of storing exactly the same data, and are capable of supporting exactly the same final business analyses. It's just that we are choosing to present the data differently. The dimensional model is a top-down model (notice that we started by talking to the CEO), and the data dependencies model is a bottom-up model.

Even if people don't think about a dimensional model so explicitly, they still have a natural sense of deconstructing our example business by the obvious components of Product, Market, and Time. They will even use the word *dimension* in such a conversation, whether or not they are visualizing a cube of data.

The central attraction of the dimensional model of a business is its simplicity. We will see in this book that simplicity is the fundamental key that allows users to understand databases, and allows software to navigate databases efficiently. In many ways the dimensional design process amounts to "holding the fort" against assaults on simplicity. By consistently returning to the top-down perspective, and by refusing to compromise on the goals of user understandability and software performance, we can maintain a coherent design of a database that serves the needs of a data warehouse.

The distinction between the dimensional model and the data dependencies model is at the very center of data warehouse design. Crudely put, if you as the reader get nothing else from this book than the conviction that your data warehouse must be built from a simple dimensional perspective rather than from a complex data dependencies perspective, then it will have served its purpose. The rest of this book systematically extends and deepens the ideas behind simple dimensional modeling.

SNATCHING DEFEAT FROM THE JAWS OF VICTORY

We are in danger of letting the relational database revolution pass by without making good on the original promise of delivering data that can be accessed every which way. Why did we begin turning our IS shops upside down in the early 1980s, replacing our flat file databases and our hierarchical databases with relational databases, if it wasn't for the dream of much more flexible access? We are now very far along with replacing all of our production database systems with relational technology, yet amazingly, we have lost track of the original "fatal attraction" that led us to relational databases in the first place.

Relational databases were supposed to provide equal access. If your sales database was built around product, market, and time entities, it wasn't supposed to matter whether you asked the product question before you asked the market question, or vice versa. Either approach was just as good. The older hierarchical databases, like IMS, forced you to ask your business questions in a fixed order, beginning with the root of the database. Freed from the shackles of asking business questions in a set way, with relational databases we were supposed to finally unlock our corporate information.

The early writings on relational databases were full of the promise of equal access. Chris Date's wonderful book, *An Introduction to Database Systems,* published in the early 1980s by Addison-Wesley, is filled with simple and compelling examples of equal access. Who can forget his examples of parts and suppliers and cities? Or is it suppliers and cities and parts? It doesn't matter . . . it's relational. It is very revealing to page through his book and see that there are no discussions of transaction processing and E/R diagrams. All of that came later.

Even though we bought the relational dream in the early 1980s, we couldn't use relational databases very effectively because there wasn't any data in them yet. So we began to use relational technology to capture primary business production data like orders, invoices, and business transactions. Almost immediately we ran into a serious problem: The early relational systems were pitifully slow for transaction processing. A typical transaction rate was about one per second. No large business could possibly run at one transaction per second. For example, today's **SABRE** system, the reservation system for American Airlines, routinely processes 4,000 transactions per second during heavy loads, and is capable of peak bursts in excess of 13,000 transactions per second.

The transaction processing performance crisis we had in the 1980s was both good news and bad news. It was good because it caused the database vendors to seriously improve and strengthen the relational database software so that transactions could be performed fast and reliably. This was a necessary precursor to making relational databases "production capable." Today it is possible to buy off the shelf a UNIX processor and a relational database that are capable of a sustained transaction rate of 1,000 per second. This is a monstrous improvement from the early 1980's that would have seemed impossible at that time. It used to be said that "the price we have to pay for the wonderful flexibility of relational databases is that they will always be slow." Fortunately, this view was wrong.

The good news of the big transaction processing performance gain, however, is tempered with the bad news that we have become fixated by transaction processing. We have become so steeped in the terminology and discipline of online transaction processing (OLTP), that we have a whole generation of IS professionals who think that the point of relational databases is to get data in rather than get data out. Actually, the opposite is true. Transaction processing is an awkward graft onto relational databases, and to do transaction processing well in this environment we have to ignore or even misuse many of the core facilities in relational databases. In Chapter 1, we will systematically explore the differences between OLTP and dimensional data warehousing, and learn how to think separately about getting the data in and getting the data out. We need to return to our roots.

The Goals of a Data Warehouse

The data warehouse is the place where people can access their data. The fundamental goals of a data warehouse can be developed by walking around the halls of any large organization and listening to management talk. The recurring themes heard from management sound like this:

"We have mountains of data in this company but we can't get access to it."
"Nothing drives senior management crazier than to have two people present the same business result but with different numbers."
"We want to slice and dice the data every which way."
"Just show me what is important."
"Everyone knows that some of the data isn't very good."

These concerns are so universal that they drive the bedrock requirements for the data warehouse. Let us turn these problems into opportunities and state them as requirements:

1. The data warehouse provides *access* to corporate or organizational data.

Access means several things. The managers and analysts of an organization must be able to connect to the data warehouse from their personal computers. This connection must be immediate, on demand, and with high performance. It is not acceptable if the access is through another person, or if the access is unreliable or slow. High-performance access means the tiniest queries run in less than one second. Access also means the tools available to the managers and analysts are very easy to use. Chapter 16 will discuss this issue in much more detail, but "easy to use" means a useful report can be run with one button click after opening the tool, and the report can be changed and rerun with two button clicks.

2. The data in a data warehouse is *consistent*.

Consistency means that when two people request the sales for the Southeast region for January they get the same number, even if they request the data at different times. Consistency also means that when these people ask the data warehouse what the definition of the "sales" data element is, they get a useful answer that lets them know what they are fetching from the database. Consistency also means that if yesterday's data has not been completely loaded, the analyst is warned that the data load is not complete and to not expect the final data load until tomorrow.

3. The data in a data warehouse can be separated and combined by means of every possible measure in the business (the classic **slice and dice** requirement.)

The slicing and dicing requirement speaks directly to the dimensional approach. We will see in Chapter 1 that a more operational definition of slicing and dicing is *row headers and constraints*. Row headers and constraints will turn out to be the fundamental building blocks of every data warehouse application and they will come directly from the dimensions in our data model.

4. The data warehouse is not just data, but also a set of tools to *query, analyze, and present* information.

The "back room" components, namely the central data warehouse hardware, the relational database software, and the data itself, are only about 60 percent of what is needed for a successful data warehouse. The remaining 40 percent is the set of front end tools that query, analyze, and present the data. The "show me what is important" requirement needs all of these components. These points are developed in detail in Chapter 16.

5. The data warehouse is the place where we *publish used data*.

The responsibility to publish is at the very core of the data warehouse. Data is not simply accumulated at a central point and let loose. Rather, data is carefully assembled from a variety of information sources around the organization, cleaned up, quality assured, and then released only if it is fit for use. If the data is unreliable or incomplete, the responsible data quality manager does not allow it to be published to the user community. The data quality manager plays much the same role as a magazine editor or a book publisher. He or she is responsible for the content and quality of the publication and is identified with the deliverable.

6. The quality of the data in the data warehouse is a *driver of business reengineering*.

   The best data in any company is the record of how much money someone else owes the company. Data quality goes downhill after that. Frequently a data element would be very interesting if it were of high quality, but it either isn't collected at all or it is optional. *Optional* is the kiss of death for data.

   The data warehouse cannot fix poor quality data. If an automobile insurer does not require the "cause of accident" data to be collected by the field adjusters, then there is nothing the data warehouse can do when this data arrives at the front door. The only way to fix poor-quality data is for both affected data entry personnel and management to return to the source of the data with better systems, better management, and better visibility of the value of good data. Interestingly, often a good way to justify such a business reengineering project is to go ahead and publish the incomplete data, and then let natural pressure arise within the organization when people see how valuable the data would be if only it was of better quality. In this way, the data warehouse can play a key role in the business reengineering efforts in an organization.

THE GOALS OF THIS BOOK

This book is a practical guide to owning and building a data warehouse. A major goal of the book is to teach the processes of (1) assembling a proper set of requirements for the data warehouse in your organization; (2) doing the logical design of the warehouse data structures; (3) planning the data extract and transformation steps down to the individual data element; (4) building a front end tool suite; and (5) managing the completed data warehouse. This book is written from years of hands-on experience designing large data warehouses and launching IS organizations in the right direction. Every one of the examples developed in Chapters 2 through 11 is an operational data warehouse in a large corporation designed by the author. All of these warehouses are in the 10 gigabyte to 1 terabyte range and the largest queryable tables range up to 1 billion records.

A second goal of this book is to communicate a set of standard techniques for data warehouse design. The OLTP side of the house has developed a powerful and precise vocabulary for OLTP design. Serious OLTP designers know that transaction systems that pass the ACID test possess the qualities of *a*tomicity, *c*onsistency, *i*solation, and *d*urability. We on the data warehouse side of the house need an equally powerful vocabulary and set of design principles. Fortunately, data warehouse design is replete with a number of powerful, consistent principles. This book names and categorizes these principles and ties each of them to characteristic businesses. In this way they are easier to remember. Appendix A of this book summarizes this data warehouse design vocabulary.

A third goal of this book is to help the reader understand where the data warehouse part of the market is going and to help the reader become an effective voice for necessary change. Data warehousing is not very mature. Although the vendors are doing their best to define what is important in this market, most of the advances have been far too technology driven and not enough user driven. It is amazing that we are being sold on the benefits of scanning billion-row tables from start to finish on parallel processors but most of the vendors don't have a STOP command for runaway queries. It is amazing that we have logically sophisticated structured query language (**SQL**) commands like EXISTS and ANY being implemented faithfully by all the DBMS vendors, but we don't have commands or tools that can effectively compare one number with another. If you don't believe this, stay tuned. A final goal of this book is to show how well (and how poorly) SQL and relational databases match with simple business analysis.

1

Two Different Worlds

Before we can develop the perspectives and techniques necessary for designing a data warehouse, we have to face an important issue. On-line transaction processing (**OLTP**) is profoundly different from dimensional data warehousing (**DDW**). The users are different, the data content is different, the data structures are different, the hardware is different, the software is different, the administration is different, the management of the systems is different, and the daily rhythms are different. In spite of all these differences, we continue to use OLTP thinking and OLTP tools to design our data warehouse databases. In this chapter we will catalog these differences very carefully, with the goal of leaving you absolutely convinced that the design techniques and design instincts appropriate for transaction processing are inappropriate and even destructive for information warehousing. We will then fill the void with a set of different techniques, called *dimensional modeling*, that are today being used by scores of successful data warehouse shops. Throughout this book, when we use the term **data warehouse**, we specifically mean a **dimensional data warehouse**. We will define this term carefully in this chapter.

CONSISTENCY

Both OLTP and data warehouse systems are greatly concerned with data consistency. However, OLTP consistency is microscopic. The point of transaction processing is to process a very large number of tiny, atomic transactions without losing any of them. The essence of a transaction is that both the sender and the receiver agree at all times as to whether the transaction has taken place. In this way, each transaction is accounted for. This view is excessively microscopic. There is nothing in this view of database consistency that asks whether Chicago was on-line while all the transactions were performed. All that we care about in OLTP consistency is whether we agree that all the transactions presented to the system have been accounted for.

In a data warehouse, consistency is measured globally. In general we don't care about an individual transaction, but we care enormously that the current load of new data is a full and consistent set of data. In this case we demand to know whether Chicago was on-line. If Chicago wasn't on-line, then the data fails the consistency test and cannot be published. Instead of a microscopic perspective, we have a quality assurance perspective. Instead of a technical calculation of data consistency, we have a manager's judgment of data consistency.

This requirement for consistency creates a new IS job role: the data quality assurance manager. Several years ago, the author was visiting the IS shop of a leading soft drink manufacturer. This company had been one of the early pioneers in information warehousing and knew how to manage a data warehouse environment. The morning of the visit, while the author was sitting in the office of a marketing manager, a loud bell went off in the hallway. Thinking it was a fire alarm, we were prepared to leave the building. But looking down the hallway, we saw people *entering* their offices. At this point, the marketing manager said, "Oh, don't worry, that was just the data bell. We ring that every morning when the data passes quality assurance, and people know they can then go to their terminals to look at yesterday's shipments and share."

Hopefully this is a glimpse of the future. The data quality assurance manager at this soft drink manufacturer not only subjected the data to a quality assurance pass every morning, but he actively took responsibility for publishing the data. Today perhaps we would use electronic mail to send a more comprehensive message, but we can't have a clearer vision of data consistency.

WHAT IS A TRANSACTION?

A serious OLTP system processes thousands or even millions of transactions per day. Each transaction contains one small piece of data. A serious data warehouse often will process only one transaction per day. But this transaction contains thousands or even millions of records. Rather than calling it a transaction, we call it the **production data load**. What we care about is the consistent state of the system we started with before the production data load, and the consistent state of the system we ended up with after a successful production data load. If we are forced to stop a production data load before it is completed, we aren't likely to roll back the data load record by record; rather we will overwrite the entire system with a **snapshot** of the system taken before the load began. Chapter 14 describes the production data load process in great detail, and tells why the most practical frequency of this production data load is once per day, usually in the early hours of the morning.

USERS AND MANAGERS

The users of an OLTP system turn the wheels of the organization. They take the orders, open and close the cash registers, sign up new customers, log complaints, make reservations, enter new data, and correct old data. Users of an OLTP system almost always deal with one account at a time. The retrievals they do from the database are almost always lookups of single records elsewhere in the database that enable them to continue their primary data entry function. OLTP users perform the same tasks many, many times. Performance is the absolute king of an OLTP system. No "optional" activity is allowed to slow down the OLTP system. Data-warehouse-like activities such as launching a query to summarize 100,000 records simply are not allowed on an OLTP system. The majority of reports done on OLTP systems are the preparation of listings of entire tables. The familiar three-inch stack of computer paper sitting on the manager's desk is actually not a report; it's a database. See Figure 1.1.

The manager of an OLTP system is driven by performance and reliability concerns. This manager rightly feels that he or she is overseeing the essential machinery of the company. If the OLTP system stops, then the company stops. If you are lucky, this manager will run a batch job for you in the middle of the

FIGURE 1.1

A data warehouse implemented on paper.

night to offload data for analysis, but don't ask for significant CPU or disk resources on this person's machine, especially during daylight hours.

The users of a data warehouse, on the other hand, are *watching* the wheels of the organization. They count the new orders, ask when the cash registers are opening and closing, ask why the new customer signed up, ask what those customers complained about, ask how many more reservations there are this year than last year, look to see what data is new, and ask that wrong data be corrected. Users of a data warehouse almost never deal with one account at a time. Rather, they ask for a page or two of summaries of accounts, usually requiring hundreds or thousands of records to be searched and compressed into a small **answer set**. Users of a data warehouse continuously change the kinds of questions they ask of a database. Although the templates of their requests may be similar from query to query, their impact on the database will vary wildly, from fetching a hundred records into their small answer set to fetching a million records into their small answer set.

Performance on a data warehouse is important, just as it is on an OLTP system, but it has a different character. Small single-table queries, called **browses**, need to be instantaneous. Large multitable queries, called **join queries**, are expected to run for seconds or minutes. The occasional query that runs for an hour or more calls for a trip to the data warehouse database administrator (**DBA**), who is expected to make the query run much faster. In Chapters 13 and 14 we will see that the modern data warehouse DBA has some powerful tools that in most cases allow the DBA to significantly improve the user's query once the query is understood.

Reporting is the primary activity in a data warehouse. In some ways it is the only activity. However, since this reporting is usually done on-line, the days of the three-inch stack of paper are over. Information users recognize a database for what it is and they leave it on the computer. Data warehouse users consume information in human-sized chunks of one or two pages at a time. The ideal data warehouse report is a single-page top-line summary shown on the screen with a few of the numbers blinking in boldface. The user is expected to touch one or more of the blinking bold numbers and ask Why. The page is then replaced with another page that contains the numbers that make up the blinking bold items. Perhaps some new numbers are blinking on this second page. See Figure 1.2.

ONE MACHINE OR TWO

Because of the significant and highly variable resource demands of the data warehouse, it is usually implemented on a machine separate from the OLTP system. The resource argument is usually sufficient reason to require a second machine, but there are two other very significant motivations. First, the data warehouse often is a centralized resource where data is integrated from multiple remote OLTP systems. In this case by definition the data warehouse machine is separate. Second, as we will see later in this chapter, the basic data structures of a data warehouse are completely different from the OLTP system. Since the data must be copied and restructured for the data warehouse, there is little motivation to keep it on the original OLTP machine.

Until about 1993, the DBMS vendors were advertising that customers

Product	Region	Sales This Month	Growth in Sales vs. Last Month	Sales as % of Category	Change in Sales as % of Category vs. Last Month	Change in Sales as % of Category YTD vs. Last Year YTD
Framis	Central	110	12%	31%	3%	7%
Framis	Eastern	179	(3%)	28%	(1%)	3%
Framis	Western	55	5%	44%	1%	5%
Total Framis		344	6%	33%	1%	5%
Widget	Central	66	2%	18%	2%	10%
Widget	Eastern	102	4%	12%	5%	13%
Widget	Western	39	(9%)	9%	(1%)	8%
Total Widget		207	1%	13%	4%	11%
Grand Total		551	4%	20%	2%	8%

FIGURE 1.2

The ideal data warehouse report.

needed only a single system to perform OLTP and **decision support**. Those claims have disappeared from the pages of the trade journals. Hopefully the reason is that the vendors now realize that OLTP and information warehousing are fundamentally different, and require two very differently configured systems. However, as one wag has suggested, the change in marketing may be due more to the realization that if they stopped making the claim for a single system, they were more likely to sell *two* licenses.

THE TIME DIMENSION

OLTP systems and data warehouses treat time very differently. The best OLTP system is an instantaneous snapshot of an organization's affairs, constantly updated as transactions pour in. Key measures of the business should be changing from minute to minute and from second to second. Status is constantly being changed and the relationships among business entities are being altered. For instance, as orders are being filled, the order backlog changes. The parts-supplier relationships may be changing as you watch the database. We call this kind of OLTP database a **twinkling database**.

Although there are a few applications and a few individuals who wish to perform data-warehouse-like queries on a live twinkling database, most applications and individuals do not want this capability. Many users are disturbed at the thought that the database may change while they are performing a query, or in between queries. This twinkling nature of OLTP databases is the first kind of **temporal inconsistency** that we avoid in data warehouses.

The second kind of temporal inconsistency in an OLTP database is the lack of explicit support for correctly representing prior history. In a data warehouse we are always asking the questions "What was my business doing last month? or last quarter? or last year?" For these kinds of questions we want to know what the order backlog and the parts-supplier relationships were at prior points in time. If we have filled the orders, or if we have overwritten the old parts-supplier relationships, we may not be able to recover an accurate picture of these prior points in time. Although it is possible to keep history in an OLTP system, it is a major burden on that system to correctly depict *old* history. A deeper and more subtle difficulty is that if all we have is a long series of transactions that incrementally alter history, it is close to impossible to quickly reconstruct the snapshot of a business at a specified point in time.

We address all of these problems in the data warehouse by making the warehouse an explicit time series. We move snapshots of the OLTP systems over to the data warehouse as a series of data layers, much like geologic layers. Every data warehouse is a times series. Like geologists we then dig down through the layers to understand what our business was like at previous points in time. In Chapter 6 we will discuss how to handle **slowly changing dimensions**, which is the primary data warehouse technique for correctly representing the past. By bringing **static snapshots** to the warehouse only on a regularly scheduled basis, we solve both of the time representation problems we had on the OLTP system. First, the data warehouse is quiet during the day when the users are querying. Twinkling is not allowed. Second, by carefully storing the information in each snapshot in the warehouse, we can represent all prior points in time correctly. Now we can ask what the difference in **average order backlog** is between last year and this year, and we can ask how many suppliers supplied a part at a previous point in time.

The model of taking regular snapshots of the OLTP system and then transferring these snapshots to the data warehouse is an extremely important way to think about data warehouses. The snapshot is called the **production data extract**, and we **migrate** this extract to the data warehouse system at the same time every day, or every week, or every month as part of the production data load. This process gives rise to the two very different phases that all data warehouses share: loading and querying. As we will see in Chapter 14, many of the required system characteristics differ between these phases.

THE ENTITY RELATION DATA MODEL

The final and most important difference between OLTP systems and data warehouses is the organization of the data in the systems, or more simply, the data model. To understand why the data is organized so differently, we need to return to the issue of transaction performance. Much of the miraculous gain in transaction performance is due to a technique called *entity relation modeling*. Entity relation modeling seeks to drive all the redundancy out of the data. If there is no redundancy in the data, then a transaction that changes any data (or adds or deletes data) only needs to touch the database in one place. This is the secret behind the phenomenal improvement in transaction processing speed since the early 1980s.

Entity relation modeling works by dividing the data into many discrete entities, each of which becomes a table in the OLTP database. For instance, a database of sales orders, which might have started off with each order being a record, turns into an astonishingly complex diagram under the entity relation model, often consisting of hundreds of tables. A simple version of such an entity relation data layout was shown in Figure I.2. Real data layouts are significantly more complex than this illustration. Often the layout diagram covers the entire wall of the designer's office. The closest analogy is to a map of Los Angeles. The entities are the cities in the Los Angeles basin, and the relations (the joins between the tables) are the freeways. Almost every table connects to every other table. No one knows how many joins (freeways) there are between all possible tables: no one has bothered to count. And more subtly, no one has bothered to see that all these freeways are paved (quality assured).

There are a number of important observations to make about this OLTP-oriented entity relation diagram. First, in a strange sort of way, this diagram is very symmetric. All the tables look the same. There is no way to tell which table is the most important or the largest. There is no way to tell which tables contain numerical measurements of the business and which tables hold static or near-static descriptors of objects. This symmetry means that one can scramble the diagram pretty much arbitrarily and it looks about the same. Diagrams like this are very hard for people (end users or designers) to visualize and keep in their heads.

Second, if two tables in the diagram are needed in a given query, there are a huge number of possible connection paths between those two tables. For example, in Figure I.2, how many pathways are there between Contract and Product? Even in this simplified diagram, there are a very large number. Many people react to this by saying "But this is a relational database. Surely the different pathways will give the same answer." This is one of those relational-database myths. Unfortunately, it does matter which pathway is chosen. To see this, recall that in a relational database we must build a "data bridge" between tables in order to link data elements in remote tables. These data bridges are almost always implemented as inner joins bridging from data element to data element. Thus, in general, each pathway gives a different answer.

The value of an entity relation diagram is to use the tables individually and in pairs. No human being and no DBMS really takes seriously large swaths of these tables at any one time. Every DBA and application designer knows that a query involving several large tables of a million rows or more simply will not return results. These professionals would consider it laughable to let end users construct their own queries in such a database. For queries that span many records or many tables, entity relation diagrams are too complex for users to understand and too complex for software to navigate. In fact, this is such an important result that we need to state it unequivocally:

> Entity relation data models are a disaster for querying because they cannot be understood by users and they cannot be navigated usefully by DBMS software. Entity relation models cannot be used as the basis for enterprise data warehouses.

There is a syndrome in large IT shops that is altogether too common. It is a kind of sickness that comes from overly complex schemas. The symptoms are: (1) a $3 million hardware and software system that is doing 50 queries per day; (2) an IT department that is forced to be a kind of priesthood writing the queries in hand-coded SQL; (3) queries that are simple in business terms, requiring one to two pages of single-spaced SQL with ten to fifteen separate constraints; (4) a marketing department that is very unhappy because they can't use the system directly and they can't ask whether they are profitable in Schenectady; and (5) a restless CIO who is determined to make some changes if things don't improve drastically. In most cases, this set of symptoms is due to one problem: overly complex schemas.

Far from this being the inevitable fate of the company, in this kind of environment it is possible, by restructuring the data and configuring the system correctly, to have an end user community of 100 users performing their own queries using reusable templates, and to have the DBMS routinely process 3,000 to 8,000 queries a day for these 100 users. Eighty percent of these queries will be single-table browses, and 20 percent will be multitable joins. (See Chapter 15 for a discussion of these query types.) The author has observed this level of performance in many IS shops that have built their systems according to the proper design principles of information warehousing. The underlying secret is the simplicity of the data structures.

THE DIMENSIONAL MODEL

IS shops, end users, and even syndicated data suppliers like **A.C. Nielsen, IRI, IMS,** and **Walsh America** have in case after case gravitated to a simple "data cube" structure that matches end users' needs for simplicity. This structure is a **dimensional model.** A typical dimensional model is shown in Figure 1.3.

Another name for the dimensional model is the **star join schema.** This is a name that database designers have long used to describe dimensional models because the diagram looks like a star, with one large central table and a set of smaller attendant tables displayed in a radial pattern around the central table.

Unlike the entity relation model, the dimensional model is very asymmetric. There is one large dominant table in the center of the schema. It is the only table in the schema with multiple joins connecting it to other tables. The other tables all have only a single join attaching them to the central table. We will

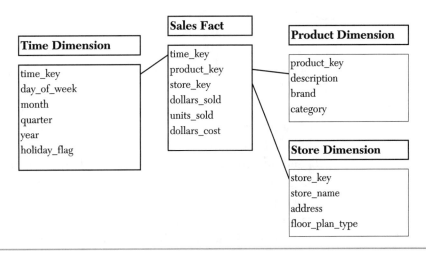

FIGURE 1.3

A typical dimensional model.

call the central table the **fact table** and the other tables the **dimension tables.**

In Figure 1.3 we are modeling a simple business that sells products in a number of markets and measures its performance over time. In the Introduction, we heard the description of this business from the CEO of the company. As the database designers, we have decided that the fact table in Figure 1.3 contains *daily item totals* of all the products sold. This is called the **grain** of the fact table. In other words, each record in the fact table represents the total sales of a specific product in a market on a day. Any other combination of product, market, or day generates a different record in the fact table.

If we have a large business, we will surely have a very large number of records in the fact table. The fact table of a typical grocery store retailer, for example, with 500 stores, each carrying 50,000 products on the shelves and measuring daily item movement for two years, could approach one billion rows. However, by using modern high-performance server hardware and any of several industrial-strength relational database software systems we can store and query such a large fact table with good performance. This is what this book is all about.

THE FACT TABLE

The fact table is where the numerical measurements of the business are stored. Each of these measurements is taken at the intersection of all the dimensions. In Figure 1.3 the numerical measurements are the number of dollars sold, the number of units sold, and the **extended cost**. The cost is how much the product costs us, as retailers, to put it on the shelf. Throughout this book we will use "dollars" for money to make the examples tangible. (Please bear with the author and substitute your own currency if it doesn't happen to be dollars!) We can imagine standing out in the marketplace watching products being sold. We write down the number of dollars, the number of units, and the extended cost each day, in each market, and for each product. The best and most useful facts are numeric, **continuously valued,** and **additive.** This is the holy grail of dimensional database design. The reason for numeric, continuously valued, additive facts is that in virtually every query made against this fact table we are going to ask for hundreds, thousands, or even millions of records to be used by the DBMS to construct the answer set. This large number of records will be compressed into a few dozen rows of the user's answer set. Overwhelmingly, the only useful way to compress these records into the answer set is to add them. Thus if the measurements are numbers and if they are additive, we can easily build the answer set.

We suggest the facts be continuously valued mainly as a guide for the database designer to help sort out what is a fact and what is a dimensional attribute. The number of dollars fact is continuously valued in this case because it can take on virtually any value within a broad range of values. As observers, we have to stand out in the marketplace and wait for the measurement before we have any idea what the value will be. In this sense, the number of dollars is continuously valued. Notice that in this database, if there is no product activity on a given day, in a market, we leave the record out of the database. It is very important that we do not try to fill the fact table with zeros representing "nothing happening." For this reason, fact tables are always **sparse**. Most fact tables are extremely sparse.

It may seem obvious that the dollars, units, and cost facts in this example are additive. All that means is that it makes sense to add the dollars and other measurements across every combination of time, product, market, and promotion. No matter what slice of the database is chosen by the user, it makes sense to add up the dollars and other measurements to a total, and the total is valid.

Additivity, however, is a precious gift that we must work to preserve. We will see later in this book that there are facts that are **semiadditive**, and facts that are **nonadditive**. Semiadditive facts can be added along only some of the dimensions, and nonadditive facts simply can't be added at all. For nonadditive facts, we are forced to use counts if we wish to summarize the records, or we are reduced to printing out the fact records one at a time. This is a dull exercise in a fact table with a billion rows.

THE DIMENSION TABLES

The dimension tables are where the textual descriptions of the **dimensions** of the business are stored. Each of the textual descriptions helps to describe a member of the respective dimension. For example, each record in the product dimension represents a specific product. In a well-designed database, the product dimension table has many **attributes** (fields). The best attributes are **textual**, **discrete**, and used as the source of **constraints** and **row headers** in the user's answer set. Since dimension attributes play the role of describing one of the items in a dimension, they are most useful if they are text. Typical attributes for a product would include a short description (10 to 15 characters), a long description (30 to 60 characters), the brand name, the category name, the packaging type, and the size. Although the size is probably numeric, it still is a good dimension attribute because it behaves more like a textual description than like a numeric measurement. Product sizes are discrete and constant descriptors of a specific product. We don't stand out in the marketplace and measure the standard size of a product.

Sometimes when we are designing a database, it is unclear whether a numeric data field extracted from a production data source is a fact or is an attribute. Often we can make the decision by asking whether the numeric data field is a measurement that varies continuously every time we sample it (making it a fact), or whether it is a discretely valued description of something that is more or less constant (making it a dimensional attribute). A common example is a standard cost for a product that seems like a constant attribute of the product but may be changed so often that we eventually decide it is more like a measured fact. Occasionally, we still can't be sure of the classification. In such cases, it may be possible to model the data field either way, as a matter of designer's prerogative.

A key role for dimension table attributes is to serve as the source of constraints in a query or to serve as row headers in the user's answer set. A typical answer set returned from a query looks like this:

BRAND	DOLLAR SALES	UNIT SALES
Axon	780	263
Framis	1044	509
Widget	213	444
Zapper	95	39

This query seeks to find all the product brands that were sold in the first quarter of 1995 and present the total dollar sales as well as the number of units. In this database, a brand is a collection of individual products. To construct this report, the user dragged the attribute Brand from the product dimension and placed it as the row header. The user then dragged Dollar Sales and Units Sold from the fact table and placed them to the right of the Brand row header. Finally, the user specified the constraint "1 Q 1995" on the Quarter attribute in the Time dimension table. At this point, the user's query is well specified, and the query tool can generate the required SQL and fetch the answer set shown above. We have used dimension attributes for the primary functions both of providing row headers and of providing constraints.

THE STANDARD TEMPLATE QUERY

Although programming in SQL is not a strong prerequisite for designing data warehouses, the SQL generated in this example is so characteristic of the use of data warehouses that it is helpful to examine its components. The SQL for this example looks like:

```
select p.brand, sum(f.dollars), sum(f.units)    <== select list
from salesfact f, product p, time t             <== from clause with aliases f,
                                                     p, and t
where f.productkey = p.productkey               <== join constraint
    and f.timekey = t.timekey                   <== join constraint
    and t.quarter = '1 Q 1995'                  <== application constraint
group by p.brand                                <== group by clause
order by p.brand                                <== order by clause
```

The components of the SQL statement are labeled in italics here for discussion purposes. The italics are not part of the SQL itself and are not sent down to the DBMS. This SQL can be thought of as the standard template for all data warehouse queries involving the fact table. The select list defines the columns that will appear in the user's answer set. Virtually every query that generates a report, like this one, contains row headers and **aggregated facts** in the select list. The row headers are the things that are not summed, in this case Brand. Normally we arrange the row headers to be the first items in the select list. Hence the name *row header*. The aggregated facts are the things that are summed, in this case Dollars and Units. Normally we arrange the aggregated facts to follow the row headers in the select list. Since we have three items in our select list, we will have three columns in our answer set.

After the select list we always have the **from clause** in the SQL. The from clause is a listing of the tables that are required in the query. Our example query requires tables named *salesfact*, *product*, and *time*. Usually when we write SQL we follow the names in the from clause with shortened names called **aliases** that make the SQL easier to write. The alias for the salesfact table is "f", the alias for the product table is "p", and the alias for the time table is "t". Whenever we use an alias in other parts of the SQL, it is the same as if we had typed the full table name.

The next two lines of the SQL are the join constraints. These lines serve to bookkeep the relationships between the fact table and the dimension tables. The first join constraint joins the salesfact table to the product table by linking the productkey field in both tables. The productkey field is the **primary key** in the product table. This means that there is a unique productkey for each record in the product table. The productkey appears in the salesfact table as many times as there are sales records. It is possible a given productkey does not appear in the salesfact table (if there were no sales of that product), or the productkey could appear millions of times. The productkey in the salesfact table is called a **foreign key**, which means that it is drawn from the product table, by definition. In every case, a productkey in the fact table must have its counterpart in the product table. This requirement is called **referential integrity** and is an extremely important requirement in data warehouses.

The fact table itself has a primary key, which is the combination of the four foreign keys. This is called a **composite key**, or sometimes a **concatenated key**. Every fact table in a dimensional database has a composite key, and conversely, every table that has a composite key is a fact table. Another way to say this is that in a data warehouse every table that expresses a **many-to-many relationship** must be a fact table. All other tables are dimension tables.

The joins in a dimensional database schema in a data warehouse play a far more important role than they do in an entity relation database schema. Typically there are only a few joins in a dimensional database. Furthermore, each of the joins expresses a fundamental relationship between items in the underlying business. The product join that we have been discussing represents the relationship between the master product list and the company's sales. The market join represents the relationship between the company's markets (or perhaps customers) and the company's sales. In virtually all such joins in a dimensional database, the keys that implement these joins are already the subject of much administration and attention by MIS. This contrasts with most of the joins in an entity relation database designed for OLTP, where the joins are usually artificially generated numeric keys that have little administrative significance elsewhere in the company. There are probably people whose job functions are to administer the two ends of the product join in the dimensional database. One person maintains the master product file and oversees the generation of new product keys and the other person makes sure that every sales record contains valid product keys. For these reasons, we call the joins in a data warehouse **MIS joins**.

After the join constraints we find an **application constraint** in our example SQL. This constraint serves to restrict the time dimension to only those records representing the first quarter of 1995. If the time dimension table in our example contains one record for each day, then this constraint would limit the valid time keys to 90 values (31 for January, 28 for February, and 31 for March).

Virtually all application constraints apply to individual dimension tables. The user creates an application constraint by *browsing* the dimension, looking at possible values and looking at the relationships among the various attributes. Browsing is described in detail in Chapters 15 and 16. It rarely makes sense and it rarely is possible to apply an application constraint simultaneously across two dimensions, thereby directly linking the two dimensions. In a dimensional database design, the dimensions are linked only through the fact table. It is possible, however, to directly apply an application constraint to a fact in the fact table. For example, we could restrict our example query to retrieve only those sales records where the number of units sold was greater than 10. This is a legitimate application constraint and can be thought of as a **filter** on the records that would otherwise be retrieved by rest of the query.

The next line in our example SQL is the **group by clause**, which tells SQL how to summarize records by the row headers. The only meaningful entry in this clause is to list the row headers exactly as they appear in the select list. SQL will complain if you leave out any of the row headers. You could theoretically put additional items in this list other than the row headers, but this would result in unlabeled rows in the answer set that could not be distinguished by the end user. For these reasons, we simply copy the row header list into the group by clause for every join query we do.

The final line in our example SQL is the **order by clause**, which determines how the answer set is sorted when it is presented to the user. In this case, it is sorted alphabetically by row header. We can use the order by clause to sort the answer set by any column or combination of columns.

Our SQL template provides us insight into how a query should be processed in a dimensional database. First, the application constraints are evaluated, dimension by dimension. Each dimension thus produces a set of candidate keys. The candidate keys are then assembled from each dimension into trial composite keys to be searched for in the fact table. All the "hits" in the fact table are then grouped and summed according to the specifications in the select list and group by clause. Although each DBMS will choose to process the SQL differently, this model of processing a dimensional query is very important from the back room perspective in a data warehouse environment. Queries that run for hours in a data warehouse are often queries where the DBMS decided not to process the dimensions first but rather is trying to process the fact table too early in the process. Much time is wasted in the back room trying to coerce the DBMS into processing the query in the proper order. These points are developed further in Chapters 14 and 16.

ATTRIBUTES ARE THE DRIVERS OF THE DATA WAREHOUSE

In the previous section we have seen how the dimension tables play off against the fact table in typical uses of the data warehouse. Using our newly developed vocabulary, we describe the use of a dimensional database in a data warehouse as follows:

The user begins by placing application constraints on the dimensions through the process of browsing the dimension tables one at a time. The browse queries are always on single-dimension tables and are usually fast acting and lightweight. Browsing is for information purposes only to allow the user to assemble the correct constraints on each dimension. The user may launch many browse queries during this phase. The user also drags row headers from the dimension tables and additive facts from the fact table to the answer set staging area (the report). The user then launches the multitable join. The DBMS groups and summarizes hundreds, thousands, or even millions of low-level records from the fact table into the small answer set and returns the answer set to the user.

We will see in Chapter 15 that this scenario is played out thousands of times per day in a typical data warehouse environment. From this perspective we see that the dimension table attributes play a vital role in the data warehouse. Since they are the source of virtually all interesting constraints, and since they are the source of all row headers in the user's answer sets, this means that the database is only as good as the dimension attributes. The more time spent providing descriptive English text attributes, the better the data warehouse is. (If your language happens not to be English, please substitute your own language!) The more time spent filling out the values in an attribute field, the better the data warehouse is. The more time spent quality assuring the values in an attribute field, the better the data warehouse is.

SPONTANEOUS EVOLUTION

The highly structured view of dimensional databases presented in this chapter and in the rest of this book is not something made up by the author. Major data suppliers such as **A.C. Nielsen, IRI, IMS,** and **Walsh America**, who can be regarded as pioneers in the business of providing text and numbers databases to end users, have for years used the dimensional approach as the primary data model. These vendors invented the "fact" and "dimension" vocabulary.

Dozens of large corporations, especially in the consumer package goods industry, learned through direct experience how to make large databases simple enough for users and software to handle successfully. Invariably these simple designs were dimensional. Rather than being a creative piece of work, this book serves mostly to collect and catalog the techniques that these pioneer data warehouse environments have used to implement successful systems.

A WORD ABOUT OLAP

OLAP (On-Line Analytic Processing) is a term invented to describe a dimensional approach to decision support. The OLAP philosophy is highly aligned with the goals and content of this book. There is a set of twelve OLAP criteria proposed by E.F. Codd that is supposed to be a yardstick by which decision support systems can be compared. However, unlike the original twelve OLTP criteria proposed by Codd in the 1980s, the twelve OLAP criteria are too vague to be a useful guideline for judging an actual system. Also, Codd's original statement of these goals was seriously compromised by an accompanying "rating" of a vendor (who scored twelve out of twelve) who later was accused of writing the evaluation. What is needed is a far more specific set of criteria for defining the OLAP philosophy. We hope that this is forthcoming.

In addition to Codd's OLAP philosophy, there is a consortium of vendors who call themselves OLAP vendors. Generally, these vendors sell proprietary, nonrelational decision support products that compete as replacements for relational databases and SQL-based front end tools. At the time of this writing, these are the most serious issues for an IS department relative to OLAP products:

1. The OLAP products are not open. That is, they do not process standard SQL.
2. The OLAP products do not scale to enterprise-sized data warehouses. These products cannot store and query the equivalent of a billion-row fact table (i.e., one billion actual records in a dimensional framework).

If the OLAP vendors will solve these two problems, they will be formidable competitors to the traditional relational database vendors, because culturally the OLAP vendors are much more aligned to the dimensional approach needed for data warehousing. We will not focus further on the OLAP movement in this book except to keep in mind that the dimensional recommendations that are so much a part of this book probably overlap the OLAP vendor's products in some interesting ways, at least for smaller, nonrelational applications.

2

THE GROCERY STORE

The best way to understand the principles of dimensional modeling is to work through a series of tangible examples. By visualizing real cases we can hold in our minds the particular design challenges much more effectively than if they are abstractly presented. In this book we will develop examples from traditional product businesses, including retail and manufacturing examples, to financial services, to transportation businesses, to government agencies, and to universities as a way to move past one's own detail and come up with the right design. It is helpful in this regard to remember that dimensional modeling is a top-down design process where we apply our end user's understanding of the business in choosing what dimensions and what facts should be in our database.

To learn dimensional modeling, please *read all of the chapters*, even if you don't manage a grocery business or work for an insurance company! Each chapter is a metaphor for a characteristic set of dimensional modeling problems that come up in nearly every kind of business. Universities, insurance companies, banks, and airlines will surely need the techniques developed in this chapter on grocery stores. Besides, it's refreshing to think about someone else's business at times. It is too easy to get derailed by historical complexities in the administration of keys or in the definition of attributes within one's own company. By stepping outside of one's own business and then returning with a well-understood design principle (or two), it is easier to remember the spirit of the design principles as one descends into the business details.

STEPS IN THE DESIGN PROCESS

Throughout this book we will approach the design of a dimensional database in a consistent way, by always considering four steps in a particular order. The meaning of these four steps will become more obvious as we proceed with the various designs, but we give their initial definitions now before we start:

1. Choose a *business process* to model. A business process is a major operational process in your organization that is supported by some kind of legacy system (or systems) from which data can be collected for the purposes of the data warehouse. Examples of business processes are orders, invoices, shipments, inventory, account administration, sales, and the general ledger.
2. Choose the *grain* of the business process. The grain is the fundamental, atomic level of data to be represented in the fact table for this process. Typical grains are individual transactions, individual daily snapshots, or individual monthly snapshots. It is impossible to proceed to step 3 without defining the grain.
3. Choose the *dimensions* that will apply to each fact table record. Typical dimensions are time, product, customer, promotion, warehouse, transaction type, and status. With the choice of each dimension, describe all discrete, textlike dimensional attributes (fields) that fill out each dimension table.
4. Choose the *measured facts* that will populate each fact table record. Typical measured facts are numeric additive quantities like Quantity Sold and Dollars Sold.

Throughout this book we will keep these four steps in mind as we develop each of the examples. Note that the perspectives necessary to actually make these decisions come from an understanding of the end user requirements and what is in the legacy data sources that are available to the data warehouse design team.

GROCERY STORE ITEM MOVEMENT

Let us start with a brief description of the grocery store business that will make our dimension tables and fact tables understandable. We will imagine we work in the headquarters of a large grocery chain. Our business has 500 large grocery stores spread over a three-state area. Each of the stores is a typical modern supermarket with a full complement of departments including grocery, frozen foods, dairy, meat, produce, bakery, floral, hard goods, liquor, and drugs. Each store has roughly 60,000 individual products on its shelves. The individual products are called *stock keeping units*, or **SKUs**. About 40,000 of the SKUs come from outside manufacturers and have bar codes imprinted on the product package. These bar codes are called **Universal Product Codes**, or **UPCs**. UPCs are at the same grain as individual SKUs. Each different package variation of a product has a separate UPC and hence is a separate SKU.

The remaining 20,000 SKUs come from departments like the meat, produce, bakery, or floral departments and don't have nationally recognized UPC codes. Nevertheless, as a grocery store we have to assign SKU numbers to these products. Since our grocery store is a modern, highly automated business, we stick scanner labels on many of the items in these other departments. Although the bar codes are not UPCs, they are certainly SKU numbers. Even with these scanner labels on many of our meat and bakery products, we still have lots of products, like apples, where the checker has to identify the SKU at the check stand. (We hope that the checker can tell the difference between a Macintosh and a Washington Delicious!) Figure 2.1 shows a typical grocery store SKU.

Those of you who are database administrators are already thinking, *hmmm, the master product key has got to be able to handle both UPCs and SKUs. I wonder how I assign SKU numbers.* We will return to the detailed issues of assigning master keys to our dimensions in Chapter 14, but for now we will cruise along at a higher level as we bring our design into focus.

There are several interesting places in a grocery store to collect data. The most useful and frequent place to collect data is at the cash register. Overwhelmingly, modern grocery stores scan the bar codes directly into the **point of sale** system, known as the **POS**. The POS is at the front door of the grocery store and is where the customer makes purchases. The back door, where vendors make deliveries, is another good place to collect data, although surprisingly, only a fraction of grocery stores use scanner technology to register deliveries in real time. Many stores do not actually know what they have received from whom until Accounts Payable at headquarters processes the vendors' invoices. In these kinds of stores, inventory is understood by gauging consumer **takeaway** through the POS and by using the old-fashioned technique of walking the aisles and seeing what shelves are empty.

At the grocery store, management is concerned with the logistics of order-

FIGURE 2.1

A typical grocery store SKU.

ing, stocking the shelves, and selling the products as well as maximizing the profit at each store. The profit ultimately comes from charging as much as possible for each product, lowering costs for product acquisition and overhead, and at the same time attracting as many customers as possible in a highly competitive pricing environment. The most significant management decisions that can be made in real time have to do with pricing and promotions. Both store management and headquarters marketing spend a great deal of time tinkering with pricing and running promotions. Promotions in a grocery store include **temporary price reductions** (called **TPRs**), ads in newspapers and newspaper inserts, displays in the grocery store including **shelf displays** and **end aisle displays**, and coupons. The most direct and effective way to create a big surge in *volume* (the amount of product sold) is to lower the price dramatically. A 50-cent reduction in the price of paper towels, especially when coupled with an ad and a display, can cause the sale of the paper towels to jump by a factor of ten. Unfortunately, such a big price reduction is usually not sustainable, because the towels are probably being sold at a loss. As a result of these issues, the visibility of all forms of promotions is an important part of analyzing the operations of a grocery store.

IDENTIFYING THE PROCESSES TO MODEL

Now that we have described our business, we want to begin the design of our data warehouse. As we proceed with the design, we will call out the design principles as we encounter them. Each design principle will be flagged with the icon ➤. These principles are collected and restated in Appendix A. Here is our first principle:

> The first step in the design is to decide what business **process(es)** to model, by combining an understanding of the business with an understanding of what data is available.

In our grocery store data warehouse we will decide to build a **daily item movement** database. This database will allow us to see in a detailed way what products are selling in which stores, at which prices, and on which days. The grain of this database will be *SKU by store by promotion by day*.

> The second step in the design is to decide on the grain of the fact table in each business process.

The grain is important because it determines the dimensionality of the database, and of course also has a profound impact on the size of the database. In our grocery business we have decided on the grain of daily item movement for several reasons. First, we could have chosen to build a database from every base-level customer ticket (transaction). However, we are discouraged from doing this because the size of the database could become astronomical. Also, in our particular grocery store chain we do not have an effective way to identify the individual customer at the cash register. Lacking the customer identification, we cannot perform some of the interesting **market basket** and shopping behavior kinds of analyses that we could otherwise do. If we had the identity of the customer, we would take a serious look at storing individual transactions.

Even though we choose not to record individual transactions, we still want a very detailed look at sales in the grocery store. We choose not to store weekly or monthly item movement at the lowest level of the database because we would be missing too many important effects that are visible only at a daily grain. For instance, we want to see the difference in sales between Mondays and Saturdays. We also want to see how our paper towels are **depleted** from the stores on a day-to-day basis when we run our 50-cents-off promotion.

We choose to track sales at the individual SKU level rather than at the package-size level or the brand level. There are many questions that we will want to ask that depend on the individual SKU, such as:

- Is it worthwhile to stock so many individual sizes of certain brands, like aspirin, or shampoo, or canned vegetables?
- Which items are **cannibalized** when I promote a particular diet cola? In other words, which products experience a decrease in sales when I promote another product?
- If I compare my own stores' sales to sales by my competitors (available through **syndicated data suppliers** providers like A.C. Nielsen), what are the top 10 items my competitors are selling that I don't sell at all?

Note that none of these questions are queries that call for one specific SKU. Rather, they are broad questions that need product detail down to the individual SKU. This observation leads to another principle:

> A data warehouse almost always demands data expressed at the lowest possible grain of each dimension, not because queries want to see individual low-level records, but because queries need to cut through the database in very precise ways.

Thus the best grain for a grocery store data warehouse is daily item movement, or SKU by store by promotion by day. Once the grain of the fact table has been chosen, the primary dimensions of time, product, and store fall out immediately. This is step three of our four design steps in every dimensional data warehouse. Within the framework of the primary dimensions, we can ask whether other dimensions can be attributed to the data, such as the promotion under which the product is sold, or the vendor who supplied the product to the store, or the name of the manager in charge that particular day. We express this as another design principle:

> A careful grain statement determines the primary dimensionality of of the fact table. It is then usually possible to add additional dimen-

sions to the basic grain of the fact table, where these additional dimensions naturally take on only a single value under each combination of the primary dimensions. If it is recognized that an additional desired dimension violates the grain by causing additional records to be generated, then the grain statement must be revised to accommodate this additional dimension.

Our schema diagram begins to take shape. See Figure 2.2. We will agree on four dimensions for our grocery store: time, product, store, and promotion.

PICKING THE BUSINESS MEASUREMENTS FOR THE FACT TABLE

Usually the fourth and final step in the design is to make a careful determination of which facts will appear in the fact table. Sometimes by examining the facts we will discover some adjustments that have to be made either in the grain assumptions or in the number of dimensions. We will return to completing filling out the dimension tables a little later.

In our grocery store data we poll each store at the end of the working day to report the product sales. Since we have hundreds of stores, this polling process is a complex application with a lot of data flowing up to headquarters. Generally, we can take one of two approaches. We can transport every individual sales transaction up to headquarters and perform the daily summarization there, or we can program the POS machine to produce the daily summaries by product and pro-

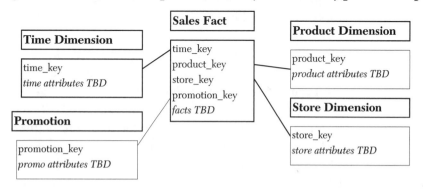

FIGURE 2.2

The grocery store schema.

motion and simply transfer the summaries to headquarters. Often it is helpful to estimate the number of records involved to see if there is a big difference. You don't have to know too much about grocery stores to do some useful analysis. To estimate the number of individual transaction line items coming from an individual store, we start with the **gross revenues** of the chain as a whole, which in this case is $4 billion per year. The only other piece of information we need is the average price of an item on a customer ticket, for example, a given can of vegetables in Mr. Jones's grocery cart. Let us assume that the average ticket line item in our grocery store is $2.00. From this we see that there will be two billion ticket line items per year ($4 billion divided by $2). By the way, this supports our decision to stay away from the individual ticket line item level of detail in the data warehouse. Three years of historical data at this level would be six billion records, which is well beyond our upper zone of comfort of one billion fact table records. This observation also generates a worthwhile design principle for sizing a data warehouse:

> The number of base sales transaction line items in a business can be estimated by dividing the gross revenue of the business by the average price of a sales item.

This principle is useful for "triangulating" the size of a data warehouse at a very early stage of the design. Now that we know the number of ticket line items per year for the whole chain (2 billion), we divide by 365 days and by 500 stores to get the average number of ticket line items per day per store. This works out to (2 billion/365/500) = 10,959. We can round this off to 11,000 for discussion purposes.

The alternate method of uploading data to headquarters each night is to let the POS accumulate the daily totals by product and just transfer the daily totals. From experience we know that in an average store stocked with 30,000 SKUs we will see about 10 percent of them, or 3,000, move through the registers each day. Thus we are about a factor of four better off creating the daily totals at the store and transferring these to headquarters each night.

The facts that our POS can report for each daily item total include the total dollar revenue, the total number of units (scannable items), the total dollar cost for the product as delivered to the store by the vendor, and the number of customer tickets that made up the daily activity for that product. Our fact table begins to take shape (Figure 2.3):

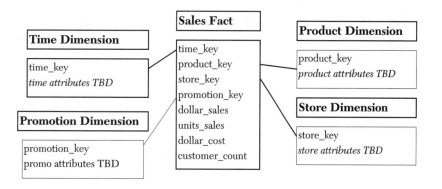

FIGURE 2.3

The grocery store schema showing the measured facts.

For the moment, let us assume that this schema is both the logical and physical design of our database. In other words, DBMS contains five actual tables: Sales, Time, Product, Store, and Promotion. Each of the dimension tables has a primary key (time_key, product_key, store_key, and promotion_key, respectively), and the fact table has a composite key made up of these four foreign keys. Perhaps the most striking aspect of the design at this point is the extreme simplicity of the fact table. If the four foreign keys are tightly administered consecutive integers, we could reserve as little as 14 bytes for all four keys (4 bytes each for time, product, and promotion, and 2 bytes for store). If the four measured facts in the fact table were each 4-byte scaled integers, we need to reserve only another 16 bytes. This would make our fact table record only 30 bytes wide. Even a billion-row fact table would occupy only about 30 GB of primary data space. Such a skinny fact table record is a very typical result in a data warehouse design. In Chapter 14, we will examine the implications of these skinny fact table records much more closely.

RESISTING NORMALIZATION

It is interesting that the design of the fact table is very compact in the keys and the data. There is no way to further **normalize** the extremely complex many-to-many relationships among the four keys in the fact table, because our four dimensions are essentially uncorrelated with each other in our business. Every store is open every day. Virtually every product is sold in every store over a period of time. Sooner or later, almost every product is sold on promotion in most or all of our stores. This leads to a design principle:

> **The fact table in a dimensional schema is naturally highly normalized.**

As we will see throughout this book, the fact table is overwhelmingly the largest table in a dimensional database. The dimension tables, by definition, are almost always geometrically smaller than the fact table. All realistic estimates of the disk space needed for the data warehouse can effectively ignore the dimension tables. This can be expressed as another design principle:

> **Efforts to normalize any of the tables in a dimensional database solely in order to save disk space are a waste of time.**

PRESERVING BROWSING

Throughout this book we will pay special attention to the design of the dimension tables to support the most flexible browsing possible. Recall that browsing is the user activity of exploring a single-dimension table for the purposes of setting constraints and choosing useful row headers. Browsing often involves constraining one or more dimensional attributes and looking at the distinct values of another attribute in the presence of these constraints. For instance, if we want to see which of our stores in Kent County, Ohio has the new upgraded floor plan, we would open our interactive browser on the store dimension and display the Store Name, County, State, and Floor Plan fields, initially with no constraints (Figure 2.4).

We select Ohio in the State list, and then we scroll the County list until we find Kent and we select it. We also select Upgraded in the Floor Plan Field. Each time we make a selection, all the fields in the browser change to reflect the selection. After making all three selections, the Store Name field contains the names of the stores we want (Figure 2.5). If we were in the process of build-

field:	Store Name	County	State	Floor Plan
constraint:				
distinct values:	Bill's Irwin's Jack's Jane's Margaret's Nelson's Tom's William's (& many more)	Arden Billton Camdale Kent McManus Newton	Ohio Pennsylvania West Virginia	Basic Deluxe Expanded Old Style Upgraded

FIGURE 2.4

Browser open with unconstrained fields.

ing a report analyzing these stores, we would press the Make Constraint command in our browser at this point.

Each time we refresh the screen in our browser, we perform a **SELECT DISTINCT** on each field displayed in the browser, subject to the constraints we picked on other fields in that same table. These SELECT DISTINCTs are a very characteristic use of a dimension table in a data warehouse. We take one or more fields in the dimension table, constrain them, and ask what the distinct values in some other field are. This is how *pick lists* are generated. The fields selected for this pick list generation may be related to each other hierarchically (like counties and states) or they may be effectively uncorrelated (like counties and floor plans). What we need in our dimension tables is equal access to all of the fields so that we can present a clean view to the user and very quickly browse the underlying data. In our example, each time we clicked a field, we launched up to four SELECT DISTINCT queries. The dimension tables should remain as flat **denormalized** tables just as shown in our dimensional schematic diagrams (see Figures 2.2 and 2.3.). If we normalize them by extracting repeating

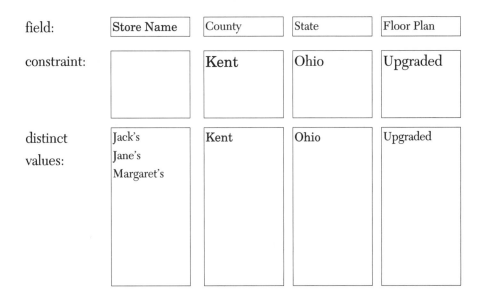

field:	Store Name	County	State	Floor Plan
constraint:		Kent	Ohio	Upgraded
distinct values:	Jack's Jane's Margaret's	Kent	Ohio	Upgraded

FIGURE 2.5

Browser showing stores in Kent County with upgraded floor plans.

data elements into separate "outrigger" tables, we make browsing and pick list generation difficult or impossible. This results in another design principle:

> The dimension tables must not be normalized but should remain as flat tables. Normalized dimension tables destroy the ability to browse. Disk space savings gained by normalizing the dimension tables are typically less than one percent of the total disk space needed for the overall schema.

THE TIME DIMENSION

Now that our fact table has taken shape, we will complete the design each of the dimension tables. We will start with the time dimension. The time dimension is the one dimension virtually guaranteed to be present in every data warehouse, because virtually every data warehouse is a time series. Time is usually the first dimension in the underlying sort order in the database because when it is first in the sort order, the successive loading of time intervals of data will load data into virgin territory on the disk.

Many data designers pause at this point in the design and ask why an explicit time dimension table is needed. They reason that if the time key in the fact table is a date data type, then any SQL query can directly constrain on the time key in the fact table and use the natural SQL date semantics to constrain on the month, or on the year. This is certainly a valid observation. If the usage of dates and time spans in the particular business being modeled needs only months or years, then the time dimension table could in theory be omitted. However, if the business wants to slice its data by workdays versus holidays, or by fiscal periods, or by seasons, or by major events like Super Bowl Sunday, then an explicit time dimension table is essential.

In our grocery store design we decided on a daily grain of data. Thus each record in our time dimension table represents a day. Unlike most of our other dimensions, we can build the time dimension table in advance. We may put five or even ten years of records representing days in the table so that we can cover all of the old history we have stored as well as the next few years. Even ten years' worth of days is only about 3,650 records, which is a relatively small dimension table. For a daily time dimension table in a retail environment, we recommend the fields shown in Figure 2.6.

The Day of Week field contains the name of the day, such as Tuesday. This field would be used to create reports comparing the business on Tuesdays with the business on Saturdays. The Day Number in Month field starts with 1 at the beginning of each month and runs to 28, 29, 30, or 31, depending on the month. This field is useful for comparing the same day each month. The Last Day in Month Flag is also used in this context to select the final days in a month. This is useful for payday analyses. The Day Number Overall field is effectively a Julian day number (i.e., a consecutive day number starting at the beginning of some epoch). This field allows simple arithmetic between days across year and month boundaries. Similar comments apply to the Week Number and Month Number fields. The Quarter and Fiscal Period fields are text fields containing the organization's designation for what quarter and what fiscal period the particular day falls into. Remember that each field in this table is defined by the particular day that the record represents.

The Holiday Flag is a Y or an N depending on whether the day is a legal hol-

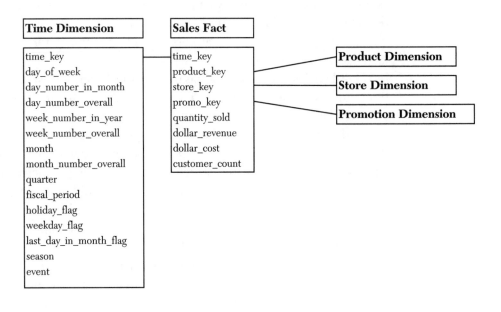

FIGURE 2.6

Time dimension detail in the grocery schema.

iday. This field would allow fast comparisons of holiday business to nonholiday business. The Weekday Flag is a Y or an N depending on whether the day is a weekday or not. Saturdays and Sundays are assigned the value N. This field allows the rapid comparison of weekdays to weekends. Of course, multiple time fields can be compounded together, so we can compare weekday holidays to weekend holidays, for example.

The Season field is set to the name of the retailing season, if any. Examples could include Christmas, Thanksgiving, Easter, Valentine's Day, Fourth of July, or None. The Event field is similar to the Season field and can be used to mark special outside events like Super Bowl Sunday, or Labor Strike, or Hurricane Hugo. Regular promotional events are usually not handled in the time table, but rather are described more completely by means of the promotion dimension. Keep in mind that promotional events are not defined only by time, but in general are defined by time, product, and store.

Most data warehouses need an explicit time dimension table even though the primary time key may be an SQL date-valued object. The explicit time dimension is needed to describe fiscal periods, seasons, holidays, weekends, and other calendar calculations that are difficult to get from the SQL date machinery.

THE PRODUCT DIMENSION

The product dimension describes every SKU in the grocery store. The product dimension is almost always sourced from the production **product master file** used by the POS systems in the stores. Most well-managed grocery stores administer their product master files at headquarters and download them to each store at frequent intervals. It is headquarters' responsibility to obtain notification of each new UPC created by packaged goods manufacturers and define the appropriate product master record for that UPC. Each new UPC is given a unique SKU number. Headquarters also defines the rules by which stores assign their own SKUs to such items as bakery goods, meat, and produce. As owners of the data warehouse, we extract the product master file into our product dimension table each time the product master changes.

An important function of the product master file is to hold the many descriptive attributes of each SKU. The **merchandise hierarchy** is an important group of attributes. Although each grocery store defines its own merchandise hierarchy, the structures are very similar. Typically, individual SKUs roll up to package sizes. Package sizes roll up to brands. Brands roll up to subcategories. Subcategories roll up to categories, and categories roll up to departments. Thus if an individual SKU is described as Green 3-pack Brawny Paper Towels, the merchandise hierarchy for this SKU may well look like this:

SKU: Green 3-pack Brawny Paper Towels, UPC # xxxxxxxxx

Package Size: 3-pack

Brand: Brawny

Subcategory: Paper Towels

Category: Paper

Department: Grocery

A typical store in our grocery chain has 30,000 SKUs. For each and every SKU, all of the levels of the merchandise hierarchy are well defined. Some attributes, such as the SKU description, are unique. In this case there are 30,000 different values in the SKU description field. At the other extreme, there are only perhaps 30 distinct values of the Department attribute. Thus, on the average there are 1,000 repetitions of each value in the Department attribute. This is all right! We do not need to separate these repeated values into an **outrigger table** to save space. Remember that space considerations in the dimension tables pale in comparison to space considerations in the fact table.

Many of the attributes in the product dimension table are not part of the merchandise hierarchy. The Package Type attribute, for example, might take values such as Bottle, Bag, Box, or Other. Any SKU in any department could have one of these values. It makes perfect sense to combine a constraint on this attribute with a constraint on an attribute within the merchandise hierarchy. For example, we could look at all the SKUs in the Cereal subcategory packaged in Bags. To put it another way, we can browse among dimension attributes whether or not they belong to the merchandise hierarchy, and we can **drill up** and **drill down** using attributes whether or not they belong to the merchandise hierarchy.

We can even have more than one merchandise hierarchy in our product dimension. We will explore this problem and some other interesting practical problems in large dimensions like the product dimension and the customer dimension in Chapter 6, on big dimensions.

A recommended typical product dimension for a grocery store data warehouse would look like Figure 2.7. A reasonable product dimension table would have 50 or more attributes. Each of these attributes is a rich source for constraining and constructing row headers. Viewed in this way, we see that drilling down is nothing more than asking for a row header that provides more information. For example, if we have a simple report whose row header is Department:

Department	Dollar Sales	Unit Sales
Bakery	$12,331	5,088
Frozen Foods	$31,777	15,565
Grocery	$100,756	48,885
Photo	$8,079	1,274

and we want to drill down, we can drag virtually any other attribute, like Brand, from the product dimension into the report next to Department and we will automatically drill down to this next level of detail. A typical drill down within the merchandise hierarchy would look like this:

Department	Brand	Dollar Sales	Unit Sales
Bakery	Fluffy	$6,024	1,993
Bakery	Light	$6,307	3,095
Frozen Foods	Coldpack	$10,022	5,564
Frozen Foods	Frigid	$21,755	10,001
Grocery	Juicy	$8,445	10,055
Grocery	Lean	$52,554	21,234
Grocery	Good	$39,757	17,596
Photo	Contrast	$4,011	499
Photo	Shiny	$4,068	775

Or, we could drill down by the Diet attribute, even though it isn't in the hierarchy.

Department	Diet	Dollar Sales	Unit Sales
Bakery	Diet	$9,864	4,070
Bakery	Non Diet	$2,467	1,018
Frozen Foods	Diet	$25,422	12,452
Frozen Foods	Non Diet	$6,355	3,113
Grocery	Diet	$80,605	39,108
Grocery	Non Diet	$20,151	9,777

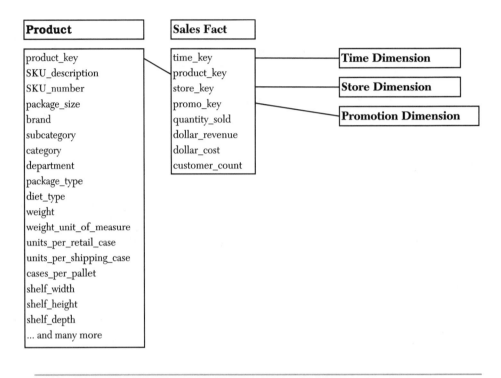

FIGURE 2.7

The grocery store product dimension.

We have belabored the examples of drilling down in order to make a point, which we will express as a design principle:

Drilling down in a data warehouse is nothing more than adding row headers from the dimension tables. Drilling up is subtracting row headers. An explicit hierarchy is not needed to support drilling down.

We also should mention:

The product dimension is one of the two or three primary dimensions in nearly every data warehouse. Great care should be taken to fill this dimension with as many descriptive attributes as possible. Retail product dimension tables should have at least 50 attributes.

THE STORE DIMENSION

The store dimension describes every store in our grocery chain. Unlike the product master file, which is just about guaranteed to be available in every large grocery business, there may not be a comprehensive store master file. The product master needs to be downloaded to each store every time a product description changes. However, the individual POS systems do not need a store master describing each of them. For this reason, the IS staff frequently must assemble the necessary components of the store dimension from multiple sources.

The store dimension is the primary geographic dimension in our grocery business. Each store can be thought of as a point in space. Because of this we can roll stores up to any kind of geography. In the United States, stores usually roll up to zip code, to county, and to state. Stores usually also roll up to sales districts and sales regions. These two kinds of hierarchies are both very comfortably represented in the store dimension, since both the geographic hierarchy and the sales region hierarchy are well defined for a single store record. A recommended store dimension table for the grocery business is shown in Figure 2.8.

The Floor Plan Type, the Photo Processing Type, and the Finance Services Type are all short text descriptors that describe the particular store. These should not be one-character codes, but should be 10- to 20-character readable standardized descriptors that make sense when viewed in a **pull down list** or when used as a row header in a report.

The First Opened Date and Last Remodel Date are actual date-valued fields that can be directly accessed by SQL or can be used as join keys to copies of the time dimension table. Such copies of the time dimension are declared in standard SQL by the **SYNONYM** construct, and are semantically distinct from the main time dimension. A typical SYNONYM declaration would look like this:

CREATE FIRST_OPEN_TIME AS SYNONYM FOR TIME

Now the system thinks that there is another physical copy of the time dimension table called FIRST_OPEN_TIME. Constraints on this new table have nothing to do with constraints on the time dimension table. This is an example of the use of the time dimension table as an **outrigger** to the store dimension.

The fields describing square feet of space for the store and the departments are numeric and additive across stores. One might be tempted to place them in the fact table. However, they are clearly a constant attribute of store,

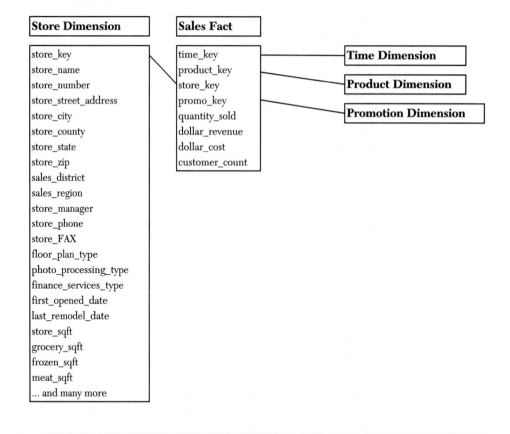

FIGURE 2.8

Recommended store dimension for a grocery store.

and are used as constraints and row headers in reports more often than they are used as additive elements in a summation. For these reasons we are confident in our placement of these attributes in the store dimension table.

THE PROMOTION DIMENSION

Potentially the most interesting dimension in our schema is the promotion dimension. The promotion dimension describes each promotion condition under which a product is sold in the grocery chain. Promotion conditions include temporary price reductions, end aisle displays, newspaper ads, and coupons. This dimension is often called a **causal** dimension (not a casual dimension!) because it describes factors that are thought to cause a change in product sales. Managers both at headquarters and the store are very interested in whether a promotion is successful or not. Promotions are judged on one or more of the following factors:

- Whether the products under promotion experienced a gain in sales during the promotional period. This is called the **lift**. The lift can be measured only if the store can agree on what the **baseline sales** of the promoted products would have been without the promotion. Baseline values can be estimated from prior sales history and, in some cases, with the help of sophisticated mathematical models. The historical data, of course, is part of the data warehouse, but the mathematical models, if any, are applications outside of the warehouse proper.
- Whether the products under promotion showed a drop in sales after the promotion, thereby canceling the gain in sales during the promotion. This is called **time shifting**.
- Whether the products under promotion showed a gain in sales but other products nearby on the shelf showed a corresponding decrease in sales. This is called **cannibalization**.
- Whether all the products in the promoted category of products experienced a net overall gain in sales taking into account the time periods before, during, and after the promotion. This is called **growing the market**.
- Whether the promotion was profitable. Usually the profit of a promotion is taken to be the incremental gain in profit of the promoted category over the

baseline sales taking into account time shifting and cannibalization, and taking into account the special costs of the promotion including temporary price reductions, ads, displays, and coupons.

The causal conditions affecting a sale are not automatically captured by the POS system. Ideally the store manager enters all of the causal conditions as they occur. It may be most convenient and manageable to change the price reduction, ad, and display status of products once per week, say on Saturday night, especially if this is accompanied by corresponding changes as to how the product is presented on the floor of the store. Coupons are a little easier to handle, because the customer either presents the coupon at the time of the sale or does not. In this case, the POS must record the presence of the coupon.

The various possible causal conditions are highly correlated. A temporary price reduction is usually associated with an ad and perhaps an end-aisle display. Coupons are often associated with ads. For these reasons it makes sense to create one record in the promotion dimension for each *combination* of promotion conditions that occur. Over the course of a year there may be 1,000 ads, 1,000 temporary price reductions, and 200 end-aisle displays, but there may only be 5,000 combinations of these three conditions affecting any particular product. For example, in a given promotion, most of the stores would simultaneously run all three promotion mechanisms, but a few of the stores would not be able to deploy the end-aisle displays. In this case, two separate promotion condition records would be needed, one for the normal price reduction plus ad plus display, and one for the exceptional price reduction plus ad only. Our recommended promotion dimension table is shown in Figure 2.9.

From a purely logical point of view we could record very similar information about the promotions by separating the four causal mechanisms (price reductions, ads, displays, and coupons) into four dimensions rather than combining them into one dimension. Ultimately this choice is the designer's prerogative. The tradeoffs in favor of keeping the four dimensions together include the following:

- Since the four causal mechanisms are highly correlated, the combined single dimension is only a little larger than any one of the separated dimensions would be.

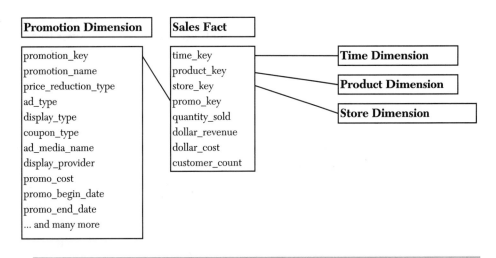

FIGURE 2.9

The recommended promotion dimension table.

- The combined single dimension can be browsed efficiently to see how the various price reductions, ads, displays, and coupons are used together. However, this browsing shows only the possible combinations. This browsing does not reveal which stores or products were affected by the promotion. Such coverage information must be found by tying the promotion dimension to the fact table.

The tradeoffs in favor of separating the four causal mechanisms into distinct dimension tables include the following:

- The separated dimensions may be more understandable to the user community if they think of these mechanisms separately. This would be revealed during the user interviews.
- Administration of the separate dimensions may be more straightforward than administering a combined dimension. The combined dimension requires the creation of an artificial key.

Regardless of the choice of one promotion dimension or four, there is one important question that cannot be answered by our grocery store schema. What products are on promotion but didn't sell? The sales fact table records only the SKUs actually sold. There is no record for SKUs that didn't sell. In Chapter 10, we will use a "factless" fact table to answer this question.

THE GROCERY STORE FACTS

The four measurable facts we have recorded in our POS sales fact include quantity sold, dollar revenue, dollar cost, and customer count. The first three of these are beautifully additive across all the dimensions. We can slice and dice the fact table with impunity, and every sum of these three facts is valid and correct. We can compute the **gross profit** by subtracting the dollar cost from the dollar revenue. Although computed, this gross profit is also perfectly additive across all the dimensions. We can calculate the gross profit of any combination of products sold in any set of stores on any set of days. The **gross margin** is calculated by dividing the gross profit by the dollar revenue. We can similarly calculate the gross margin of any set of products, stores, or days by remembering to add the revenues and costs before dividing. This can be stated as a design principle:

A nonadditive calculation, such as a ratio like gross margin, can be calculated for any slice of the fact table by remembering to calculate the *ratio of the sums*, not the sum of the ratios. In other words, the computation must be distributed over the sums, not the other way around.

This design principle shows how to calculate the gross margin in a break row in a report. The gross margin break row is not the sum of the gross margins appearing in the detail rows above the break row, but rather is the ratio of the sum of the dollar revenue and the sum of the gross profits from each of the detail lines. Every report writer in the data warehouse marketplace should automatically perform this function correctly. Surprisingly few handle this computation gracefully.

The fourth fact, customer count, however, is not additive across the product dimension. To visualize this, consider two item movement records representing the sales of paper towels and tissue paper in a particular store on a particular day. In the first record we have recorded 20 customers. In the second record we have recorded 30 customers. Unfortunately, in looking at these records, we cannot tell how many customers bought either paper towels or tissue paper. The number could be anywhere between 30 and 50. We effectively discarded this information when we summarized up from the individual transactions to the daily item movement totals. The customer count, because it is additive across three of the dimensions, but not the fourth, is called *semiadditive*. Care must be taken in the final end user applications to either warn users or prohibit them from adding customer counts. Any analysis using the customer count must be restricted to a single product key to be valid. There is no approximation, such as average, minimum, or maximum that is worth very much analytically in trying to combine customer counts across the product dimension.

This particular semiadditive problem can arise whenever *time snapshots* include transaction counts. We state this as a design principle:

> Customer counts are usually semiadditive when they occur in time snapshot fact tables because they double count activity across products during the customer event. In these cases they can be used correctly in user applications only by restricting the keys in the nonadditive dimensions to single values.

Correct customer counts over time for higher-level aggregations in the nonadditive dimensions (such as the customer count for the overall Paper category in our grocery store example) can be achieved. The most obvious solution is to change the grain of the database to the individual transaction. In the grocery store POS case this means the individual customer ticket line item. Customer counts are then performed on the fly. The applications to do this calculation are somewhat complicated because at the transaction line item grain, separate products purchased by a customer on a ticket are stored in separate records. The application must group line items together and find those groups where the desired products coexist. This can be done with the COUNT DISTINCT operator in SQL.

A less obvious and less complete solution is to store brand, subcategory, category, department, and all merchandise customer counts in explicitly stored **aggregates**. Thus far in our database design, we have not considered these explicitly stored aggregate records. They are a very important part of data warehouse database design, and are discussed in detail in Chapter 13. In order to store the correct customer counts in these aggregate records, we must maintain running totals of these customer counts by brand, subcategory, category, department, and all merchandise as we process each customer ticket. When we have completed scanning each ticket, we can add the unduplicated customer count for these product aggregates within the customer's ticket into the explicit product aggregate record we are accumulating for that store for that day. We don't have to maintain this running total across anything bigger than an individual customer ticket because the customer count is additive across all the other dimensions.

In claiming that customer counts are additive across all the dimensions except product, the alert reader may question whether customer counts are additive across the promotion dimension. Customer counts will be additive across the promotion dimension if it is impossible for a customer to simultaneously purchase the same product both on promotion and off promotion. This is almost certainly the case for price reductions, ads, and displays, because these are factors set by store management for all sales of a product in a single stroke. However, it may be possible for a customer to buy an item with a coupon and to buy another identical item without a coupon. In this case, we have the added complexity that customer counts will not be additive across different coupon conditions. If store management believes this is very infrequent, then the distortion in the data may be ignored. Alternatively, the coupon promotion condition can be handled as a separate dimension in order to allow the other promotion conditions to be perfectly additive.

DATABASE SIZING FOR THE GROCERY CHAIN

In each of the industry example chapters, starting with this one, we include a reasonable estimate for the size of the database we have designed. A detailed discussion of the field width assumptions is given at the beginning of Chapter 13.

Time dimension: 2 years × 365 days = 730 days
Store dimension: 300 stores, reporting sales each day

Product dimension: 30,000 products in each store, of which 3,000 sell each day in a given store

Promotion dimension: a sold item appears in only one promotion condition in a store on a day

Number of base fact records = $730 \times 300 \times 3000 \times 1 = 657$ *million records*

Number of key fields = 4; Number of fact fields = 4; Total fields = 8

Base fact table size = 657 million $\times$ 8 fields $\times$ 4 bytes = *21 GB*

3

THE WAREHOUSE

In Chapter 2 we developed a dimensional model for retail sales in a large grocery chain. In this chapter we will move up the **value chain** to a typical warehouse. Perhaps this warehouse is a distributor that serves the grocery industry. In this case, the distributor serves as middleman between the package goods manufacturer and the grocery retailers. However, the design developed in this chapter on inventory analysis should apply to a broad set of warehouse inventory situations both inside and outside the grocery industry.

INVENTORY LEVELS: ANOTHER SEMIADDITIVE FACT

The interesting issues in modeling inventory arise from the traditional static nature of inventory snapshots. In the last chapter, we modeled the flow of product past a point. Only the products that actually sold were measured. By the nature of product sales, once a product was sold it couldn't be counted again in a subsequent sale. This made most of the measures in the grocery store sales perfectly additive across all the dimensions, including time. Traditional inventory levels, however, are not additive across time, because they represent snapshots of a level or a balance. It is not possible to tell whether yesterday's inventory is the same or different from today's inventory solely by looking at inventory levels. Inventory levels (and all forms of financial account balances) are thus a second kind of semiadditive fact.

Inventory levels and account balances are nonadditive across time. However, unlike the transaction count measure in Chapter 2, we can usefully combine inventory levels and account balances across time by averaging. We are all familiar with our bank telling us what our average daily balance is on our monthly account summary. These observations lead to a design principle:

> **All measures that record a static level, such as inventory levels, financial account balances, and measures of intensity such as room temperatures, are inherently nonadditive across time. However, in these cases the measure may be usefully aggregated across time by *averaging over the number of time periods*.**

The last few words in this design principle contain a trap. Notice that you cannot use the SQL AVG function to perform the averaging over time. The SQL AVG function averages over all the records received by the query, not just the number of time periods. For example, if a row in a query result is supposed to contain the combined inventory level for a cluster of 3 products, 4 stores, and 7 time periods (i.e., what is the average daily inventory of a brand in a geographic region during a given week), using the SQL AVG function would divide the summed inventory value by 3*4*7 = 84. The correct answer is to divide the summed inventory value by 7, which is the number of time periods. This is an unfortunate complexity in inventory calculations because SQL has no AVG_TIME_SUM operator that would compute the average over just the time dimension. A proper inventory application must isolate the time constraint (in this case the seven days comprising the requested week) and retrieve the cardinality of this constraint by itself. Then the application must divide the summed inventory value by the time constraint cardinality. This can be done with an embedded SQL call within the overall SQL statement, or by querying the time dimension separately and then storing the resulting value in an application that is passed to the overall SQL statement.

INVENTORY MODELS

In the remainder of this chapter we will explore three separate inventory models. The first is the *inventory snapshot*. Every day, or every week, we measure the inventory levels and place the numbers in the database in separate records.

The second is the *delivery status* model. In this case we build one record for each delivery of product to the warehouse, and then in this single record track the disposition of all the items in the delivery until they have left the warehouse. The delivery status model is only possible if we can reliably distinguish the products delivered in one shipment or a related series of shipments from those products delivered at a later time. The third inventory model is the *transaction* model. Here we record every change of status of delivered products as they arrive at the warehouse, are processed into the warehouse, go through inventory status changes in the warehouse, and eventually leave the warehouse in various ways. Each of the three inventory models tells a different story. In some inventory-intensive applications, two or even all three models may be simultaneously appropriate.

THE INVENTORY SNAPSHOT MODEL

Inventory dimensions are usually simpler than retail sales dimensions. In a standard inventory snapshot fact table, there are three primary dimensions: time, product, and warehouse. Warehouse inventory normally does not have a Customer or Store dimension unless the inventory has been **allocated**. Warehouse inventory usually is not attributed with a promotion dimension either. Although a promotion may be going on while the products are sitting in inventory, the promotion really cannot be associated with the product until the product is actively sold. After the promotion has ended, the products may still be sitting in inventory. Warehouse inventory may possibly have a supplier dimension, but in those cases where a supplier changes or where there are multiple sources for a product, it may be impossible to tell which products are assigned to which supplier, and when those products have been taken off the shelf or out of the bin.

The simplest view of inventory uses only a single fact: Quantity on Hand. This leads to an exceptionally clean dimensional design, as shown in Figure 3.1. Even a database as simple as this one can be very useful. If there are many products and many warehouses, and the inventory is measured frequently (even daily), many useful insights can be derived. For example, if the warehouse dimension is actually a Store dimension, and the inventory is the on shelf inventory of a mass merchandiser, this database may be the central logistics

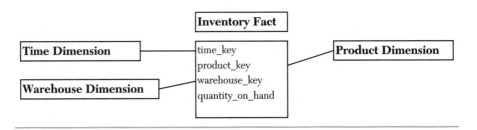

FIGURE 3.1

The simplest inventory schema.

database for a multi-billion-dollar company. Such a database could be used to balance store inventories each night after the stores close.

However, this inventory fact table has a serious problem that the retail sales fact table in Chapter 2 did not have. The retail sales fact table was reasonably *sparse*, because only about 10 percent of the products in each of our hypothetical grocery stores actually sold each day. If a product didn't sell in a store on a given day, then there was no record in the fact table for that combination of keys. On the other hand, inventory by nature generates fairly dense fact tables. The mass merchandiser inventory example is the worst. Virtually every product must be represented in every store every day. A mass merchandiser with 100,000 products in each of 2,000 stores would generate 100,000 × 2,000 × 1,100 = 220 billion records over a three-year period if daily measurements were kept. Even with a potentially tiny record width of 12 to 16 bytes, the data portion of the database would swell to an unmanageable 2.64 terabytes to 3.52 terabytes. Although the problem is not nearly this severe in most businesses, the denseness of inventory databases requires some compromises be made.

Perhaps the most obvious compromise is to increasingly space out the time measurements for old history. It may be acceptable to keep the last rolling 30 days of inventory at the daily level, and then revert to weekly inventory for the next most recent 11 months, and then revert to monthly inventory snapshots for the prior two years. In this way, instead of 1100 time snapshots, the number would be reduced to 30 + 48 + 24 = 102 snapshots. We have reduced the database by more than a factor of 10.

GROSS MARGIN RETURN ON INVENTORY (GMROI)

The very simple view of inventory we developed in our inventory snapshot fact table only allows us to see the time series of inventory levels for each product. There is no way using only Quantity On Hand to measure the velocity of inventory movement and develop other interesting inventory measures such as the *number of turns*, the **days supply**, and the gross margin return on inventory (**GMROI**, pronounced *jem-roy*).

If we add Quantity Shipped, or equivalently Quantity Depleted, or Quantity Sold, to each inventory fact record, we can calculate the number of turns and the days supply. For daily inventory snapshot records, the number of turns measured each day is (Quantity Shipped)/(Quantity On Hand). For an extended time span, such as a year, the number of turns is (Total Quantity Shipped)/(Daily Average Quantity on Hand). The days supply is a similar calculation and over a time span is equal to (Final Quantity On Hand)/(Average Quantity Shipped).

If we have the Quantity Shipped available, we probably can supply the Value at Cost as well as the Value at Latest Selling Price. The difference between these two Values is, of course, the Gross Profit. The Gross Margin is equal to (Gross Profit)/(Value at Latest Selling Price).

Finally, we can multiply the number of turns by the Gross Margin to get the Gross Margin Return on Inventory, which can be expressed as a formula:

$$\text{GMROI} = \frac{(\text{Total Quantity Shipped})*(\text{Value at Latest Selling Price} - \text{Value at Cost})}{(\text{Daily Average Quantity on Hand})*(\text{Value at Latest Selling Price})}$$

Although the formula is complicated, the idea behind the GMROI is simple. By multiplying the gross margin by the number of turns, we create a measure of the effectiveness of our inventory investment. A high GMROI means that we are moving the product through the warehouse quickly (lots of turns) and are making good money on the sale of the product (high gross margin). A low GMROI means that we are moving the product slowly (low turns) and aren't making very much money on it (low gross margin). The GMROI is a standard powerful metric used by inventory analysts to judge a company's quality of investment in its inventory.

If we want to be more ambitious than our initial simple design in Figure 3.1, then we should include the Quantity Shipped, Value at Cost and Value at Latest Selling Price fields in our inventory snapshot fact table. We can call this the advanced inventory snapshot (Figure 3.2).

Notice that although the Quantity On Hand is semiadditive, the other three measures are all fully additive across all three dimensions. The Quantity Shipped amount applies to the particular grain of the fact table, which in this case we have assumed is daily. Remember that the Value fields are extended amounts. Although it should be obvious, we must make sure not to store the GMROI values themselves in the table. The GMROI numbers are not additive. We can quickly calculate the GMROI from the constituent fields in the above table across any number of records by adding the fields up before performing the calculation, but we are dead in the water if we store the GMROIs explicitly, because we can't usefully combine GMROIs across multiple records.

THE DELIVERY STATUS MODEL

The delivery status model creates one record for a complete shipment of a product to a warehouse. It is often useful if the record corresponds to a particular line item on a vendor purchase order. In this way we are looking at the complete inventory history of a particular SKU. This model is especially useful in inventory situations where a large quantity of a particular SKU arrives in a short period of time, and the SKU is then completely sold or otherwise de-

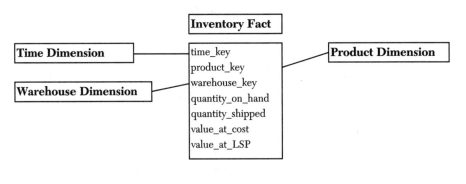

FIGURE 3.2

Advanced inventory snapshot supporting GMROI analysis.

pleted from the warehouse. In this way it makes sense to track a series of well-defined events from start to finish. This model is not appropriate for products that arrive in a continuous flow over a long period of time, and under a number of purchase orders.

To create a typical delivery status model, let us assume that in our warehouse operation inventory normally goes through the following steps:

1. Received
2. Inspected
3. Placed into inventory
4. Authorized to sell
5. Picked from inventory
6. Boxed
7. Shipped

A routine product with no problems would progress through these steps in order. Of course, there are exception conditions, including the following:

- Failed inspection
- Returned to vendor
- Damaged in handling
- Lost
- Returned from customer
- Returned to inventory
- Written off
- Refunded

The philosophy of the delivery status fact table is to provide a continually updated status of the products received on a given purchase order. A given record may be updated each day until all the inventory has reached its final disposition. The delivery status fact table looks quite different from the inventory snapshot (Figure 3.3).

The delivery status fact table is worth examining closely. It is a relatively wide table, with 26 fields in addition to the primary dimensional keys. These 26 fields can be classified into four characteristic groups:

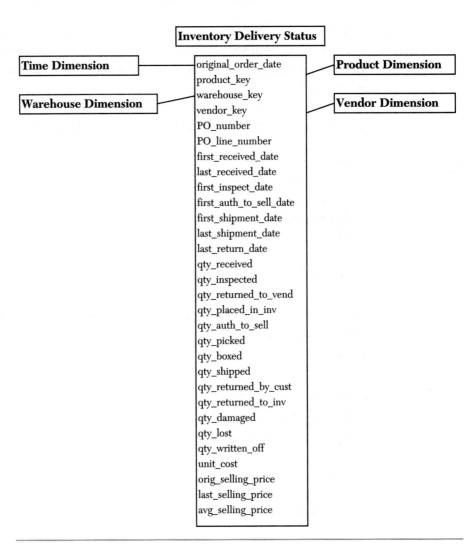

FIGURE 3.3

The delivery status model of inventory.

- **degenerate dimension** fields (2 fields) : PO_number and PO_line_number
- auxiliary date fields (7 fields)
- additive, numeric quantities (13 fields)
- unit prices and costs (4 fields)

Degenerate Dimensions

The PO_number and PO_line_number fields together would appear to form a dimension. In a traditional **parent-child** database, the PO_number would be the key to the purchase order header record, which would contain all the information valid for the purchase order as a whole, such as the vendor name, the original order date, and the destination warehouse. However, in our dimensional model we have already extracted all of this interesting information into other dimensions. The PO_number is still useful to us because it serves as the grouping key for pulling together all the products ordered on one purchase order. Also in some rare instances it may be interesting to actually print out the PO numbers in order to reference the actual paperwork. A number of organizations are using "optical jukeboxes" to store images of actual paper documents so that the PO_number can be used to bring up an image of the signed document.

Although the PO_number is a legitimate element of the fact table, we have stripped off all of the items that would otherwise make the PO_number a dimension key. For this reason, we call the PO_number a *degenerate dimension*. In nearly every case where the grain of a fact table represents an actual working document, this situation arises. Order numbers, invoice numbers, and bill of lading numbers almost always wind up as degenerate dimensions in a dimensional model.

Document control numbers such as order numbers, invoice numbers, and bill of lading numbers usually are represented as degenerate dimensions (i.e., dimension keys with no corresponding dimension table) in fact tables where the grain of the table is the document itself or a line item in the document.

Auxiliary Date Fields

Status tracking fact tables, such as the inventory status table we are discussing, usually have a lengthy list of interesting date fields. It is often helpful if one of the dates is used as the primary date. In our example the primary date is the original order date. This is the date field that will most often be constrained. The primary date is used as the date component of the master composite index on the fact table.

The set of date fields in a status tracking fact table are mainly of use in measuring the spans of time over which the product is processed through the warehouse. The numerical difference between any two of these dates is a number, which can usefully be averaged over all the dimensions. It would probably make sense to build a view on this fact table that calculated a large number of these date differences and presented them to the user as if they were stored in the underlying table. These view fields could include such measures as Product Delivery Time, Receipt to Authorized Time, Receipt to First Shipped Time, and First to Last Shipped Time.

Unit Prices and Costs

The last four fields in the inventory status fact table are unit costs and prices. Even though these numbers are not additive, it is much more efficient to store these measures as unit values, because we want to use these four numbers in virtually every combination with the thirteen quantity fields. For example, it makes sense to value the shipped inventory at cost, at original selling price, at last selling price, and at average selling price. To literally present all of these combinations in the physical fact table would require 4 costs and prices times 13 quantities, or 52 fields. Instead, we store just the unit costs and prices, and then we create a view in SQL to present the 52 combinations to the user as fully additive facts. This leads to a design principle:

Exceptions to absolute additivity in the fact table can be made where the additive measures are more conveniently delivered in a view. Examples include computed time spans from a large number of date fields, as well as extended monetary amounts derived from unit costs and prices. In such a case it is important to have all users access the view instead of the underlying table.

Note that the extra computation involved in multiplying prices or costs by quantities in every record fetch is negligible compared with other overheads in the DBMS. Intrarecord computations are very efficient.

The alert reader may note that explicitly storing unit prices also makes **price point analysis** quite simple. By including the observed unit price in the select list without summing it, we are forced by SQL to include the unit price in the group by clause as well. This creates a separate row for each price. Within each of these price point rows in the answer set we can count the number of transactions, add up total sales, and perform any computation we wish.

THE TRANSACTION MODEL

The third way to model inventory is to record every transaction that affects inventory. Inventory transactions include the following:

- Receive shipment line item
- Place SKU into inspection hold
- Release SKU from inspection hold
- Place SKU into inspection failed with reason
- Mark SKU for return to vendor with reason
- Place SKU in bin
- Authorize SKU for sale
- Pick SKU from bin
- Package SKU for shipment
- Ship SKU to customer
- Bill customer
- Receive SKU from customer with reason
- Return SKU to inventory from customer return
- Remove SKU from inventory with reason

Each of these transaction types is accompanied by the identification of the SKU, the warehouse, the time, and in most cases, a single amount representing the quantity of the SKU affected by the transaction. The fact table representing inventory transactions is quite simple (Figure 3.4).

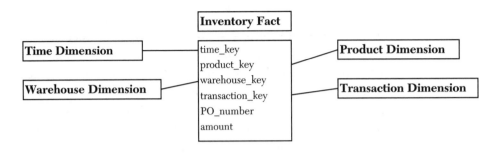

FIGURE 3.4

The inventory transaction model.

The transaction dimension has one record for every possible transaction type as well as every possible reason code for those transactions with reasons. Even with every possible reason code, the number of transaction types will be quite small, typically less than 100.

The single amount field is typical of a transaction level fact table, since the target of a single transaction is usually a single naked amount. Since transaction level fact tables are important, we state this as a design principle:

 Transaction-level fact tables have a characteristic structure, with as much surrounding context as possible expressed in conventional dimensions. Frequently, a degenerate dimension such as a purchase order number is present. The list of facts is almost always a single amount field.

It is important not to limit oneself to the literal transaction record that may be downloaded during the extract process. It is almost always possible to deduce more context, and hence more dimensionality, from other factors that are known about the transactions being processed. The warehouse identification might well be an example.

Even though the transaction-level fact table is very simple, it contains the most detailed information possible about inventory since it is by definition a mirror of the fine-scale inventory manipulations. Even so, it is impractical to use this table as the sole basis for tracking inventory. Although it is theoretically possible to reconstruct the exact inventory position at any moment in time by rolling all possible transactions forward from a known inventory position, this approach is simply too complicated for broad-scale data warehouse questions that span time or products. This leads to a design principle:

> **A transaction-level fact table must in most cases be accompanied by some form of snapshot table to give a practical view of a process.**

The transaction-level fact table is very valuable for measuring the frequency and timing of specific transaction types. For instance, only this table can answer the following questions:

- How many times have we placed a product into an inventory bin on the same day we have picked the product from the same bin at a different time?
- What is the clustering in time of customer returns of a particular SKU?
- How many separate shipments did we receive from vendor X and when did we get them?
- On which SKUs have we had more than one round of QA inspection failures that caused the return of the product to the vendor?

Inventory is one of the most important processes to measure in many businesses. In this chapter we have developed dimensional models for the three most important views of inventory. Either the inventory snapshot model or the delivery status model will serve as a good standalone depiction of inventory. Advanced applications will want to augment one or both of these models with the transaction model. Additionally, we will see in Chapter 5 how we may build a whole succession of inventory snapshot models as separate fact tables. This would be appropriate when inventory is moved from an unallocated state to an allocated state. The first inventory fact table would not have the customer dimension while the second inventory fact table would.

DATABASE SIZING FOR INVENTORY SNAPSHOT (assuming a food distributor)

Please see the discussion at the beginning of Chapter 13 for detailed assumptions.

Time dimension: 2 years × 365 days = 730 days

Product dimension: 60,000 products in each warehouse

Warehouse dimension: 8 warehouses

Number of base fact records: 730 × 60,000 × 8 = *350 million records*

Number of key fields = 3; Number of fact fields = 1; Total fields = 4

Base fact table size = 350 million × 4 fields × 4 bytes = *5.6 GB*

Base fact table size (advanced inventory fact with 4 fact fields) = *9.8 GB*

DATABASE SIZING FOR INVENTORY DELIVERY STATUS (assuming a garment retailer)

Time dimension: 2 years

Product dimension: 400,000 products in each warehouse

Warehouse dimension: 4 warehouses

Vendor dimension: 1 vendor for each product

Number of purchase orders per product per year: 10

Number of base fact records: 2 × 400,000 × 4 × 1 × 10 = *32 million records*

Number of key fields = 4; Number of fact fields = 26; Total fields = 30

Base fact table size = 32 million × 30 fields × 4 bytes = *3.8 GB*

DATABASE SIZING FOR INVENTORY TRANSACTION (assuming a garment retailer)

Time dimension: 2 years

Product dimension: 400,000 products in each warehouse

Warehouse dimension: 4 warehouses

Transaction dimension: 1 vendor for each product

Number of deliveries per product per year: 10

Number of transactions per product delivery: 20

Number of base fact records: $2 \times 400{,}000 \times 4 \times 1 \times 10 \times 20 = \textit{640 million records}$

Number of key fields = 5 (including PO); Number of fact fields = 1; Total fields = 6

Base fact table size = 640 million $\times$ 6 fields $\times$ 4 bytes = *15.4 GB*

4

SHIPMENTS: THE MOST POWERFUL DATABASE

The shipments process in a business is where the product leaves the company and is sent to the customer. Upon delivery, title passes to the customer and the customer owes the company money. A large number of businesses, especially manufacturers, have shipments as a dominant and recognizable process. Many forms of financial services and other services fit this model well enough that this chapter will be relevant to those businesses as well. For a number of reasons this central shipments process is the most effective process to track in a data warehouse. In many ways the resulting database is the most powerful database possible in a business.

We will visualize the shipments process as if we were standing at the loading dock and watching boxes of product being loaded on a truck destined for a particular customer address. Accompanying each shipment is a *shipment invoice*. The shipment invoice governs the current shipment of products on that truck on that day to a particular customer address. The shipment invoice has multiple **line items**, each corresponding to a particular SKU being shipped. Different line items are different SKUs. With each line item are various prices, discounts, and allowances. The extended total amount for each line item, including taxes and shipping charges, is shown.

THE MOST POWERFUL DATABASE

Although we don't show it on the invoice to the customer, a number of other interesting facts are known about each SKU at the time of shipment. We know list prices, manufacturing costs, distribution costs, and marketing costs as well. Thus, at the moment of shipment we know a lot about the state of our business. We call the shipments database the most powerful database because this is the one place in the business where we can see:

- All the company's products
- All the company's customers
- All the contracts and deals under which the company sells products
- All the off-invoice discounts and allowances
- All the money actually owed to the company by customers
- All the variable and fixed costs associated with manufacturing and delivering products
- All the money left over after delivery of product (the "incremental contribution")
- Important measures of customer satisfaction such as on-time delivery, and complete orders

This is worth a design principle:

> For any company that ships products to customers, or performs a similar function, the best place to start a data warehouse is with shipments.

We will choose the grain of the shipments fact table to be the individual shipments invoice line item. An ideal shipments fact table looks like the one in Figure 4.1. The shipments database contains a number of interesting new dimensions we have not seen yet in any of the designs. After describing these dimensions, we will look closely at the facts themselves, which comprise a **P&L**, or profit and loss statement.

The time and product dimensions should be identical in scope and intent to the time and product dimensions we developed both for retail sales and in-

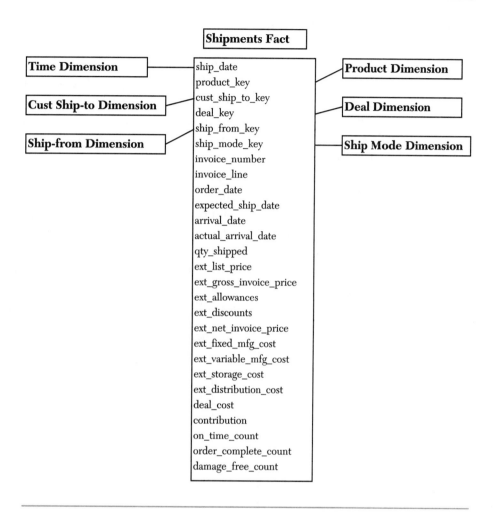

FIGURE 4.1

The ideal shipments fact table.

ventory. In fact, in Chapter 5 we will see that it is essential these dimensions be literally identical so that we can **drill across** from fact table to fact table.

THE SHIP-TO DIMENSION

The customer ship-to dimension contains one record for each possible customer ship-to location. This physically corresponds to every discrete location to which we can ship a product. Customer ship-tos can range from moderately large (10,000 to 50,000 records) to extremely large (millions of records) depending on the nature of our customers. A large packaged goods manufacturer shipping to grocery store chains and distributors might have 30,000 customers. A large catalog retailer might have 30,000,000 customers.

The customer ship-to dimension usually contains more than one hierarchy. From a manufacturer's point of view there are at least three separate and independent hierarchies that are interesting. A typical customer ship-to dimension is shown in Figure 4.2.

The first hierarchy is the natural geographic hierarchy defined by the ship-to location. Since the ship-to location is a point in space, any number of geographic hierarchies may be defined by nesting ever larger geographic entities

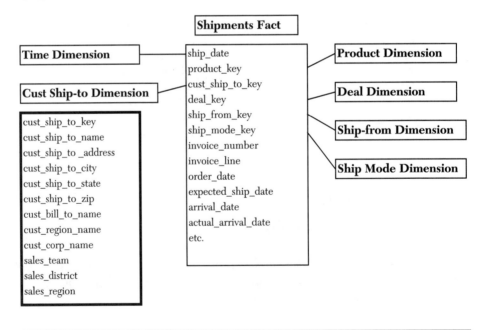

FIGURE 4.2

A typical customer ship-to dimension.

around the point in space. In the United States, the usual geographic hierarchy is City, County, State. Another geographic hierarchy could be five-digit ZIP codes, which by definition have five levels. From this we derive a design principle:

Any dimension whose records define a point in space automatically is capable of supporting multiple independent geographic hierarchies.

A second kind of hierarchy is the customer's organizational hierarchy, assuming that the customer is a corporate entity. We could possibly have customer bill-to, customer region, and customer corporate. Notice that this hierarchy is not necessarily geographic. However, for every base-level record in the customer ship-to dimension, both the physical geography and customer organizational affiliation are well defined. These two hierarchies may roll up differently, but they are always well defined for every ship-to. This leads to a very important design principle:

It is natural and common, especially for customer-oriented dimensions, for a dimension to simultaneously support multiple independent hierarchies. Drilling up and drilling down within each of these hierarchies must be supported in a data warehouse.

The alert reader may have a concern with the assumption previously given that ship-to rolls up to bill-to, which rolls up to customer region. In most large businesses we want each ship-to associated with a single bill-to in a many-to-one relationship. However, the real world rarely is quite this clean. There are always a few exceptions involving some ship-tos that for complex reasons can be associated with more than one bill-to. This breaks the simple hierarchical relationship that we have assumed in the customer ship-to dimension. If, as in most cases, this is a fairly unusual occurrence, it would be reasonable to generalize the customer ship-to dimension so that the grain of this dimension is actually the ship-to-bill-to combination. If this is done, all the other comments regarding hierarchies remain valid. If, for some reason, most of the ship-tos are associated with many bill-tos in a robust many-to-many relationship then ship-to and bill-to probably need to be made into separate dimensions. This might happen if the ship-to identity was purely geographic and the bill-to was determined by the nature of the product shipped, independent of the geography. We can summarize this in another design principle:

 Two loosely correlated attributes that have a many-to-many relationship can be modeled either as a single compound dimension, such as the ship-to-bill-to example, or they can be modeled as separate dimensions, at the designer's discretion.

In both cases, exactly the same information is preserved at the *shipment line item* level. If the attributes are highly correlated (i.e., if the relationship is mostly a **one-to-many relationship**) it is recommended that a single compound dimension be used, since the two attributes can then be browsed against each other much more efficiently than if they intersect only in the fact table, and the total number of keys in the single dimension will only be a little larger than the cardinality of the more numerous attribute. If the attributes are very loosely correlated or have no correlation, then it is best to model them as separate dimensions, because otherwise the number of records in a combined dimension will probably be the product of the numbers of the separate attributes.

A third independent hierarchy in the customer ship-to dimension is the manufacturer's own sales organization. It is appropriate to embed one's own sales organization in the customer dimension if that is the way your company organizes sales. The advantage of doing this is that the relationships between sales teams and customers can be efficiently browsed in the single dimension without traversing the fact table. If, on the other hand, the sales organization maps confusingly onto the geographic customer list, then Sales should be its own independent dimension. In this case it makes sense to navigate through the fact table to discover all the relationships between the sales organization and the customers.

THE DEAL DIMENSION

The deal dimension is similar to the promotion dimension in Chapter 2. The purpose of the deal dimension is to describe the incentives that have been offered to the customer that affects the customer's desire to purchase the products, and to explain the discounts, allowances, and deal dollars that appear in the P&L. Companies frequently call this dimension "promotion," even though it is not a consumer promotion like the grocery store examples. Sometimes this dimension is called "contract." A typical deal dimension is shown in Figure 4.3.

The deal dimension describes the full combination of terms, allowances, and incentives that pertain to the particular invoice line item. The same issues arise here that we faced in the grocery store promotion dimension. If the terms, allowances, and incentives are usefully correlated, then it makes sense to package them into a single deal dimension. If the terms, allowances, and incentives are quite uncorrelated, and we find ourselves generating the Cartesian product of these factors in the dimension, then it probably makes sense to split such a deal dimension into its separate components. Once again, it is not an issue of gaining or losing information, since the database contains the same information in both cases, but rather it is the issues of user convenience and administrative complexity that determine whether to represent these deal factors as multiple dimensions. In a very large fact table, with tens of millions or hundreds of millions of rows, the desire to reduce the number of keys in the fact table composite key would favor keeping the deal dimension as a single

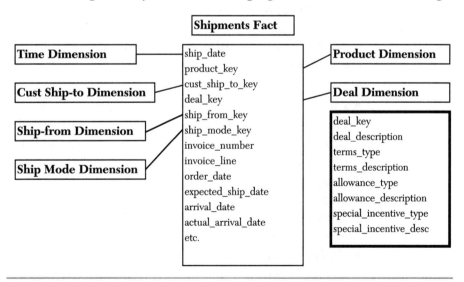

FIGURE 4.3

A typical deal dimension.

dimension. Certainly any deal dimension smaller than 100,000 rows would be tractable in this design.

THE SHIP-FROM DIMENSION

The Ship-from dimension contains one record for manufacturer warehouse or shipping location. This is usually a simple dimension with name, address, contact person, and storage facility type.

THE SHIP MODE DIMENSION

Until recently, a shipments database would have contained a rather simple carrier dimension, which would have recorded the identity of the transportation company taking the product from the loading dock to the customer's ship-to location. In most cases there was only one "mode of delivery," namely "truck to customer" where the customer location was usually a customer distribution center. The customer then took responsibility for transporting the product to its final destination. However, in recent years there has been tremendous interest in tracking alternative and more efficient delivery modes. The new delivery modes include the following:

- *Direct Store Delivery*—where the carrier bypasses the customer's distribution center and takes the product all the way to the retail outlet.
- *Cross Docking*—where the carrier delivers the product to a docking facility but another carrier is waiting to immediately load the product onto a truck. The product does not enter the warehouse.
- *Back Hauling*—where the carrier arranges to make sure that the truck carries product, possibly at a reduced rate, on a return trip from a drop-off point in cases where the truck would otherwise be traveling empty.
- *Custom Pallet Creation*—where multiple products are custom assembled and shrink-wrapped on a pallet destined to go all the way to a retail outlet without being unloaded. Custom pallet creation is often associated with *Electronic Data Interchange* (EDI) between the manufacturer and the customer, where the manufacturer sends the customer an *Advance Ship Notice*

(ASN) describing each custom pallet so that its bar code can be recognized at the receiving dock.

As manufacturers invest in these alternative shipping modes, they are interested in analyzing their businesses along the shipping mode dimension. Figure 4.4 shows a typical ship mode dimension.

PROFIT AND LOSS (P&L)

At the time of shipping product to the customer, most businesses are in a position to identify many of the incremental revenues and costs associated with doing business. This is why the shipments database can be the most powerful database in a business. It is traditional to arrange these revenues and costs in sequence from the "top line," which represents the undiscounted value of the products shipped to the customer, all the way to the "bottom line," which represents the money left over after discounts, allowances, and costs. This list of revenues and costs is called a *profit and loss statement*, or simply, a P&L.

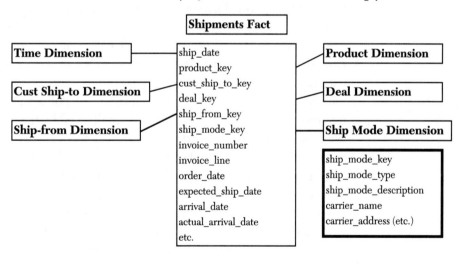

FIGURE 4.4

A typical ship mode dimension.

In the shipments database we are usually in a position to capture only the revenues and costs that are obviously attributable to the sales of specific products. We don't usually make an attempt to carry the P&L all the way to a complete view of company profit, including general and administrative costs. For this reason, we will call the bottom line in our P&L the Contribution.

Keeping in mind that each record in the shipments fact table represents a single line item on the shipments invoice, the elements of our P&L, as shown in Figure 4.1, have the following interpretations:

- *Quantity Shipped*—the number of cases of the product named on the particular line item of the invoice. If this quantity is being compared to other quantities further up or down the value chain, such as cases manufactured or scanned items sold to the consumer, care must be taken to provide for the conversions among these different quantities. The product dimension table is a reasonable place to store case conversion rates but there is some danger in this approach. The case conversion rates must then be tracked very accurately over time, and all user applications will need to find the correct rates and multiply them by the different quantities in the different fact tables. A more brute force but simpler approach is to carry two or even three versions of the quantity shipped directly in the fact table. This reduces the risk of miscalculating the correct equivalent quantity.
- *Extended List Price*—a target or *par* price that may exist only on an internal price sheet, or may be the price shown to the customer and printed at the top of the invoice. This and all subsequent dollar values are extended quantities or, in other words, unit rates multiplied by the quantity shipped. This insistence on actual additive values may seem artificial but it simplifies most applications. Remember that it is very rare for the user to ask for the price from a single row of the fact table. When the user wants an average price drawn from many rows, the extended prices are first added and then the result is divided by the sum of the shipped quantities.
- *Extended Gross Invoice Price*—the price that is printed at the beginning of the entries for this line item. In most cases this is the same as the extended list price.
- *Extended Allowances*—the total amount subtracted on the invoice for promotional and deal-related allowances. The explanation of which allowances are granted is found in the promotion dimension record that joins to this fact table record. These allowance amounts, shown on the invoice, are called

off invoice allowances. The actual invoice may have several allowances under a given line item. In this schema we lump the separate allowances together. If the allowances need to be tracked separately and there are potentially many simultaneous allowances on a given line item, then a different dimensional structure that is not a P&L must be used. Such an *allowance detail* fact table could be used to augment the P&L fact table, and could serve as a drill-down target for a detailed explanation of the allowance bucket in the P&L fact table.

- *Extended Discounts*—the amount subtracted on the invoice for volume terms or payment terms. The explanation of which discounts are taken is also found in the promotion dimension record that points to this fact table record. As discussed in the section on the promotion dimension in this chapter, the decision to code the explanation of the promotion allowances and the discount types together is the designer's prerogative. It makes sense to do this if allowances and discounts are correlated and the users wish to browse within the promotion dimension to study the relationships between allowances and discounts. Note that the discount for payment terms is characteristically a forecast that the customer will pay within the time period called for in the terms agreement. If this does not happen, or if there are other corrections to the invoice, then the finance department will probably back out the original invoice in a subsequent month, and post a new invoice. In all likelihood, the data warehouse will see this as three transactions. Over time, all the additive values in these records will add up correctly, but care must be taken in performing records counts not to impute more activity than actually exists. Large manufacturers process corrections on between 10 percent and 40 percent of all their invoices. Representing the time series of these transactions, of course, is the classic financial reporting dilemma.

Note that all allowances and discounts in this database are represented at the line item level. Of course, some allowances and discounts are calculated at the invoice level, not the line item level. Nevertheless, a heroic effort should be made to allocate all such allowances and discounts, as well as other costs, down to the line item. Only in this way is a complete P&L possible. Although a P&L is quite possible at the invoice level, it must necessarily be independent of the product dimension. This is a serious limitation on the ability of the data warehouse to present P&L slices of a business. For example, brand, category and possibly even divisional P&Ls could not be produced if product were missing. By making the investment to allocate allowances, discounts, and costs to the line item level, the data warehouse will then be able to turn around and present much more useful P&L pictures of the company. We can summarize this in a design principle:

> **A significant effort should be made to allocate allowances, discounts, and activity-related components of cost down to the line item (i.e., product) level in businesses that ship products to their customers.**

- *Extended Net Invoice Price*—the amount the customer is expected to pay for this line item before tax.
- *Extended Fixed Manufacturing Cost*—the amount identified by manufacturing as the pro rata fixed manufacturing cost of the product. This and subsequent items in the P&L are not presented on the invoice to the customer!
- *Extended Variable Manufacturing Cost*—the amount identified by manufacturing as the variable manufacturing cost of the product. This amount may be more or less **activity based,** reflecting the actual location and time of the manufacturing run that produced the product in the box being shipped to the customer. Conversely, this number may be a standard value set by a committee of executives. If the manufacturing costs or any of the other storage and distribution costs are too much "averages of averages," then the detailed P&Ls in the data warehouse may be meaningless. For example, a specific product may go from being profitable to being unprofitable because of a decision elsewhere in the company not to launch a new product line. If the new product launch is postponed, then existing products may be saddled with mindlessly calculated pro rata shares of overhead rather than being judged on a true incremental basis. This is a painful dilemma for most manufacturers. The existence of the data warehouse tends to illuminate this problem and tends to accelerate the adoption of activity-based costing methods and incremental as opposed to fully burdened decision making.
- *Extended Storage Cost*—the cost charged to the product for storage prior to being shipped to the customer.
- *Extended Distribution Cost*—the cost charged to the product for transportation from the point of manufacture to the point of shipment. This cost is notorious for not being activity based. Sometimes a company doesn't want to see that it costs more to do business in Seattle because the manufacturing plant is in Alabama. The distribution cost can possibly include freight to

the customer if the company pays the freight, or the freight cost can be presented as a separate line item in the P&L.

- *Accrued Deal Cost*—the estimated cost, at the invoice line item level, of the special payments made to the customer as part of the overall deal relationship. This is not the off-invoice allowance, but is rather a special payment, usually made directly out of Accounts Payable, to the customer on a quarterly or annual basis in recognition of the overall relationship. Since these payments occur months after the products are shipped, they are normally missed in an invoice-oriented summary. But the potential for these payments is well understood at the time of product shipment, and an estimated, or accrued, value should be supplied to make the P&L accurate. Of course this amount must be allocated down to the product level. It would be possible to leave an additional *actual* field in the P&L blank for many months until the actual payments are known. Such a blank field could be filled in by updating the old records.

- *Contribution*—the final calculation of the Extended Net Invoice less all of the P&L costs discussed above. This is not the true bottom line of the overall company because general and administrative expenses and other financial adjustments have not been made, but it is a very important line in the overall P&L of a company. This line has more names than other lines, depending on the company culture. The most common alternate name is Margin. In some companies, Contribution is called Pocket Profit, apparently because these business people visualize the Contribution as being the money left over in the pocket after selling the product to the customer. Other companies call Contribution the Brand Available, because this is how much money is left over for the brand teams at headquarters to spend on national advertising and product research.

CUSTOMER SATISFACTION

Below the P&L it is very useful to include some simple measures of delivery. At the invoice line item level we insert a 1 or a 0 in separate fields depending on whether the delivery was On Time, Complete, and/or Damage Free. These measures should be made from the customer's perspective, and may need to be collected via an EDI link with the customer's delivery dock. These 1's and

0's are additive across all the dimensions, and yield interesting measures of customer satisfaction for every slice of the business.

THE INVOICE NUMBER: A DEGENERATE DIMENSION

Our shipments fact table contains the original invoice number in every line item record. In a traditional parent-child database design, the invoice number would be associated with a header record that would contain all the information common to the invoice as a whole. However, in our dimensional design, we have systematically extracted all the information from the invoice header and placed this information in the various dimension records. This is a natural consequence of arranging the invoice information dimensionally. Still, the invoice number is useful, and belongs in the database. It serves as the grouping mechanism for the separate line items on the actual invoice, and it is occasionally directly useful for the user moving between a decision support and operational perspective in the data warehouse. In the previous chapter we defined a field like this as a degenerate dimension. Our invoice number is a good example of a degenerate dimension.

If the designer decides that certain data elements actually do belong to the invoice itself, and do not usefully fall into another natural business dimension, then Invoice Number becomes a normal dimension with its own dimension table. However, those designers with a strong parent-child design background should try very hard not to lump the traditional information in the invoice header into an invoice dimension. In most cases, all of the invoice header information belongs to other dimensions.

DATABASE SIZING FOR SHIPMENTS
(assuming a packaged goods manufacturer)

Please see the discussion at the beginning of Chapter 13 for detailed assumptions.

Time dimension: 3 years

Number of shipping invoices per month: 40,000 => 480,000 per year

Number of line items per invoice: 20

Deal dimension: 1 deal per line item on a given invoice

Ship-from dimension: 1 ship from per line item on a given invoice

Ship Mode dimension: 1 ship mode per line item on a given invoice

Number of base fact records: $3 \times 480,000 \times 20 \times 1 \times 1 \times 1 = 28.8$ *million records*

Number of key fields = 8 (including degenerates); Number of fact fields = 19; Total fields = 27

Base fact table size = 28.8 million $\times$ 27 fields $\times$ 4 bytes = *3.1 GB*

5

THE VALUE CHAIN

In the previous three chapters we have developed schemas for various steps in supplying and selling products. In many manufacturing and retail businesses several if not all of these databases would be useful views of the business. By following the progress of products from the point where they are manufactured to point where they are sold, we build a series of databases that represent the value chain of the product flow. This particular value chain is often called the **demand side** of the business, since it represents the steps needed to satisfy the customer's demand for the product. The **supply side** of the business consists of the steps needed to manufacture the products from original ingredients or parts and is modeled separately from the demand side. The supply side of a business feeds the demand side of the business. In this chapter we will discuss designs for both the demand and supply sides.

THE DEMAND VALUE CHAIN

A typical product demand scenario consists of at least six databases, arranged in order from where products originate to where they pass to the ultimate consumer (Figure 5.1).

In examining the list of steps we see that the six databases alternate inventory and flow, inventory and flow, inventory and flow. Specifically, the identities of the above databases are as follows:

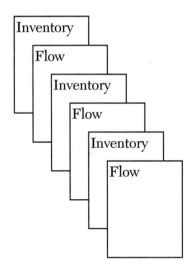

FIGURE 5.1

The demand value chain.

- Finished Goods Inventory
    dimension: Time
    dimension: SKU (Product)
    dimension: Warehouse

- Manufacturing Shipments to Distribution Center (Flow)
    dimension: Time
    dimension: SKU (Product)
    dimension: Warehouse
    dimension: Distribution Center
    dimension: Contract (or Deal or Promotion)
    dimension: Ship Mode (including Carrier)

- Distribution Center Inventory
    dimension: Time
    dimension: SKU (Product)
    dimension: Distribution Center

- Distribution Center Depletions to Retail Stores (Flow)
    dimension: Time
    dimension: SKU (Product)

> dimension: Distribution Center
> dimension: Retail Store
> dimension: Contract (or Deal or Promotion)
> dimension: Ship Mode (including Carrier)

- Retail Store Inventory
    dimension: Time
    dimension: SKU (Product)
    dimension: Retail Store

- Retail Store Sales (Flow)
    dimension: Time
    dimension: SKU (Product)
    dimension: Retail Store
    dimension: Promotion (sometimes called Store Condition)
    dimension: Customer (maybe)

The physical products move sequentially through this value chain. In some cases a single company owns all of these steps including the warehouses and vehicles needed to move the product down the chain. In most cases, however, a manufacturer contracts with a carrier to ship the products to the distribution center operator, who may be a separate middleman. The distribution center may then deliver the product to the potentially independent retail stores through yet another carrier. When all these entities are separate businesses, it is more difficult to collect the data representing the entire value chain, although in the grocery and drugstore trades most of these steps are accessible, either through internal data sources or external syndicated sources.

All six databases share the product dimension as well as the time dimension. The second and the fourth databases have ship mode (carrier) dimensions, although it is likely that the actual carriers identified are mostly different. The second, third, and fourth databases have distribution center dimensions. The fifth and sixth databases have store dimensions. The second, fourth, and sixth databases, which represent the flows or movements in the value chain, all may have promotion (or deal or contract) dimensions.

The attraction of assembling a value chain of databases is that several of the databases can be combined in a single report by drilling across. A drill-across report can show a snapshot or a slice of the entire value chain that shows how far the **bulge of product** has moved from manufacturing to the final customer. The specific techniques needed to build drill across applications are discussed in detail in Chapter 16, although from an overall schema perspective it is worthwhile to discuss the following requirement. It is very important in those cases where the dimensions that span multiple databases mean the same thing that the respective physical dimension tables be exactly the same. We state this more precisely as a design principle:

> In order to support drill-across applications, all constraints on dimension attributes must evaluate to exactly the same set of dimensional entities from one database in the value chain to the next database in the value chain.

In other words, a constraint on lemon-flavored products at any point in the value chain must mean exactly the same set of products at all points in the value chain. In this way constraints and row headers can be applied to the common dimensions up and down the value chain. The design principle will obviously be satisfied if a given common dimension table is, in fact, implemented as a single physical table that all the fact tables share. However, there are two subtle generalizations of the design principle that are possible in advanced situations.

Dimensions with Reduced Detail

Sometimes the product dimension may be known by the manufacturer at a finer level of detail than it is known further down the value chain. For instance, the manufacturer may be able to track finished goods inventory and manufacturing shipments by manufacturing lot number, which is at a finer grain than the SKU number visible to the distribution center and retail store. The manufacturer thus possesses a product dimension table that has more rows and columns than the distribution center or retail store. In this case it will not be possible to do a value chain analysis that depends on an individual lot number. However, if the smaller product dimension tables at the distribution center and retail store are properly constructed rollups of the manufacturer's SKU table, then drill-across applications can be constructed that only rely on attributes that legitimately exist in all the versions of the dimension, such as Lemon. "Relying on" means that the attribute is constrained or is used as a row header in the application. These points are discussed in more detail in Chapter 16.

Derived Dimensions that Support Aggregates

Although we have not developed the architecture for aggregates yet, it is worth noting this second generalization of our drill-across design principle because it is similar to the first generalization. We will see in Chapter 13 that it is extremely important to build derived (summarized) fact tables at various high levels to improve the performance of queries that would otherwise fetch a large number of detailed fact records. In our product dimension, for example, we could build aggregate records representing flavor totals, such as Lemon. We recommend in Chapter 13 that in this case, a derived product dimension table and derived fact table be created that contain only data that logically rolls up from the level of flavor. If this has been done for some, but not all, databases in the value chain, the question arises whether a drill-across application can opportunistically use a derived aggregate dimension table if such a table is encountered in one of the databases. The answer, under this generalization of the design principle, is Yes. If the constraints and rows headers of the overall drill-across application are consistent with the derived aggregate dimension table then the derived aggregate dimension table may be used even though it may not have been created for all the databases in the value chain. We will see in Chapter 16 that any application that supports drill-across and automatic aggregate navigation must handle this case.

SUBDIVISIONS WITHIN THE VALUE CHAIN

It is certainly possible to have more than the six steps we have proposed in the value chain. Another common step is **transshipments** that occur within the manufacturer's operations before shipment to the distribution center. This would happen if the manufacturer had multiple manufacturing plants and shuffled finished goods around to various holding points before servicing the orders from the distribution center. Frequently, these transshipments can be put in the same database as the manufacturing shipments.

Another common subdivision of the value chain is breaking the inventory steps into multiple pieces. It makes sense to do this when inventory passes from unallocated status to allocated status, since when inventory is allocated it has gained a new dimension representing the destination of the upcoming shipment.

Finally, the second and fourth flow steps are usually broken down into Orders and Shipments. In most cases Shipments have a many-to-one relationship to Orders. All of these businesses must contend with Returns, which are a kind of reverse Shipment. Businesses that track Returns carefully almost always represent Returns in a separate database so that special attributes such as Return Reason and Disposition can be represented in new dimensions. Also, it is likely that the production system that records Returns is separate from the production system that records Shipments.

THE SUPPLY VALUE CHAIN

Supply-side analysis and supply-side data are fundamentally different from the demand side. The supply side represents the manufacturing process and is concerned with acquiring ingredients or parts and assembling them into finished goods. Supply-side data includes measurements of continuous flow processes as well as the discrete document-oriented processes we encountered on the demand side. Typical databases in the supply value chain include the following:

- Purchase Orders
    dimension: Time
    dimension: Ingredient (or Part)
    dimension: Supplier
    dimension: Deal (or Contract)

- Deliveries
    dimension: Time
    dimension: Ingredient (or Part)
    dimension: Supplier
    dimension: Plant
    dimension: Ship Mode (including Carrier)
    dimension: Deal (or Contract)

- Materials Inventory
     dimension: Time
     dimension: Ingredient (or Part)
     dimension: Plant

- Process Monitoring
     dimension: Time
     dimension: Ingredient
     dimension: Process
     dimension: Plant

- Bill of Materials
     dimension: Time
     dimension: Ingredient
     dimension: SKU (Product)

- Finished Goods Inventory
     dimension: Time
     dimension: SKU (Product)
     dimension: Warehouse

- Manufacturing Plans
     dimension: Time
     dimension: SKU (Product)

Unlike the demand value chain, where the product dimension is usefully threaded through the entire chain, in the supply value chain there is no dimension except time that is directly common to all of the databases. This is a natural consequence of the manufacturing process, in which there is a many-to-many relationship between ingredients (or parts) and finished goods SKUs. Although it is relationally possible to link an ingredient all the way through to the finished goods SKUs, it always boils down conceptually to a two-step process, where first the ingredient is presented to the bill of materials fact table, and all the possible values of the product dimension are discovered (i.e., which SKUs contain the ingredient). Then the list of finished goods SKUs can be used further down the value chain. It is not normally feasible to keep the ingredient dimension directly connected to the finished goods inventory fact table because that would force the grain of the finished goods inventory fact table to be SKU by ingredient, and no standard demand-side production databases handle data this way.

6

THE BIG DIMENSIONS

Now that we have designed several serious product-oriented databases and we are about to design some serious customer-oriented databases, it is worthwhile to discuss in detail the characteristics of the two dominant dimensions in these databases, namely product and customer.

THE PRODUCT DIMENSION

The product dimension describes the complete portfolio of what a company sells. In most cases, this turns out to be a number that is surprisingly large, at least from an outsider's point of view. A prominent manufacturer of dog and cat food in the United States, for example, tracks no less than 17,000 manufacturing variations of all its products, including retail products everyone (or every dog and cat) is familiar with, as well as many special products sold through commercial and veterinary channels. The product dimension in the data warehouse in most companies is derived directly from product master files maintained on a production system, usually an inventory tracking system. The product dimension we developed in Chapter 2 looks like Figure 6.1.

The existence of the product master is a tremendous help to the maintenance of the data warehouse's product dimension table, but a number of transformations and administrative steps must take place to convert the production product master file into the product dimension table. These steps include the following:

```
┌─────────────────────────────┐
│ Product Dimension           │
├─────────────────────────────┤
│ product_key                 │
│ SKU_description             │
│ SKU_number                  │
│ package_size                │
│ brand                       │
│ subcategory                 │
│ category                    │
│ department                  │
│ package_type                │
│ diet_type                   │
│ weight                      │
│ weight_unit_of_measure      │
│ units_per_retail_case       │
│ units_per_shipping_case     │
│ cases_per_pallet            │
│ shelf_width                 │
│ shelf_height                │
│ shelf_depth                 │
│ ... and many more           │
└─────────────────────────────┘
```

FIGURE 6.1

The grocery store product dimension.

- Possible remapping of the production product master key to avoid duplicate use of the product key over time. It is usually the case that the data warehouse has a longer time perspective than the inventory system, and where the reuse of a product key may be acceptable within the inventory system, it will raise havoc in the data warehouse. A production product master key may well be an industry UPC. Even UPCs get reused by manufacturers who either make administrative mistakes or do not understand the need to avoid duplicate use.
- Possible remapping of the production product master key to create a much shorter and more efficient join key to be used in the data warehouse. Even an industry-standard UPC code is an 11-digit alphanumeric key in the United States, and a 12-digit alphanumeric key internationally. If the key is this long or especially if it is even longer, it begins to raise questions as to whether performance will be compromised by the need to perform millions of multiple-word string comparisons in the inner loop of large queries.

- Generalization of the production product master key to track changing descriptions or formulations of the product in those cases where the production system has not changed the master key but has changed the description of the product. This is an instance of a *slowly changing dimension*, discussed later in this chapter.
- Generalization of the production product master key to describe aggregate products in the aggregate summary tables that are a part of every data warehouse. In other words, what is the SKU code for a brand or a category? The procedures for doing this are discussed in detail in Chapter 14.
- Addition of readable text strings to augment or replace any numeric code existing in the production product master file. Usually the excuse is that "the marketing people are familiar with the codes." The only reason marketing people are familiar with numeric codes is that they have been forced to use them! Remember that the fields in a dimension table are the sole source of constraints and report breaks in a data warehouse. The candidates for a possible constraint are presented to the user by enumerating the distinct values of the field from the dimension table. Codes are unfriendly and virtually useless compared to readable text. There are an amazing number of reports produced even today whose row and column headers consist entirely of cryptic numbers. No normal person can decipher such a report. If the readable text is not supplied with the production product master file download, then it is essential that the data warehouse team provide an attribute completion function that supplies this text every time the production product master file is copied to the data warehouse. Keep in mind that cryptic abbreviations of readable text are nearly as bad as outright numeric codes. Cryptic abbreviations should also be augmented or replaced with readable text.
- Quality assurance of all the text strings supplied from the production product master to eliminate variations in product descriptions based on trivial punctuation or spelling differences. SQL will gleefully produce a new line in a report if it is using an attribute for a row header in which the attribute differs in any way between products. However, a word of warning must be given here. If the data warehouse team succeeds in cleaning up the production product master file, then the data warehouse dimension table may well become the new company product master file, and the flow of responsibility will be reversed! Perhaps this is not all bad news.

These administrative steps result in the following design principle:

> Although the production product master file is the source of product identification, it must be transformed and augmented on a continuing basis in order to serve as the product dimension in the data warehouse. The primary steps needed are the generalization and/or replacement of the primary product key, and the completion and quality assurance of the descriptive attributes.

A good rule of thumb for a serious product dimension for a large manufacturer or retail company is that there should be at least 50 descriptive text fields, and 100 fields is not a foolish number. Of course, in these 50 fields we include useful standard numeric descriptions of products, such as the size, the weight, and the dimensions. Even though such fields are numeric, they are not confused with facts in the fact table. Facts in the fact table vary continuously every time or nearly every time we observe the marketplace. Dimension table attributes naturally describe the item in the dimension, do not vary because of the influence of another dimension, and are virtually constant over time.

THE MERCHANDISE HIERARCHY

In Chapter 2, we described a typical merchandise hierarchy. Our example typical grocery store product had the following merchandise hierarchy attached to it:

SKU:	Green 3-pack Brawny Paper Towels, UPC # xxxxxxxxx
Package Size:	3-pack
Brand:	Brawny
Subcategory:	Paper Towels
Category:	Paper
Department:	Grocery

The merchandise hierarchy is simply a collection of attributes describing a product that happens to be administered so that they each have a many-to-one relationship as we ascend the hierarchy. For example, there are several SKUs with Package Size = 3-pack. All of these SKUs also have Brand = Brawny, Subcategory = Paper Towels, Category = Paper, and Department = Grocery.

THE TRUE MEANING OF DRILL DOWN

There is a tendency for relational database tool vendors to think too much like computer scientists, and to insist that drilling down means descending the product hierarchy. Actually, drilling down really means "show me more detail," usually to explain something remarkable in the data. In this context we see that drilling down simply means "add another row header to the report." *Any* row header will do! Adding a row header to an existing report will almost always break the existing rows of a report down into constituent rows distinguished by the values of the new row header. For instance, say our existing report looks like this:

BRAND	PACKAGE SIZE	SALES
Brawny	2-Pack	$50
Brawny	3-Pack	$110
Brawny	6-Pack	$75

Then by adding Color as an additional row header the same report expands into this:

BRAND	PACKAGE SIZE	COLOR	SALES
Brawny	2-Pack	White	$8
Brawny	2-Pack	Brown	$5
Brawny	2-Pack	Green	$37
Brawny	3-Pack	White	$22
Brawny	3-Pack	Green	$88
Brawny	6-Pack	White	$14
Brawny	6-Pack	Pink	$12
Brawny	6-Pack	Brown	$4
Brawny	6-Pack	Green	$45

From this we see that the green paper towels are the big sellers and it is really questionable whether we should keep selling the brown color. The addition of Color as a drill-down step was the key insight into this business analysis. In Chapter 2, we stated the design principle that drilling down is simply the addition of a row header to a report, and drilling up is simply the removal of a row header from a report.

MULTIPLE HIERARCHIES

There is a strong temptation to call the merchandise hierarchy previously described "the hierarchy." In fact, some query tool vendors reserve a button called Drill Down to be used to descend "the hierarchy." It is very possible in the product dimension, as well as the customer dimension, for there to be more than one hierarchy. For instance, Sales and Finance could think of the merchandise as belonging to two dissimilar hierarchies. Finance could organize the product space according to inventory classifications such as Storage Type (Regular Shelf, Refrigerated, and Bulk Bin), followed by Shelf Life Type (Stackable/Nonstackable for Regular Shelf, No Freeze/Hard Freeze for Refrigerated, and Regular/Sanitary for Bulk Bin). Sales and Finance could each separately drill down and drill up within their hierarchies. Most interestingly, either group could start drilling down in their hierarchy, and then continue by adding row headers from the other hierarchy! Under paper towels, we would find interesting values for Storage Type and Shelf Life Type.

We summarize this discussion with a design principle:

A typical dimension contains one or more natural hierarchies, together with other attributes that do not have a hierarchical relationship to any of the attributes in the dimension. Any of the attributes, whether or not they belong to a hierarchy, can freely be used in drilling down and drilling up.

RESISTING THE URGE TO SNOWFLAKE

Dimensions with hierarchies are often decomposed by well-meaning database designers into a **snowflake** structure. Each of the many-to-one relationships is celebrated as a separate table. For example, our product dimension with Sales and Finance hierarchies would end up looking like Figure 6.2.

The computer scientists among us think that this looks beautiful. Unfortunately, our average user is intimidated by this diagram. All other technical objections aside, this impact on our end users is enough to recommend against using a snowflake structure to represent hierarchies.

The usual reason given for adopting a snowflake structure is to save storage. In a typical large product table 100 MB in size, it is possible to imagine saving several MB by not copying the most highly repeated text fields thousands of times. However, in the disk space calculation for the data warehouse we are likely to be looking at the following:

Fact table data size:	30 GB
Fact table index size:	20 GB
Largest dimension table size (product):	0.1 GB
Savings by snowflaking:	0.005 GB (perhaps)
Total database size without snowflaking (rounded to reasonable accuracy):	50 GB
Total database size with snowflaking (rounded to reasonable accuracy):	50 GB

In other words, snowflaking is irrelevant to the issue of planning the disk capacity of a data warehouse.

THE THREAT TO BROWSING PERFORMANCE

Even if we thought that snowflaking was otherwise benign and couldn't hurt, we would be in danger of destroying browsing performance. Remember that browsing is the act of navigating around in a dimension, either to gain an intuitive understanding of how the various attributes correlate with each other or to build a constraint on the dimension as a whole. It is very misleading to think about browsing in a small dimension table, where all the relationships

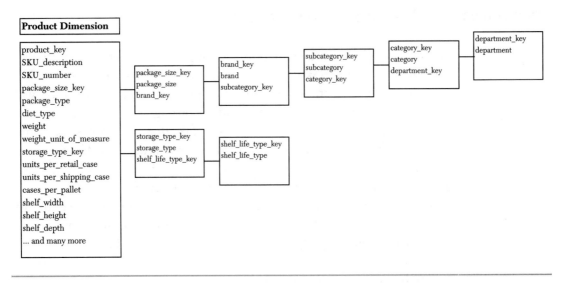

FIGURE 6.2

A snowflaked product dimension.

can be imagined or visualized by the reader of a textbook. Real dimension ta-bles have thousands of entries, and the typical user does not intimately know the relationships. In order to discover the relationships among the attributes, they often need to be queried together in pairs or groups of three or more. If there are 17,000 dog and cat foods in the product dimension, it is not too help-ful to ask for a pull down list of the product descriptions. It might actually be bad news if the computer succeeded in displaying the list of 17,000 dog and cat foods. It is essential in this case to be able to constrain on a first attribute, such as flavor, and then maybe another attribute such as package type, before attempting to display the pull down list of product descriptions. Notice that the first two constraints were not drawn strictly from a product hierarchy.

If a large product table has been split apart into a snowflake, and robust browsing is attempted among widely separated attributes, possibly lying along various tree structures, it is inevitable that browsing performance will be com-promised, if not destroyed. The best hope for general-purpose browsing in a large dimension table is a flat table implementation, both to preserve the best measure of performance and to present the simplest view to the end user.

The only defendable exception to the prohibition on snowflaking a dimen-sion comes when a large block of repeated demographic data is attached to the customer dimension. The demographic data may describe the demographics of the customer's zip code, and such data is probably sourced from an outside third party. In some cases the demographic data may consist of 50 or more numerical attributes describing population cluster counts in that zip code. If your customer file has hundreds of customers in each zip code, it may make sense in this extreme case not to duplicate such a large block of data so many times. We end this section with a design principle:

> Do not snowflake your dimensions, even if they are large. If you do snowflake your dimensions, be prepared to live with poor browsing performance.

REALLY BIG CUSTOMER DIMENSIONS

In Chapter 4 we discussed a medium-sized customer dimension (ship-to) appropriate to a manufacturing company that might have 20,000 customers. Such a customer dimension is quite similar to the product dimension we have been discussing in this chapter. It could have 50 to 100 attributes, and would certainly have two or more naturally occurring hierarchies embedded within the dimension. In the customer dimension, these hierarchies would include the ship-to/bill-to/Corporate Customer hierarchy, as well as the Location/City/County/State hierarchy, and possibly the manufacturer's Sales Team/Sales Territory/Sales District/Sales Region hierarchy. Just as in the product dimension, all of these customer hierarchies could exist simultaneously. Again, we recommend that the customer dimension be implemented as a flat table, to preserve browsing performance and simplicity of presentation to the end user.

In a number of businesses, however, the customer dimension is based on individual human beings. Financial service institutions, telephone companies, and catalog supply retailers all have customer dimensions with millions or even tens of millions of entries. Such large dimensions require special treatment. Even if a very clean flat table implementation has been achieved, it generally takes too long to browse among the relationships in such a big table. Certainly the standard relational database approach with separate B-Tree indexes on the dimension table attributes is inadequate. A number of vendors are returning to some of the ideas pioneered by the CCA Model 204 database, which used elegant bit-vector indexes to query the relationships among attributes in very large customer lists.

As exciting and useful as new indexing technology may prove to be in the future, it is possible today to attack large customer dimensions and get usable performance. The first insight is that there are a number of fields in a large customer dimension that will almost never be the source of constraints, and hence do not need to be indexed. These mostly include the first name fields and the street address fields. Last name fields are mildly useful in a data warehouse, and the state and zip code fields are quite useful.

The fields that get used heavily in a customer dimension are the demographic fields, such as age, sex, number of children, income level, education level, and behavior scores related to purchasing or the use of credit. Not only are these the fields that get used heavily, but these are the fields that get compared together in order to select an interesting subset of the customer base.

DEMOGRAPHIC MINIDIMENSIONS

The most effective technique for using these demographic attributes in a large customer dimension is to separate one or more sets of these attributes into separate **demographic minidimensions**. Although logically these attributes should remain in the primary customer dimension, we can get very significant gains in performance by creating the minidimensions. If five or six of the demographic variables are isolated into a separate table, we need only store the distinct combinations of demographic attributes that actually occur. For continuously valued attributes such as age or income level, we must group the distinct values of the attributes into bands. Although this restricts the use of this attribute to a set of predefined bands, this technique drastically reduces the number of combinations of this demographic variable with the other demographic variables. The minidimension should be designed to have less than 100,000 distinct combinations in order to preserve high performance for browsing.

The demographic minidimension can be joined either directly to the fact table or to the customer table itself, as shown in Figure 6.3. Note that the demographics key can exist as a foreign key in both the fact table and customer dimension table. The demographics key should be part of the composite key

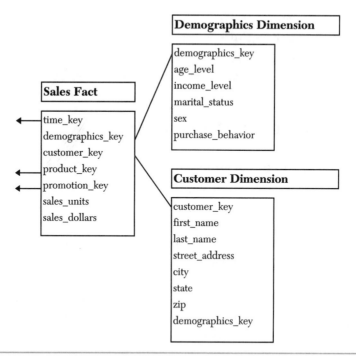

FIGURE 6.3

A typical demographic minidimension together with a customer dimension.

of the fact table in order to provide most efficient access to the fact table through the demographics attributes. The demographics key can also be used effectively directly with the customer dimension table when demographics attributes need to be browsed interactively with the customer dimension attributes. The demographics attributes can also be used with the customer dimension to produce mailing lists.

A single demographics minidimension can be generalized into several minidimensions, where each minidimension is a package of attributes that can be efficiently browsed. It is not necessary to make these minidimensions logically disjoint. In other words, the State field describing the location of a customer can be part of a purely geographic minidimension as well as a mixed behavioral and demographic minidimension. All of these constructs are artifices to allow rapid browsing and rapid access to the fact table. We summarize this section with a design principle:

The best approach for tracking changes in really huge dimensions is to break off one or more minidimensions from the dimension table, each consisting of small clumps of attributes that have been administered to have a limited number of values.

SLOWLY CHANGING DIMENSIONS

Up to this point in the design of dimensional databases, we have pretended that each of the dimensions is logically independent from all the other dimensions. In particular, dimensions like product and customer have been assumed to be independent of time. In the real world this is not strictly true. Over time the descriptions and formulations of real products slowly evolve. Customers in particular are constantly changing. Humans change their names, get married and divorced, have more children, and modify their addresses. Sales forces periodically change the names of their districts and regions, but may continue to employ the same people to call on the same customers. As database designers we must make a decision about how to handle these changes. Early in this book we made the claim that one of the main responsibilities of the data warehouse was to correctly represent prior history status. For example, in an insurance company it is essential that the description of the insured party be correctly represented as of the time of a claim, and not simply be the current description of the insured party.

The answer is not to put everything in the fact table or to make every dimension time dependent. We would rapidly talk ourselves back into a full-blown entity relation diagram with consequential disastrous loss of understandability and performance. We instead exploit the fact that most dimensions are *almost* constant over time and that we can preserve the independent dimensional structure with only relatively minor additions to capture the time-changing nature. We call these almost constant dimensions *slowly changing dimensions*.

When we encounter a slowly changing dimension we face making one of the following three fundamental choices. Each choice results in a different degree of tracking changes over time:

- Overwriting the old values in the dimension record and thereby losing the ability to track the old history.

- Creating an additional dimension record at the time of the change with the new attribute values, and thereby segmenting history very accurately between the old description and the new description.
- Creating new "current" fields within the original dimension record to record the new attribute values, while keeping the original attribute values as well, thereby being able to describe history both forward and backward from the change either in terms of the original attribute values or in terms of the current attribute values.

For specificity, we call these three choices Type One, Type Two, and Type Three slowly changing dimensions. To be more concrete, let us assume that in our customer dimension we have a record describing Mary Jones. Up until January 15, 1994, Mary was not married and thus the Marital Status field in her customer record had the value Single. Mary then got married on January 15, 1994. We will focus on the how to handle the change in the Marital Status field, and ignore possible changes to other fields that might have taken place at the same time, including Last Name and Address.

Type One

We may choose to implement this change as a Type One slowly changing dimension. In other words, we overwrite the Marital Status field in Mary Jones' record with the value Married. No changes are needed elsewhere in the dimension record and no keys are affected anywhere in the database. In this case we have decided that there is no value in keeping the old description. We can only determine this by understanding the end user's analysis needs and how important the tracking of history is. The advantage of overwriting, obviously, is that it is the easiest to implement. Of course, the use of the Type One slowly changing dimension avoids the real goal, which is to accurately track history. The use of Type One is not always crazy, however. If we had discovered that our original data on Mary Jones was in error and that she had been married all along, then we almost certainly would overwrite the Marital Status field in order to correct it.

Type Two

More frequently we would decide that we need two correct descriptions of Mary Jones. The original description with Marital Status = Single would apply to all fact records up to January 15, 1994 and a new description would apply to all fact records on or after January 15, 1994. We accomplish this by creating a second customer dimension record for Mary Jones with Martial Status = Married. The second customer dimension record must also have a new customer key since the customer key defines uniqueness in the customer dimension. This leads to an important design principle:

> The use of the Type Two slowly changing dimension requires that the dimension key be generalized. It may be sufficient to take the underlying production key and add two or three version digits to the end of the key to simplify the key generation process.

In other words, Mary Jones' actual customer Number, which may be found on her credit card, cannot continue to be used as the literal key for the customer dimension. If we are going to have multiple copies of records describing Mary Jones as a customer, then we need a generalized key. Two version digits at the end of the original customer key would allow up to 100 snapshots of Mary Jones' changing status, while three digits would allow 1,000 snapshots.

Notice that the production system probably does not create or maintain the generalized key. That is typically the responsibility of the data warehouse team and must be implemented in the data extract system, which will be discussed in detail in Chapter 14. In any case, we have another design principle:

> The creation of generalized keys is usually the responsibility of the data warehouse team, and always requires metadata to keep track of the generalized keys that have already been used.

The use of the Type Two slowly changing dimension inevitably **partitions history**. We use Mary Jones' first (Single) description up to January 15, 1994 in any fact table records that we create for her, presumably involving sales. Beginning January 15, 1994, we use the second (Married) dimension table record to tie to the fact table. This results in an exceptionally smooth transition across the marriage event. If we are simply constraining the customer dimension on the name Mary Jones, then we will pick up both customer dimension records and attempt to join them to the fact table. The first Mary Jones record will happen to join only to sales fact records before January 15, 1994. The second Mary Jones record will happen to join only to sales fact records on or after January 15, 1994. There is no intrinsic need to place an effective date for the change in Mary Jones' customer record, and there is absolutely no need to constrain the dimension table by time values in order to get the right answer. This is often a point of confusion in the design of Type Two slowly changing dimensions. It is worth a design principle:

> **The Type Two slowly changing dimension automatically partitions history and an application must not be required to place any time constraints on effective dates in the dimension.**

The avoidance of the extraneous time constraints for Type Two slowly changing dimensions is intended to reduce applications complexity and unnecessarily redundant constraints. But even further, in some cases an effective date is meaningless and an attempted constraint on an effective date will yield the wrong business result! This can happen in cases where the dimension record does not represent a single unique thing like Mary Jones, but rather represents a class of things like cans of soup. In the case of cans of soup, we imagine that a product dimension record represents a particular UPC. At some point in time, say January 15, 1994, the salt content formulation for newly manufactured cans of soup changes from salty to salt free, reflecting a real change in the soup's ingredients. In real grocery stores, this situation occurs frequently, and the grocery industry routinely issues a new UPC code to describe the altered product. We see that in this context, the UPC code is nothing more than a glorified generalized key, maintained by the manufacturer of the soup.

Now when we look at the database of grocery store sales, we don't see such an abrupt partitioning of history. The old cans of soup will continue to sell in stores past January 15, 1994 until they are depleted. This will vary from store to store. The new soups will appear on the shelves no earlier than January 15, 1994, and will gradually supersede the old soups. There will be a transition period where in any given store, both types of cans will be moving past the cash registers. The cash registers will recognize both UPC codes and will have no difficulty handling the sale of either type of soup. Again, the use of the separate dimension records automatically partitions the fact table and the user doesn't need to be concerned with whether there are two formulations of the soup unless the user is using the Salt Content field. The important point here is that although we could put a Manufacturing Effective Date in the product dimension record, we don't dare constrain on it to partition sales because it has no physical relevance, and would give us the wrong answer. Perhaps for this reason, commercial syndicated data describing consumer packaged goods does not typically have effective dates in the product dimension.

Since we see that the Type Two slowly changing dimension partitions history, we will not be able use the new value of a changed attribute on old history or vice versa. Returning to the Mary Jones example, if we constrain on Marital Status = Married, we will not see Mary Jones before January 15, 1994. In most cases this is just what we want. In a few cases we want to see what history "would have been like if it had been that way all the time." This happens most frequently when describing sales force changes. There is an abrupt point in time where the names of all the sales districts are changed. For a few months however, there is a desire to track old history in terms of the new district names, and conversely to track new history in terms of old district names. Usually the rationalization is to be able to compare performance across the transition. However, these kinds of comparisons cannot be done with the Type Two slowly changing dimension. This is where Type Three is needed. Because of the complexity of Type Three applications we try to stall on implementing this solution. Usually after a few months people lose interest in the old sales district names anyway, and the requirement goes away.

Type Three

When a dimension value changes, roughly half of the time a Type One solution is chosen and the other half a Type Two solution is chosen. Occasionally there is a legitimate need to track both the old and the new values of a changed attribute both forward and backward across the time of the change. This is the Type Three slowly changing dimension. In this case we do not issue a new dimension record, but rather we add a new field for the affected attribute. In Mary Jones' case, we would add a new attribute called Current Marital Status. We probably would rename the old Marital Status field to be Original Marital Status. In this case it makes some sense to also add a Current Marital Status Effective Date field as well. Now every time Mary Jones' marital status changes, we overwrite the Current Marital Status field and change the Effective Date. We always leave the Original Marital Status field alone. Now we can track all of history involving Mary Jones using either the Original Marital Status field or the Current Marital Status field. Since the fact table sees only a single customer key value, the only way we can partition history on the basis of the change is to use the Effective Date field.

The Type Three slowly changing dimension cannot be used to describe accurately the change in a class of objects like the can of soup. We would not be able to see when the individual cans of the old formulation were actually depleted from the stores. This situation arises once in a while when a manufacturer forgets and changes a product formulation without making sure that the UPC code changes. Sales reported back from the field in this case cannot distinguish the formulations.

The Type Three slowly changing dimension is equipped to handle only the original and the current values of the changed attribute. Intermediate values are lost. Of course, if there is a need to accurately partition history, then Type Two should be used instead, and all the myriad changes can be tracked. It would be theoretically possible to mix Type Two and Type Three but all of this results in increased applications complexity, which will rapidly not be worth the effort. End users are not impressed with complexity.

SLOWLY CHANGING MINIDIMENSIONS

Earlier in this chapter we discussed introducing artificial minidimensions in cases where we had a very large dimension like individual customers. The reason for doing this was to drastically improve browsing and constraining performance. These minidimensions also have a salubrious effect on the slowly changing customer dimension. Often the very attributes isolated in the minidimension are the same attributes that change over time and whose distinct values need to be tracked. If we assume that the minidimension already contains every possible combination of the demographic variables, then when a given customer's profile changes we simply switch to a different demographics key as we continue to load fact table records on a periodic basis. We don't need to create a new customer dimension record in this case because we already have created all the demographic profiles we need in the minidimension.

The alert reader will object that if we also have embedded the demographics key in the customer table as shown earlier in this chapter, then we still need to issue a new customer record to track the correspondence with the changing demographics. In this case, to avoid creating new customer records, we recommend a hybrid approach. Instead of creating a new customer record, we overwrite the demographics key in the customer record whenever it changes. In this way we can browse the current demographic profile with the rest of the customer attributes at any time. Old historical demographic profiles can be constructed at any time by referring to the fact table and picking up the simultaneous customer key and its contemporary demographics key, which in general will be different from the current demographics key.

7

FINANCIAL SERVICES, ESPECIALLY BANKS

The first part of this book has been concerned with tangible product businesses where an elaborate value chain exists to manufacture, ship, and sell products, which we called SKUs. Using the intuition gained from tangible product businesses, we move to financial services where we can use many of the same ideas with a few modifications.

In this chapter we will design a data warehouse for a large bank. We will imagine the bank to offer a significant portfolio of services including checking accounts, savings accounts, mortgage loans, investment loans, personal loans, a credit card, and safe deposit boxes. Our goal will be to build a household data warehouse where we can track all the accounts owned by the bank, and see all the individual account holders, as well as the residential and commercial household groupings to which they belong. A major goal of the bank is to market more effectively to its households, and offer additional services to households that already have one or more accounts.

As a result of conducting user interviews with managers and analysts around the bank, we have developed the following set of special requirements:

1. We want to see five years of historical data on every account. For all prior months it will be sufficient to see the end-of-month snapshot.
2. For the current month, we want a valid snapshot as of yesterday. We don't need the other prior days in the current month.

3. Every type of account has a primary balance. There is a significant need to group different kinds of accounts in the same analyses and compare primary balances.

4. Every type of account has a list of custom dimension attributes and custom numeric facts that tend to be quite different from account type to account type.

5. Every account is deemed to belong to a household. Upon studying the historical production data, we conclude that accounts and the individuals who own the accounts come and go from households as much as several times per year for each household.

6. Since some of the accounts were created many years ago, and by different production systems, we find that our records of the individual account holders' names and addresses differ from account to account in many cases.

7. In addition to the household identification, we are very interested in demographic information as it pertains to both the individual account holders and the households. We also capture and store behavior scores relating to the activity in each of the accounts.

As a result of these requirements, the grain and dimensionality of the bank's household data warehouse begins to emerge. In this chapter we will develop the design in two steps, beginning with a simple and somewhat incomplete view and then extending the design to deal with the major issue of **heterogeneous products**.

We start by designing a **core** fact table that records the primary balances of every account. As a result of studying the bank's environment, we choose the following dimensions:

Account, Household, Branch, Product, Status, and Time.

At the intersection of these six dimensions we take a monthly snapshot and record the primary balance and any other metrics that make sense across all account types. For example, transaction counts, although they are semiadditive, are useful in financial service applications. The grain of the fact table will be account by month.

The decision to treat account and household as separate dimensions is a matter of the designer's prerogative. In spite of the fact that they are intuitively correlated, we decide to treat them separately because of the size of the account dimension and because of its volatility. In a large bank the account dimension is huge. A large bank could easily have 10 million accounts and 3 million households. For this very large dimension, we must guard against using the Type Two slowly changing dimension approach where we generate a new account record every time a meaningful account attribute changes. Since we saw that the definition of household constituents was rather volatile, we choose to record the correspondence between account and household in the fact table rather than in the account dimension table by modeling them as separate dimensions.

The product dimension contains those attributes used to describe all possible bank products. Typically this would include a simple product hierarchy under which all bank products could be described, such as the name of the product, the type, and a high-level category. The need to construct a generic product categorization in the bank is the same need that causes grocery stores to construct a generic merchandise hierarchy. The main difference in this case between the bank and grocery store is that the bank also develops a large number of custom product attributes for each product type. We will defer putting these custom attributes into the design for the moment.

The product dimension could be embedded with the account dimension. Again, after some thought, we decide to separate them because they slowly change on different rhythms, and the end users think of them as basic, separate dimensions of the banking business.

The status dimension is a useful dimension to record the condition of the account. The status records whether the account is active or inactive, and whether a status change occurred in this particular time period. The status dimension is used to mark new accounts as well as accounts that have just been closed. The status dimension also includes reasons where they make sense, such as the reason for the account being closed.

DIRTY DIMENSIONS

Our first cut at the household data warehouse schema takes the form shown in Figure 7.1. In this database we have not identified the individual customer as a dimension. The closest dimension to individual customer is account, which

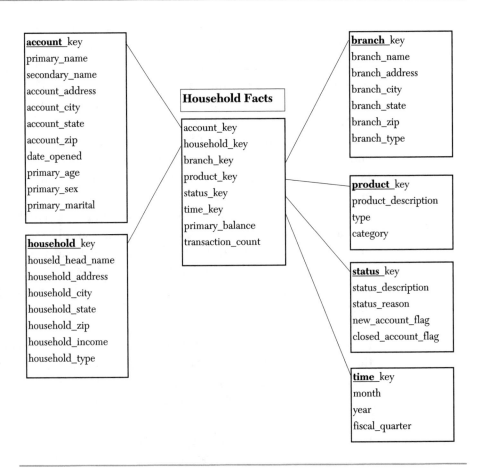

FIGURE 7.1

The household data warehouse, version 1.

can have one, two, or more individuals as account holders. In our hypothetical bank we have the typical situation where there is only a poor account-to-account correlation of individuals' names. This situation arises in real financial services environments partly for historical reasons and partly for cultural reasons. The bank's emphasis is on the account, not the individual. The marketing perspective that would pay more attention to the individual has come to many banks after the production systems and procedures were installed. As a result, there is relatively poor quality assurance on the names and addresses of the account holders. A typical bank is doing well if it can find more than 80 percent of the actual instances where the same individual has multiple accounts. In the design shown in Figure 7.1, we have not called out the individual account holder as a separate dimension for these reasons. If we had, we would call this a **dirty dimension** because it would surely contain many duplicates and extraneous entries.

Since the individual account holder is a dirty dimension, this raises questions about how good the identification of the household is in these banking databases. The truth is that the household dimension is equally dirty. In most banks and insurance companies, the household dimension is about 80 percent accurate. A number of specialist companies have sophisticated software that performs "household matching" and endeavors to do better than 80 percent.

SEMIADDITIVE ACCOUNT BALANCES

Account balances are exactly like inventory balances. They are not additive across time. In order to usefully combine account balances across multiple time periods, the application must divide the sum of the account balances by the number of periods being measured. In this case of our household data warehouse, this will always yield an average monthly balance. As we pointed out in Chapter 3, an application cannot use the SQL AVG function to perform this calculation, because the AVG function divides by the number of record instances in the fetched data, not by the number of time periods. The application must separately evaluate the cardinality of the time constraint and use that cardinality as the divisor of the sum of the account balances. It would be very helpful if SQL system vendors would extend the aggregate function set from the current five SQL aggregate functions to include Average Period Sum, and possibly Average Period Count as direct function calls. Without this functionality, standard SQL query tools cannot usefully manipulate inventory balances and account balances. We recommend the following design principle:

Average period balances in financial data warehouses and in inventory data warehouses can be calculated by generalizing the SQL AVG function to instead compute Average Period Sum. Until the DBMS vendors provide the functionality, Average Period Sum must be computed in the end user's application.

HETEROGENEOUS PRODUCTS

A central problem in the design of our household data warehouse and virtually every financial services database is the highly varied nature of the financial service products. Although every account type at the bank has a primary balance associated with it, each account type has a number of special attributes and measured facts that are not shared by the other account types. For instance, checking accounts have minimum balances, overdraft limits, service charges, and links to credit cards. Savings accounts have some of the same checking account facts plus interest paid, direct deposit options, and chargeable debits. Time deposits like CDs have few overlaps with checking or savings but have renewal dates, maturity dates, compounding frequencies, and current interest rate. Credit cards have credit levels, payment scores, number of cards issued, and number of delinquent months. Even safe deposit boxes have box type and price. From a logical design perspective, we could simply extend the product dimension table and the fact table to include these extra attributes and facts. Our design would look like Figure 7.2.

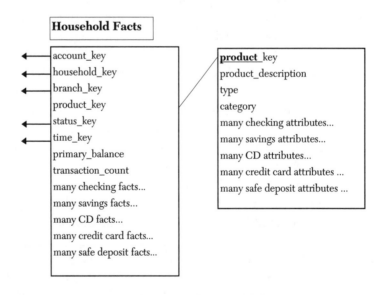

FIGURE 7.2

The logical design for heterogeneous products in a bank.

A bank could easily have a dozen or more attributes and facts for each product type. A full-service bank could have at least ten major product types. Imagine actually expanding Figure 7.2 with a dozen facts and a dozen attributes for each product type! Although it is logically correct, physically it is a disaster. Both the fact table and the product dimension table would have more than 100 fields, almost all of which would be empty for any single record.

The answer, of course, is to physically split both the fact table and the product dimension table by product type. We create a core fact table with just the primary balances and transaction counts, and we link to a core product dimension table with just the product hierarchy information. This is, in fact, what we began with in Figure 7.1. Then we create **custom** fact tables and custom product dimension tables for each product type, as shown in Figure 7.3.

> In data warehouses where a dimension must describe a large number of heterogeneous items, the recommended technique is to create a core fact table and a core dimension table in order to allow queries to cross the disparate types, and to create a custom fact table and a custom dimension table for querying each individual type in depth.

Figure 7.3 shows just two of the custom subschemas, for checking and savings. The complete database design would contain a custom subschema for each product type. Although this looks complex, only the DBA sees all the tables at once. From the perspective of the user, either an analysis is a cross-product analysis, and therefore the attention must be focused entirely on the core fact table and its attendant core product dimension table, or else the analysis is of a particular product type, and the attention must be focused on one of the custom fact and custom product subschemas. In general it does not make sense to combine data from two or more custom subschemas, because by definition the facts and attributes are disjoint or are nearly so.

If there are 500 million records in the core fact table then there will be exactly 500 million records in the sum of all the custom fact tables, because the custom fact tables can be thought of as the "tails" of respective records in the core fact table. We have duplicated all the keys exactly once. Notice that we have also duplicated the core facts (primary balance and transaction count) in every custom fact table. This is not logically necessary, but is a huge convenience because it keeps an application from trying to join a custom fact table

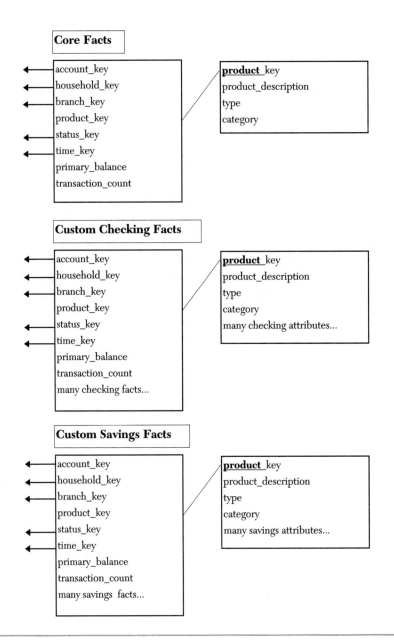

FIGURE 7.3

The physical design for heterogeneous products in a bank showing checking and savings.

to the core fact table. This approach of duplicating the core facts makes most sense when there are a small number of core facts. If there are a large number, then it may be expensive to duplicate the data, but it is still probably advisable because of the immense applications overhead of linking two fact tables. We will see in Chapter 16 that the only workable approach for linking two large fact tables together is to perform separate SQL queries and then join the resulting answer sets in the client tool.

> The primary core facts should be duplicated in the custom fact tables. This virtually eliminates the need to access two fact tables in a single query in a heterogeneous product schema.

The keys for the custom product dimension tables are the same keys used in the corresponding dimension records in the core product dimension tables, which contains all possible product keys. Each custom product dimension table is a subset of the core product dimension table, and each custom product dimension table contains extra product attributes specific to the particular product type.

INTERACTION WITH TRANSACTION GRAIN FACT TABLES

The household data warehouse we have built in this chapter is a monthly snapshot. The heterogeneous product techniques we have developed are appropriate only for fact tables where a single logical record contains many facts. Snapshots usually fit this pattern.

However, transaction-grained fact tables almost always have only a single fact. We examined one of these transaction-grained fact tables briefly in Chapter 3, and we will see several more in later chapters. Generally, all of these transaction-grained fact tables have the single Amount fact, which is generically the target of the particular transaction. These fact tables must have an associated Transaction dimension, which interprets the Amount field.

In the case of transaction-grained fact tables, we do not need the custom fact tables. There is only one fact table (the core fact table) because there is only one fact. However, we still can have a rich set of heterogeneous products with diverse attributes. In this case, we would generate the complete portfolio of custom product dimension tables, and use them as appropriate depending on the nature of the application. In a cross-product analysis we would use the core product dimension table, because it would be capable of spanning any group of products. In a single product type analysis we could optionally use the custom product dimension table instead of the core product dimension table if we wanted to take advantage of some of the custom attributes specific to that product type.

USING BIG-DIMENSION TECHNIQUES

Although we have not illustrated it specifically, our account and household dimensions both qualify as big dimensions in the sense discussed in Chapter 6. We would expect to break off the browsable and changeable attributes into minidimensions, whose keys we would introduce into the core fact table and all of the custom fact tables.

DATABASE SIZING FOR HOUSEHOLD BANKING (assuming a large multibranch bank)

Please see the discussion at the beginning of Chapter 13 for detailed assumptions.

Account dimension: 12 million
Time dimension: 3 years => 36 monthly snapshots
Other dimensions (household, branch, product, status): 1 for each account per month
Number of base fact records: 12,000,000 × 36 = *432 million records*
Number of key fields = 6; Number of fact fields = 2; Total fields = 8
Base fact table size (core fact table) = 432 million × 8 fields × 4 bytes = *13.8 GB*
Total custom fact tables sizes assuming 6 custom facts in each: *20.7 GB*

8

SUBSCRIPTION
BUSINESSES

In this chapter we will examine a cable TV supplier for a large metropolitan area, which is an example of a subscription business. Subscription businesses are an important service industry example because the relationship between when money is received by such a company and when money can be taken as income is indirect and complicated. All pay-in-advance businesses, whether they are subscription or insurance businesses, have the same characteristic problem.

SUBSCRIPTION TRANSACTIONS

The company we will model in this chapter is a large metropolitan cable TV supplier with more than one million customers. We capture all the customer-sales-oriented transactions that are taken over the phone. These transactions include the following:

- Open New Account, Change Account Type
- Purchase Package, Upgrade Package, Renew Package
- Purchase Pay Per View
- Cancel Package (with Reason)

- Cancel Pay Per View (with Reason)
- Downgrade Package (with Reason)
- Refund Purchase (with Reason)
- Close Account (with Reason)

A package is the right to watch a collection of channels for a period of months. Packages are sold with durations of 3 months, 6 months, 9 months, and 12 months. The same channel, such as HBO or Cinemax, may be part of several different packages. Customers call the cable TV supplier's office and speak to a customer sales representative. During the call, one or more transactions may take place. The ability to actually watch a channel is controlled via a descrambler located in the customer's home. During the call, the customer identifies himself or herself unambiguously so that the right authorization codes can be created to enable the channels to be watched. The cable TV supplier uses the word *product* to describe both packages and pay-per-view offerings.

The marketing department at the cable TV company is anxious to understand who is purchasing which packages and which pay-per-view offerings. The packages and pay-per-view offerings are periodically promoted with special discounts to attract new customers and encourage customers to upgrade or extend their services. Marketing wants to know whether its promotions are profitable, whether the promotions attract new business, and which customers are most likely to respond to a promotion. Once someone responds to a promotion, marketing wants to track that person indefinitely into the future.

Marketing wants to count the number of new subscribers each month, as well as the number who upgraded and the number who renewed their packages. Marketing wants to count the number who canceled or downgraded their services, and wants to see why. Marketing wants to see the time gap between initial service purchase and the first upgrade.

Operations wants to see what the call load is, potentially down to the grain of the individual minute for certain pay-per-view offerings. Operations also wants to analyze and predict call traffic in order to plan staffing.

Marketing, finance, and senior management want to see how much revenue was earned each month. The revenue numbers need to be rapidly sliced and diced by customer types, by package, by broadcast time of day (for pay per view), and by promotion.

With these requirements in mind, we extract every base-level transaction from the production customer sales system. The first database we build has the grain of every sales transaction. The dimensions of this database are as follows:

- Transaction Entry Date/Time
- Effective Date/Time
- Customer
- Sales Representative
- Product
- Promotion
- Transaction

Since this is a transaction-grained database, there will only be one fact, namely Amount. For each transaction type, Amount has a different interpretation. For Open New Account, Amount is the monthly service charge. For Close Account, Amount is the partial service charge due for the last fractional month. For Purchase Package, Amount is the monthly charge for the duration of the package if the customer pays on a monthly basis, or it is the full amount paid in advance if the customer chooses that option. The two payment options are booked as separate packages by the Cable TV supplier. For Upgrade Package, Amount is the new monthly charge for the remaining duration of the package. For Cancel Package, Amount is the amount the company owes the customer for the unused portion of the package subscription. Our database schema is shown in Figure 8.1

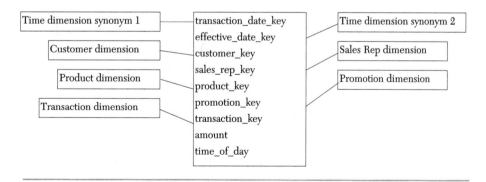

FIGURE 8.1

The cable TV sales transaction database

The transaction date and the effective date are equally interesting to the cable TV company. We only need to actually build one time dimension table however. In SQL we can pretend syntactically that there are two time dimension tables by using the SQL SYNONYM construct. The two synonyms can be constrained separately as if they were two independent tables.

Both the transaction date and the effective date are denominated in days. Most analyses will want this granularity. The time of day, to the minute, is stored separately, as if it were a fact. Although SQL can define a date/time-valued object to the precision of minutes as a single key, we would still need an explicit dimension to describe fiscal periods and holidays. At the grain of minute, this dimension would be unwieldy. An interesting extension of the separate minute field would be to construct a dimension for it as well, with 1,440 values (24 hours × 60 minutes). This dimension could contain useful minute groupings such as hour names or work shift names.

The customer dimension in this database is somewhat cleaner than the customer dimension in the bank. It really only makes sense for a person to have one cable TV account, so the issue of tying together multiple accounts by person is a nonissue for the cable TV company. Generally in this kind of business there is no problem identifying a succession of transactions on a given customer's account since we are really talking about the customer's descrambler ID, not the true identity of the person behind the account.

PAYMENTS IN ADVANCE

The most interesting issue in this database is how to handle the payments made in advance for the packages, and to a lesser extent, the payments made in advance for pay per view. For any company, a payment received in advance must be booked as a **liability**, not an **asset**. This is because, in most cases, the money received must potentially be paid back until and unless the promised service is provided. All companies that receive payments in advance deal with this, including companies that sell subscriptions to cable TV packages, magazines, and newspapers, as well as insurance companies that collect premiums in advance in payment of insurance coverage. In a similar vein, banks must book deposits as liabilities because, of course, they must pay the customer back any time the customer demands payment. A loan, on the other hand, is a bank's asset, because the bank is legally entitled to get its money back from the customer.

The reason that this is an interesting issue for the cable TV company and other companies that take payments in advance is that the sequence of transactions does not provide a clear indication of the company's income. Income can be booked by these kinds of companies only when it is **earned**. Income is earned when the service is provided. In the case of the cable TV company, the income from a package is earned month by month as long as the customer doesn't cancel the service. If we only have a transaction-grained database, the calculation of the earned income can get quite complicated. In the simplest case, where the customer signs up for the package, and pays the fee in advance, only a single transaction exists in the database. To calculate the company's income from this purchase, a database application would have to find the transaction and roll forward the monthly earned income calculation to the current month. If the customer has modified or extended the package terms in the intervening months, then any such modification transactions would also have to be found and incorporated into the calculation.

Depending on how the cable TV company calculates its earned income, some or all of the following things can happen that would make on-the-fly calculation of earned income very complicated:

- Earned income may be calculated based on the number of days in a given month, rather than dividing the subscription fee equally across all months. If this is true, then leap-year calculations enter the picture.
- The original subscription transaction may have taken place in the prior year, making date arithmetic a little more tricky. In cases where the payment in advance was a very long time ago, it may even be the case that the original transaction is not part of the data warehouse's maintained time series. This can happen if the data warehouse has just been placed on-line, and not all of the historical extracts are available. There is always the problem of how to calculate the earned income for the first available month in the database where, by definition, the originating transactions precede the first available month.
- A potentially complicated series of upgrade or downgrade transactions may exist after the originating transaction, which must be taken into account. Each kind of transaction that could affect the income stream must be interpreted separately. It is almost certainly not the case that the Amount values in the time series of such transactions can be algebraically added together. Rather it is probably the case that each Amount value in each in-

tervening transaction implies a time series of earned incomes for the remaining months of the subscription. Only after calculating these time series separately can they be added algebraically for a given month.

Because of these complexities, it is not practical to use the transaction-grained fact table to calculate earned income. The transaction-grained fact table is a good source for answering more than half of the business questions listed above, but a monthly snapshot table must be built to store the earned incomes. At the end of each month, a batch job is run, probably on the production system, that carefully calculates the month's earned income for every account. Other activity summaries for the month can be accumulated at this time. This monthly summary is then explicitly stored in a separate fact table. This leads to a design principle:

> Pay-in-advance business scenarios typically require the combination of a transaction-grained fact table as well as a monthly-snapshot-grained fact table in order to answer questions of transaction frequency and timing as well as questions of earned income in a given month.

The monthly snapshot fact table is derived from the transaction fact table. Not surprisingly, the resulting table looks very much like the monthly snapshot table we developed in the previous chapter on banking. The transaction dimension is removed and the list of facts extended to include all monthly summaries of interest. The time dimension is simplified and the second time dimension is removed because, in this database, time is simply a designation of the monthly bucket. We introduce the useful status dimension to allow the user to rapidly pick out accounts where something interesting has happened in the current month, such as a new customer, a new package signup, a modification, or a cancellation. Our derived monthly snapshot fact table for the cable TV supplier now looks like Figure 8.2.

In most pay-in-advance situations where both the transaction grained fact table and the monthly snapshot fact table must be created, there are enough transactions occurring throughout the year that the two databases are of roughly comparable size. In the extreme case where every package purchase had only one breath-of-life transaction, then the monthly snapshot database

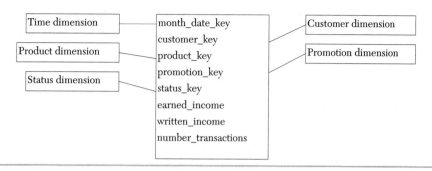

FIGURE 8.2

The cable TV sales monthly snapshot database.

could contain as much as 12 times as many records, assuming all the packages purchased were 12-month packages.

In this chapter we have developed the techniques necessary for handling pay-in-advance businesses. An important example of such a business is insurance, which we develop in the next chapter. We will be able to use the design developed in this chapter as an important component of the insurance database design. It is certainly the case in insurance that the number of transactions against a given coverage is large enough to balance the two fact tables, especially for claims.

DATABASE SIZING FOR CABLE TV SALES TRANSACTION

Please see the discussion at the beginning of Chapter 13 for detailed assumptions.

Customer dimension: 1,000,000
Product dimension: 4 packages purchased per customer per year
Transaction dimension: 3 transactions per customer per package per year
Time dimension: 3 years
Other dimensions (effective date, sales rep, promotion): 1 for each transaction
    event
Number of base fact records: 1,000,000 × 4 × 3 × 3 = *36 million records*

Number of key fields = 7; Number of fact fields = 2; Total fields = 9
Base fact table size = 36 million $\times$ 9 fields $\times$ 4 bytes = *1.3 GB*

DATABASE SIZING FOR CABLE TV SALES MONTHLY SUMMARY

Customer dimension: 1,000,000
Product dimension: 4 packages purchased per customer per year
Time dimension: 3 years => 36 monthly summaries
Other dimensions (status, promotion): 1 for each monthly summary
Number of base fact records: 1,000,000 $\times$ 4 $\times$ 36 = *144 million records*
Number of key fields = 5; Number of fact fields = 3; Total fields = 8
Base fact table size = 144 million $\times$ 8 fields $\times$ 4 bytes = *4.6 GB*

9

INSURANCE

In this chapter we bring together ideas from nearly all the previous chapters to build a data warehouse for a typical insurance company. If you are in the insurance industry and you have jumped directly to this chapter for a quick fix, please accept the author's apologies, but this chapter depends heavily on ideas from the previous chapters. You need to read the previous chapters!

We will imagine that our insurance company is a $3 billion property and casualty insurer for automobiles, home fire protection, and personal liability. There are two main production data sources: all transactions relating to the formulation of policies, and all transactions involved in processing claims. Based on extensive interviews of claims processing managers, field sales managers, financial managers, and senior management, we conclude that the insurance company wants to analyze both the written policies as well as the claims. They want to see which coverages are most profitable and which are least profitable. They want to measure profit over time by covered item type (i.e., which kinds of houses and which kinds of cars), state and county, demographic profile, underwriter, sales broker and sales region, and event. Events are usually called *catastrophes* in this industry. The desire to see profit implies that both revenues and costs can be identified and tracked.

The insurance company wants to understand what happens during the life of a policy, particularly when a claim is processed. The time from when a claim is first made to when the first payment is made is an important measure of the efficiency of the claims handling process. This can be measured only by looking at the detailed transactions.

In this chapter we will develop the design in the same way we developed the household data warehouse for the bank. We will start with the central dimensional schemas for policy creation and claims processing and then embellish them to handle monthly snapshots, heterogeneous products, and demographic minidimensions.

POLICY CREATION

We will assume that a policy is a "header" for a set of coverages sold to the insured party. Coverages are really the products that insurance companies sell. Homeowner coverages include fire, flood, theft, and personal liability. Automobile coverages include comprehensive, collision damage, uninsured motorist, and personal liability. In a property and casualty insurance company, such as the one we are modeling, coverages typically apply to a specific covered item, such as a particular house or car. Both the coverage and covered item are identified carefully in the policy. A particular covered item will usually have several coverages listed in the policy. We will assume that a policy can contain multiple covered items.

A policy is sold to an insured party by an agent or a broker. Agents are either employees of the insurance company or may be independent. Brokers are independent. Before the final policy can be created, a rater in the insurance company determines the rate that will be charged, given the particular coverages, the particular covered items, and the qualifications of the insured party. The final step of approval is made by an underwriter, who takes the ultimate responsibility for doing the business with the insured party. Typically the agent (or broker), rater, and underwriter are all different people.

We assume we capture the following transactions in the production policy creation system:

- Create Policy; Alter Policy; Cancel Policy (with Reason)
- Create Coverage on Covered Item; Alter Coverage; Cancel Coverage (with Reason)
- Rate Coverage; Decline to Rate Coverage (with Reason)
- Underwrite Policy; Decline to Underwrite Policy (with Reason)

In general, a given transaction comes with a lot of context. For example, when a Create Coverage on Covered Item transaction is processed, many things are known, including the insured party, the agent, the policy number, the coverage identification, and the covered item identification. If rating and underwriting have not happened yet, then the rater and underwriter are not known. It is important when designing the production extract system not to take the data found in the atomic transaction record so literally that some of the context is treated as unknown. Or, to state it more positively, a given atomic transaction must be embellished with as much context as possible, to create a full-dimensional description of the transaction.

The dimensional framework for the policy transaction fact table consists of the following:

- Transaction date
- Effective date
- Insured party
- Employee
- Coverage
- Covered item
- Policy
- Transaction

The transaction date is the date when the transaction was entered into the production system. The effective date is when the transaction is legally effective. These two independent dimensions can be implemented via a single physical table, which is declared via the SYNONYM construct to be two different tables as far as SQL is concerned, as described in Chapter 2.

The insured party is the customer. In all probability, the insured party dimension is a *dirty customer dimension*, in that no really serious attempt is made to identify previous instances of an insured party on other policies. The insured party can be multiple people, such as a person and their spouse, or the insured party can be a business entity. In general, insured party is a big dimension, which in the case of our $3 billion insurance company probably has a million or more entries. Later in this chapter we will definitely be using the big-dimension techniques on insured party that we developed in Chapter 6.

The employee is the responsible individual who is creating the transaction. For Create Policy and Create Coverage transactions, the employee is the agent or the broker, although "employee" is a misnomer in the case of a broker. For rating transactions, the employee is the rater, and for underwriting transactions the employee is the underwriter.

The coverage is the product that the insurance company sells on a given kind of covered item. Large insurance companies will have dozens or perhaps hundreds of separate coverages available. If the coverage has specific limits or deductibles, we generally treat these numeric parameters as facts, rather than creating a distinct coverage for every different possible value. For example, a basic limit on homeowner's fire protection is the appraised value of the house. Since the appraised value can be thought of as a continuously valued, numeric quantity that is measured each time we look at a different policy and can even vary for a given policy over time, we can be confident that such limits are legitimate facts.

The covered item is the house, the car, or some other specific insured item. The covered item dimension contains one record for each actual covered item. In general it is not desirable to capture the variable descriptions of the many covered items as facts, because most of the facts describing physical objects are textual facts that are not numeric or continuously valued. Thus we see that covered item is another big dimension. Usually the covered item dimension is somewhat larger than the insured party dimension.

The policy dimension may be a degenerate dimension if we have extracted all the header information associated with the physical policy off into the other dimensions, or there may be one or two attributes that we believe belong to the policy and not to one of the dimensions. For example, if the underwriter establishes an overall risk grade to the policy as a whole, based on the totality of the coverages and covered items, then this risk grade probably belongs uniquely to the policy dimension.

The transaction dimension is a small dimension with the transaction types listed above, together with all the possible reason descriptions for those transactions that have reasons. Usually the transaction dimension contains a hundred or fewer entries.

Because this fact table is a classic transaction-grained fact table, we have a single numeric fact, which we name Amount. As always, the interpretation of the Amount field is provided by the transaction dimension.

We are now able to present the policy transaction schema. Since we are developing this schema in the same way we developed the banking schema, this first view of the database does not yet address the issue of heterogeneous products, monthly snapshots, or the need for minidimensions. The grain of this policy transaction fact table is the individual transaction (Figure 9.1).

CLAIMS PROCESSING

After a policy is created and its associated coverages and covered items are registered and in effect, then it is possible for a claim to be made against a specific coverage and covered item. A claim is made by a claimant who may be a new party not previously known to the insurance company. In the claim, the claimant describes the claim. The nature of the claim description obviously depends on the coverage and the covered item. When the claim is received, the first step is to open the claim. Usually at this time a reserve is established that

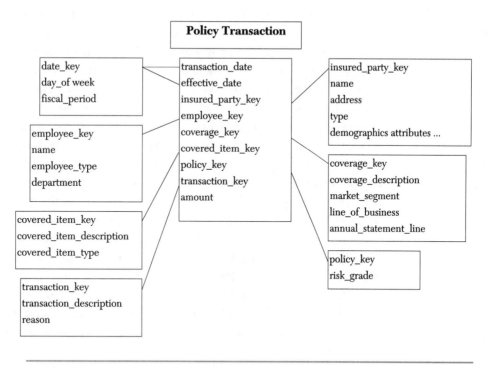

FIGURE 9.1

The initial policy transaction schema.

is a preliminary estimate of the insurance company's eventual liability for the claim. As further information develops, this reserve can be adjusted.

Usually before any claims are paid by the insurance company, there is an investigative phase where the insurance company sends out an adjuster to examine the covered item and interview the claimant, the insured party, or other involved individuals. Witnesses, claimants, and other people are sometimes called **loss parties** as a general category. The investigative phase produces a whole stream of transactions. In complex claims various outside experts may be required to pass judgment on the claim or on the extent of the damages. These can include medical personnel, fire inspectors, and automotive body shop operators. In British countries, automotive body shop operators are called "panel beaters."

In most cases, after the investigative phase, a number of payments are made by the insurance company. Many of these payments go to third parties such as doctors, lawyers, or automotive body shop operators. Some of the payments go to the claimant. Each payment is an important claim transaction.

The insurance company may take possession of the covered item after replacing it with the insured party or a claimant. In many such cases, there is a salvage value to the item, which is eventually realized by the insurance company. Salvage payments received are a credit against the claim accounting.

In some sense, an insurance company is in a vulnerable position when a claim is open and the running total of payments made to various parties is below the established reserve. In this case it is easier for money to be paid out on the authorization of many people within the insurance company. A large insurance company may have more than 1,000 individuals who are authorized to create payments against open claims. For this reason, it is desirable to identify clearly the responsible employee for every payment made against an open claim.

Eventually, the payments are finished, and the claim is closed. If nothing unusual happens, then this is the end of the transaction stream generated by the claim. However, in complex cases, further claims are made at later times, or lawsuits by the claimants may force a claim to be reopened. In this case the reserve must usually be reset as well. An important measure for an insurance company is how often and under what circumstances are claims reopened and reserves reset.

Toward the end of processing a complex claim, the insurance company may believe that further money may flow back to the insurance company when pending lawsuits or counterclaims are eventually resolved. The insurance company may choose to sell the rights to all such further recoveries to specialist third parties who are prepared to wait out the resolution of the lawsuits or counterclaims. Although such sales probably take place at a discount, this allows the insurance company to get cash immediately, and to close the books on the claim. This option is known as **subrogation** and generates its own special transaction.

The transactions associated with claims processing include the following:

- Open Claim; Reopen Claim; Close Claim
- Set Reserve; Reset Reserve; Close Reserve
- Set Salvage Estimate; Receive Salvage Payment
- Adjuster Inspection; Adjuster Interview
- Open Lawsuit; Close Lawsuit
- Make Payment; Receive Payment
- Subrogate Claim

The dimensional framework for the claims transaction fact table (Figure 9.2) consists of nearly all the dimensions associated with the coverage and covered item, together with the new dimensions needed to describe the claim transactions. These include the following:

- Transaction date
- Effective date
- Insured party (from policy)
- Employee
- Coverage (from policy)
- Covered item (from policy)
- Policy (from policy)
- Claimant
- Claim
- Third party
- Transaction

Employee in this fact table is the responsible employee for authorizing the transaction. As mentioned previously, this is particularly interesting for payment transactions. Claimant is the party making the claim, usually an individual. Claimant is usually a dirty dimension because of the difficulty of reliably identifying and tracking claimants across different claims, although there would be value in this being a clean dimension.

Claim is a codified description of the claim. Generally it must map to the coverage and the covered item in order to be valid and to make sense.

Third party is a witness, an expert, or a payee. Again, this is almost certainly a dirty dimension because of the difficulty of identifying and tracking these parties. Additionally, unscrupulous potential payees will go out of their way to not identify themselves in a way that would make it easy to tie them to other claims

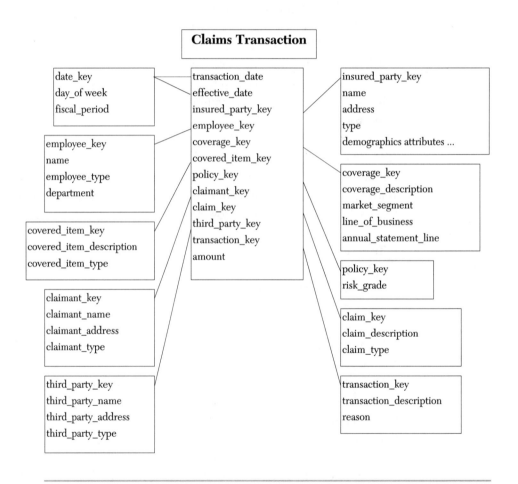

FIGURE 9.2

The initial claims transaction schema.

in the insurance company's system. The total number of payments made to various parties is huge.

MONTHLY SNAPSHOTS FOR POLICIES AND CLAIMS

The two schemas we have developed thus far are very useful for answering a whole range of questions about the insurance company. Timings of transactions and counts of transactions of various types can be done with great precision. However, as in the cable TV subscription business example developed in Chapter 8, the blizzard of transactions makes it difficult to quickly determine the status of a policy or a claim at any given point in time. All of the necessary detail certainly lies in the transaction record, but a snapshot view would require rolling the transactions forward from the beginning of history. Not only is this nearly impractical on a single policy or claim, but it is ridiculous to think about generating summary top-line views of the insurance company this way.

We take the same approach for the insurance business that we took for the cable TV subscription business. Each month after closing the previous month's transaction activity, we roll forward all the transactions and create a monthly snapshot. The previous month's snapshot for the same coverage and covered item and for the same claim is used as the base for incrementally calculating this month's snapshot. We carefully compute and store the earned income for the month, which is used as the primary measure of policy revenue.

As in Chapter 8, the monthly snapshot fact tables for policies and claims are systematic derivations from the transaction fact tables. The time dimension becomes the month designation. The transaction specific dimensions like employee, claimant, third party, and transaction are all suppressed. We introduce a status dimension to call attention to coverages or claims in specific months that are in interesting states, such as Just Opened, Just Reopened, Claim Pending, or Just Closed. The single Amount field is replaced with a potentially long list of summary facts.

The policy monthly snapshot schema is shown in Figure 9.3. The grain of this fact table is policy by coverage by covered item by month. Figure 9.4 shows the claims snapshot schema.

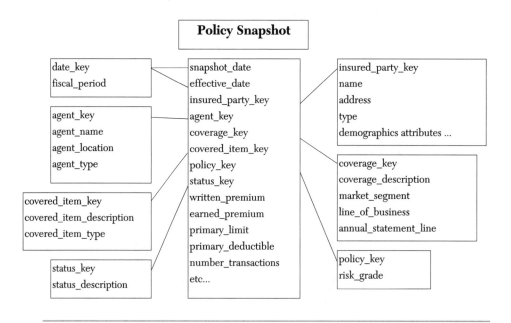

FIGURE 9.3

The initial policy snapshot fact table.

TRANSACTION SCHEMAS WITH HETEROGENEOUS PRODUCTS

Insurance companies typically carry a number of lines of business that may be quite varied. The detailed parameters of homeowner coverages differ significantly from automobile coverage. These both differ substantially from personal article coverage, general liability coverage, and life insurance. Although all coverages can be coded into the generic structures we have used so far in this chapter, insurance companies will want to track many specific attributes and facts that make sense only for a particular coverage and covered item. We can generalize the initial schemas we have developed in this chapter using the same techniques we used in the banking example of Chapter 7. For the policy transaction schema, we show the custom attributes and facts for each coverage type in Figure 9.5.

Again, we remind ourselves that although this logical schema is the correct design for representing the heterogeneous products, it is unworkable physically if there are many custom attributes, each of which makes sense only in

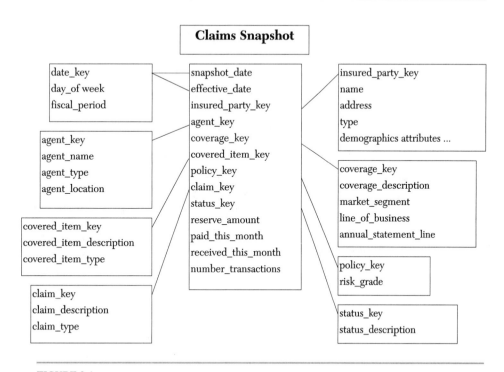

FIGURE 9.4

The initial claims snapshot schema.

the context of a specific coverage type. The answer for both the policy and claims transaction tables is to create multiple copies of the covered item and coverage dimension tables. The core versions are the ones we use in Figures 9.1 and 9.2. For each coverage type we then create custom dimension tables for both covered item and coverage. These are extended, as appropriate, for each coverage type. When an application needs the specific attributes of a single coverage type, it uses the appropriate custom dimension tables. For example, if specific attributes for automobile coverage were needed, the application would use the schema shown in Figure 9.6.

Notice that we don't need a custom transaction fact table. We need only introduce custom dimension tables to handle the special automobile attributes. No new keys need to be generated, because logically all we are doing is extending existing dimension records. We build a custom covered item dimension table and a custom coverage dimension table for each coverage type. It would be reasonable to have between four and 25 such sets of custom dimension tables.

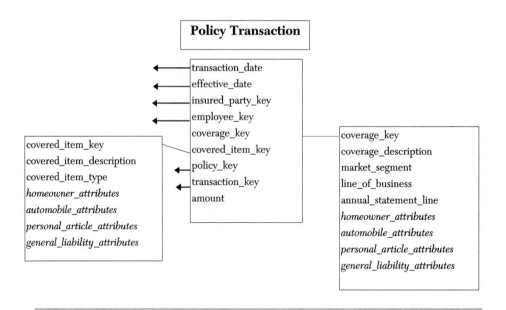

FIGURE 9.5

Logical policy transaction schema with heterogeneous products.

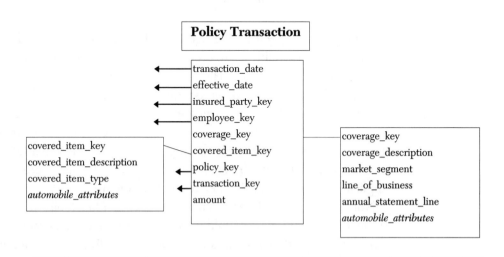

FIGURE 9.6

The policy transaction schema with a custom automobile dimension table.

The claims transaction schema is generalized in the same way. The only difference is that we probably want to extend the claims dimension table in addition to the covered item and coverage dimension tables, since it seems plausible that there could be special claim attributes dependent on the coverage type. The resulting schema would look like Figure 9.7.

SNAPSHOT SCHEMAS WITH HETEROGENEOUS PRODUCTS

The Snapshot schemas are generalized for heterogeneous products in much the same way as the transaction schemas, except that in addition we will almost certainly have a number of special numeric facts. The special numeric facts mean that we have to build a custom snapshot fact table for each coverage type. We can use the same custom dimension tables we built for the transaction schemas. The automotive custom snapshot schema is shown in Figure 9.8. The custom claims snapshot schema for automobile coverages would be generalized in a similar way, as in Figure 9.9.

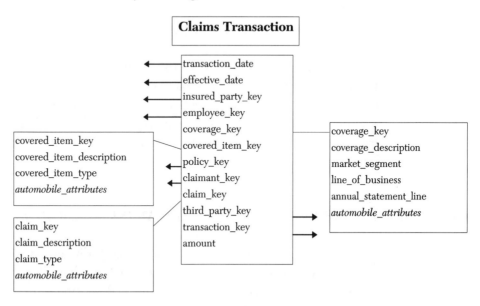

FIGURE 9.7

The claims transaction schema with a custom automobile dimension table.

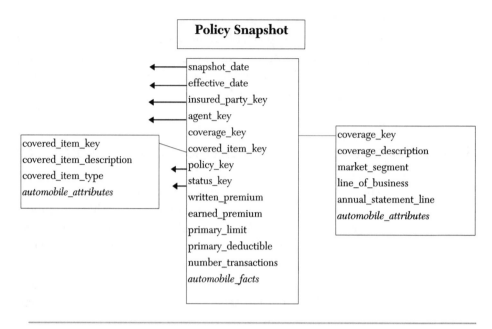

FIGURE 9.8

The custom policy snapshot schema for automobile coverages.

To summarize, recall from Chapter 7 that each of the custom snapshot fact tables is a complete copy of a segment of the core fact table, for just those coverage keys and covered item keys that correspond to a particular coverage type. We copy the core facts as a convenience so that analyses within a coverage type can use both the core facts and the custom facts without having to access two large fact tables.

MINIDIMENSIONS IN INSURED PARTY AND COVERED ITEM

These insurance schemas have a number of large dimensions, including especially insured party and covered item. For both of these dimensions, it is important to track accurately contemporary descriptions of the dimension entities. It is usually extremely important to have an accurate description of the insured party and of the covered item at the time of coverage creation, and at the time of any claim. We saw in Chapter 6 that the only practical way to track changing attributes in huge dimensions was to split the changeable at-

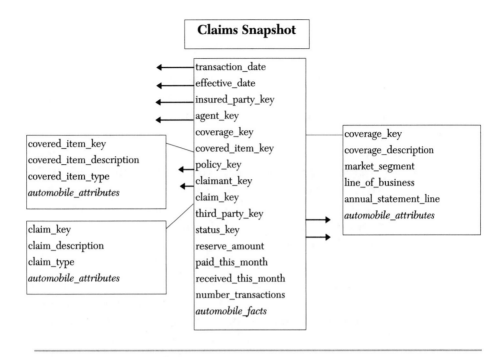

FIGURE 9.9

The custom claims snapshot schema for automobile coverages.

tributes off into one or more minidimensions, directly linked to the fact table with an artificially generated key. The use of minidimensions made a big difference in the efficiency of browsing these attributes (the changeable attributes being the very attributes one usually wants to browse and constrain upon), and made a big difference in the ease of updating. In those cases where all possible combinations of the attribute values in the minidimension have already been created, updating a demographic description in a customer minidimension simply means placing a different key in the fact table record from a certain point in time forward. Nothing else needs to be changed or added to the database.

DESIGN SUMMARY

The dimensional design of insurance databases represents the culmination of most of the important ideas we have developed. We have a reasonable vocabulary and shorthand for describing what we have done. We can compress the design into the following design principle:

An appropriate design for a property and casualty insurance data warehouse is a short value chain consisting of policy creation and claims processing, where these two major processes are represented both by transaction fact tables and monthly snapshot fact tables. This data warehouse will almost certainly need to represent a number of heterogeneous products (coverage types) with appropriate combinations of core and custom dimension tables and fact tables. Finally, the large insured party and covered item dimensions will need to be decomposed into one or more minidimensions in order to provide reasonable browsing performance and in order to accurately track these slowly changing dimensions.

DATABASE SIZING FOR INSURANCE POLICY TRANSACTIONS

Please see the discussion at the beginning of Chapter 13 for detailed assumptions.

Number of policies: 2,000,000
Number of covered item coverages (line items) per policy: 10
Number of policy transactions (not claim transactions) per year per policy: 12
Number of years: 3
Other dimensions: 1 for each policy line item transaction
Number of base fact records: 2,000,000 × 10 × 12 × 3 = *720 million records*
Number of key fields = 8; Number of fact fields = 1; Total fields = 9
Base fact table size = 720 million × 9 fields × 4 bytes = *26 GB*

DATABASE SIZING FOR CLAIM TRANSACTIONS

Number of policies: 2,000,000
Number of covered item coverages (line items) per policy: 10
Yearly percentage of all covered item coverages with a claim: 5%
Number of claim transactions per actual claim: 50
Number of years: 3
Other dimensions: 1 for each claim transaction
Number of base fact records: $2,000,000 \times 10 \times 0.05 \times 50 \times 3 = 150\ million$ *records*
Number of key fields = 11; Number of fact fields = 1; Total fields = 12
Base fact table size = 150 million $\times$ 12 fields $\times$ 4 bytes = *7.2 GB*

DATABASE SIZING FOR CORE POLICY SNAPSHOT

Number of policies: 2,000,000
Number of covered item coverages (line items) per policy: 10
Number of years: 3 => 36 months
Other dimensions: 1 for each policy line item monthly snapshot
Number of base fact records: $2,000,000 \times 10 \times 36 = 720\ million\ records$
Number of key fields = 8; Number of fact fields = 5; Total fields = 13
Base fact table size = 720 million $\times$ 13 fields $\times$ 4 bytes = *37 GB*
Total custom policy snapshot fact tables assuming an average of 5 custom facts: *52 GB*

DATABASE SIZING FOR CLAIMS SNAPSHOT

Number of policies: 2,000,000
Number of covered item coverages (line items) per policy: 10
Yearly percentage of all covered item coverages with a claim: 5%
Average length of time a claim is open: 12 months
Number of years: 3 => 36 months
Other dimensions: 1 for each policy line item monthly snapshot

Number of base fact records: 2,000,000 × 10 × 0.05 * 3 * 12 = *36 million records*

Number of key fields = 11; Number of fact fields = 4; Total fields = 15

Base fact table size = 36 million × 15 fields × 4 bytes = *2.2 GB*

Total custom policy snapshot fact tables assuming an average of 5 custom facts: *2.9 GB*

10

FACTLESS FACT TABLES

In all the examples developed in the previous nine chapters, the fact tables have had a very characteristic structure. Each fact table has had at least three and as many as ten key fields, followed by one to potentially a dozen or more numeric, continuously valued, additive facts. The facts can be regarded as measurements taken at the intersection of the key values. From this perspective, the facts are the justification for the fact table, and the key values are simply administrative structure that serves to identify the facts.

There are, however, a number of business processes that are very worthwhile to represent in a data warehouse that seem like the fact tables we have already built but for which there are no measured facts! We call these `fact-less fact tables`. We will discuss two major variations of factless fact tables: event tracking tables, and coverage tables.

EVENT TRACKING TABLES

There are many situations where a large number of events need to be recorded as the simultaneous coming together of a number of dimensional entities. For example, we can model daily class attendance at a college with a fact table with the following dimensions:

Course
Professor

- Student
- Facility
- Date/time

A fact table is a reasonable place to represent the robust set of many-to-many relationships among these five dimensions. This table could be queried to answer any number of interesting questions, such as which courses were the most heavily attended? Which courses suffered the least attrition over time? Which students attended which courses? Which facilities were used most heavily? Which facilities in which departments were used by the most students from other departments? What was the average occupancy rate of the facilities as a function of time of day?

The only peculiarity in this example is that it is hard to think of a fact. The existence of the records is not in question, but we may have to content ourselves with the reality of no measured facts. This means that applications will perform mostly counts. If, at any time during the design, a measurable fact surfaces, then it can be added to the schema, assuming it is measurable at the grain of daily attendance, which we have assumed for this example. Our daily attendance data warehouse is shown in Figure 10.1.

The SQL for performing the counts in this database is asymmetrical because of the absence of any facts. When counting the number of attendance events, any one of the five keys can be used identically as the argument to the COUNT function, for example:

SELECT PROFESSOR, COUNT(DATE_KEY)
. . .
GROUP by PROFESSOR

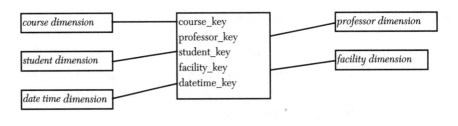

FIGURE 10.1

A factless fact table representing daily attendance at a college.

This gives the simple count of the number of student attendance events by professor, subject to any constraints that may exist in the WHERE clause. This SQL does *not* count the number of dates on which the professor taught classes. That would be accomplished by:

SELECT PROFESSOR, COUNT(DISTINCT DATE_KEY)

. . .

GROUP by PROFESSOR

This ugliness of the SQL, while not a serious semantic problem, causes some designers to create an artificial little field called ATTENDANCE that is always populated by the value 1. Now the SQL can use either COUNT or SUM and it is a lot more readable:

SELECT PROFESSOR, SUM(ATTENDANCE)

. . .

GROUP by PROFESSOR

At this point the table is no longer strictly factless, but most would agree that the 1 is an artifact.

MORE EVENT EXAMPLES

Daily attendance tracking at a college is an example of event tracking. The purpose of the fact table is to register the event of the five keys being in the same place at the same time. There are many situations in which this can occur. An analogous event is a patient in a hospital being given a specific procedure by a doctor and assistant. Again, there is a fine line between factless and factful in this example, but the point of discussing it here is to legitimize the factless fact table as a way of representing these events. The hospital patient procedure schema might look like Figure 10.2.

Another example might come from insurance where we need to register all the many-to-many correlations between loss parties and loss items, or to put it less euphemistically, all the correlations between people involved in an accident and vehicles involved in an accident. This accident parties schema might look like Figure 10.3.

The purpose of the accident parties schema is to collect in one place all the

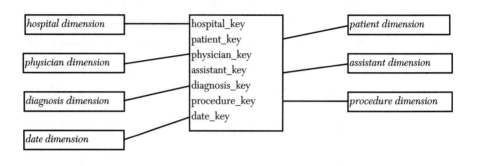

FIGURE 10.2

The hospital patient procedure schema.

miscellaneous people and vehicles involved in a complex claim, regardless of their involvement in the accident. The first six dimensions in the fact table in Figure 10.3 are the standard dimensions needed for an insurance company to track any claim. The seventh dimension, loss party, describes other individuals who were in some way involved in the accident, possibly as passengers in one of the cars, or possibly as witnesses who were not in an involved car. If the particular loss party was associated with a vehicle involved in the accident, then the loss vehicle would have a nonnull value. If the loss party was not in a loss vehicle, then the loss vehicle key would point to a no vehicle entry in that di-

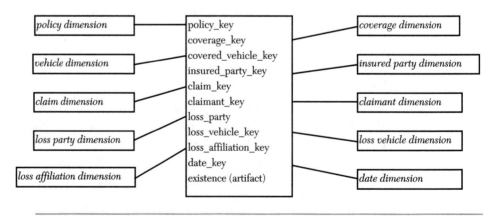

FIGURE 10.3

The accident parties schema.

mension. The loss affiliation is a kind of status that explains the role of the loss party and loss vehicle to the claim. The Existence field is a 1, like the Attendance field in the first example. This factless fact table is capable of representing extremely complex accidents with many involved vehicles, involved parties, and witnesses because the number of involved parties with various roles is open ended. This schema could answer such questions as how many bodily injury claims did we experience in which the ABC Legal Partners represented claimants and in which there were no recorded witnesses to the accident?

Events are often modeled by a fact table containing a number of keys, each representing a participating dimension in the event. Such event tables often have no obvious numerical facts associated with them, and hence are called factless fact tables.

COVERAGE TABLES

Factless fact tables arise in another context that is something like events but that is more a description of something that didn t happen than something that did happen. From the grocery store data warehouse in Chapter 2 recall that our primary sales fact table registered the sales of products past the checkout stand in grocery stores. One of the powerful applications was the ability to study the behavior of items on promotion. However, our grocery store database contained a trap. Only the items that actually sell on a given day make it into the database. Since less than 20 percent of a grocery store s SKUs actually get sold on any given day, there will be many promoted items that don t appear in the database for an individual store on an individual day. Thus we can t use the existence of records in the fact table as the basis for answering the question *What items were on promotion that didn't sell?*

In order to record the complex many-to-many relationships involved in describing the promotion coverage, we must invoke a fact-table-like structure, whether we call it that or not. In general, even under a promotion with a well known name like Spring Markdown, the actual products on promotion will vary from store to store, and will be on promotion at different times. Thus it isn t possible to mark the product dimension table with items that are on promotion. Remember that any time a many-to-many relationship is being modeled we automatically and unavoidably have a fact table.

The answer to the promotion question is to build a *coverage* table that records which items are on promotion in which stores at which times. The promotion coverage schema is shown in Figure 10.4.

The Existence field, again, is always filled with the value "1" in order to make the SQL more readable. Some care must be taken with coverage tables, such as this one, to make sure that they don't balloon uncontrollably, since they can be very dense in their keys. In many grocery store chains, items are put on promotion and taken off promotion at weekly intervals, such as Saturday night. If this is the case, the grain of this coverage table should clearly be weekly. Another ameliorating factor is that only the promoted items need actually be stored in the coverage table. A coverage table is, in effect, an inventory snapshot table for a specially chosen subset of the inventory.

Note that this table contains the information about which products were on promotion. To determine which didn't sell, the item movement fact table is also needed. A **behavioral group** could be defined from the item movement table of all those products that sold on promotion in a given store. A second behavioral group could then be defined from the coverage table of those products that were on promotion. The set difference of these two behavioral groups would then be the set of products that were on promotion but didn't sell. If this final set difference were also stored as a behavioral group, then this group could be used in subsequent queries to determine whether those products sold well at other times or in general were poor sellers. The Star Tracker demonstration reporting tool and database included with the CDROM can be used for this kind of behavioral analysis.

Another case where a coverage table may be needed is in sales tracking applications where the product being sold is a big expensive product and only

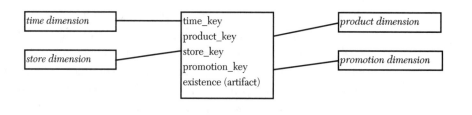

FIGURE 10.4

The promotion coverage schema.

some of the customers actually buy anything. In this case we have the same problem as in promotion coverage. The product sales database will not be able to answer the question *What customers assigned to the sales team did not purchase any products?*

Again, we need to model events that didn t happen. The coverage table for big product sales is shown in Figure 10.5. If the sales teams are not product specific, then the product dimension could be omitted.

These questions involve a complex pattern of matching on some keys and not matching on others. In Chapter 16, we will describe the architecture of these complex applications. The modelling of events that didn t happen is a design principle:

> Coverage tables are often tables of events that didn't happen. Coverage tables are usually factless in the same way as event tracking tables.

DATABASE SIZING FOR COLLEGE COURSE FACTLESS FACT TABLE

Please see the discussion at the beginning of Chapter 13 for detailed assumptions.

Course dimension: 500 courses
Professor dimension: 2 per course per semester
Student dimension: 100 per course per semester
Facility dimension: 2 per course per semester
Date dimension: 100 days per course per semester, 9 semesters => 900 days
Number of base fact records: $500 \times 2 \times 100 \times 2 \times 900 = 180$ *million records*

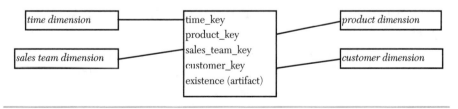

FIGURE 10.5

The big product sales coverage schema.

Number of key fields = 5; Number of fact fields = 0; Total fields = 5
Base fact table size = 180 million ×5 fields ×4 bytes = *3.6 GB*

DATABASE SIZING FOR HOSPITAL PATIENT PROCEDURE FACTLESS FACT TABLE

Patient dimension: 1,000,000 total patient stays
Procedure dimension: 10 procedures recorded per patient stay
Other dimensions: 1 each per procedure performed
Number of base fact records: 1,000,000 ×10 = *10 million records*
Number of key fields = 7; Number of fact fields = 0; Total fields = 7
Base fact table size = 10 million ×7 fields ×4 bytes = *0.28 GB*

DATABASE SIZING FOR ACCIDENT PARTIES FACTLESS FACT TABLE

Number of policies: 2,000,000
Number of covered item coverages (line items) per policy: 10
Yearly percentage of all covered item coverages with a claim: 5%
Average number of loss parties per claim: 10
Number of years: 3
Other dimensions: 1 each per claim loss party
Number of base fact records: 2,000,000 ×10 ×0.05 ×10 ×3 = *30 million records*
Number of key fields = 10; Number of fact fields = 0; Total fields = 10
Base fact table size = 30 million ×10 fields ×4 bytes = *1.2 GB*

DATABASE SIZING FOR PROMOTION COVERAGE FACTLESS FACT TABLE

Time dimension: 2 years ×365 days = 730 days
Product dimension: 30,000 products in each store
Store dimension: 300 stores
Percentage of products on promotion any given day: 10%
Number of base fact records: 730 ×30,000 ×300 ×0.10 = *657 million records*
Number of key fields = 4; Number of fact fields = 0; Total fields = 4

Base fact table size = 657 million ×4 fields ×4 bytes = *10.5 GB*

DATABASE SIZING FOR BIG PRODUCT SALES FACTLESS FACT TABLE

Time dimension: 2 years ×365 days = 730 days
Sales Team dimension: 100 sales teams
Customer dimension: 50 customers assigned to each sales team
Number of base fact records: 730 ×100 ×50 = *3.65 million records*
Number of key fields = 4; Number of fact fields = 0; Total fields = 4
Base fact table size = 3.65 million ×4 fields ×4 bytes = *0.1 GB*

11

Voyage Businesses

The last major schema type we will explore in this book involves businesses that want to track voyages. These businesses include airlines, shippers, and the travel-oriented segment of credit card businesses. We will carefully develop a schema for airline frequent flyer tracking and then we will illustrate schemas for a traditional shipper as well as a travel-oriented credit card.

THE FREQUENT FLYER DATA WAREHOUSE

In the airline frequent flyer application, the airline wants to track all the journeys taken by every member of its frequent flyer program. The airline marketing department wants to see what flights the frequent flyers take, which planes they fly, which seats they sit in, what the base fare they pay is, how often they upgrade their tickets, how they pay for their upgrades, how they redeem their frequent flyer miles, whether they respond to special fare promotions, how many overnight destinations they stay in, how long the overnight stays are, what other airlines are used on the same trips, and what proportion of these flyers have Platinum, Gold, or Aluminum status. It is assumed that the airline owns or has access to the airline reservation system on which the entire ticket is booked.

From the production system we are able to extract data with the following basic dimensionality for the flight segments:

153

- Customer (frequent flyer #)
- Leg origin (a city)
- Leg destination (a city)
- Flight
- Fare class
- Date flown
- Date purchased
- Sales channel
- Status
- Ticket #
- Segment #

In all of the voyage-oriented databases we find early in the design that the most meaningful grain of the database is the individual leg of the journey. At the leg level we have specific information about the individual airplane, the fare class, and other circumstances of the flight that cannot be ascribed to a multiple leg view of the trip. If we viewed the trip as a multiple-leg event, we would have to suppress all of these details. Although the flight identification generally would determine the origin and the destination, we call these key dimensions out separately to simplify the user's view of the database and to make access through the city table more efficient. The city airport table is joined alternately to the leg origin key and the leg destination key by using the SQL SYNONYM construct.

The flight dimension contains information about the flight, such as its scheduled takeoff and departure times, and the aircraft used. We assume that slowly changing dimension technique #2 is used to track changes to the flight description over time. In other words, we create an additional flight record each time a flight description changes. This would be tractable as long as the flight dimension did not grow bigger than a few hundred thousand records.

The fare class dimension describes the type of seat purchased (economy, business class, or first class), whether the seat was upgraded, and whether the ticket was purchased on a promotion, deal, or award. In the case of the airline, we decide not to separate the notion of promotion from the notion of fare class because after interviewing end users and database administrators at the airline, we conclude that fare class and promotion are inextricably linked and it does not make sense to separate them in the database.

The sales channel dimension identifies how the ticket was purchased, whether through a travel agency, directly from the airline, or via an on-line service. The date flown and date purchased keys link to a date table in the obvious way. The status dimension describes the customer's status at the time of the flight, including the frequent flyer classification. The ticket # and segment # are degenerate dimensions that serve to group and order the segments of a particular ticket.

In spite of the powerful dimensional framework we have set up, we are unable to answer easily one of the most important questions about our frequent flyers: *Where are our customers going?*

If we fetch all the legs of the airline voyage and put them in order by sorting on the segment #, we still have a hard time figuring out what the point of the trip is. Most complete voyages will start and end at the same airport. If an overnight stop is used as a criterion for a meaningful destination, we would need to do some expensive and tricky processing whenever we tried to summarize a large number of voyages by the meaningful stops. This is reminiscent of the earned income problem for subscription businesses.

The answer is to introduce two more airport SYNONYM dimensions, trip origin and trip destination. These are determined at extract time by looking on the ticket for overnight stops. This could be refined further to any stop of more than four hours, which is the official airlines definition of a stopover. In any case, our revised schema is shown in Figure 11.1. This schema is capable of answering all the questions posed at the beginning of this section.

SHIPPING DATA WAREHOUSE

The shipper business we will model is a transoceanic shipping company transporting bulk goods in containers from foreign ports to domestic ports. The voyages have multiple stops at intermediate ports. It is possible that the container may be offloaded from one ship to another at a port, and it is possible that one or more of the legs may be by truck rather than ship. Items in containers are being shipped from an original shipper to a final consignor. We use the same technique of representing both the legs as well as the trip in four port dimensions. Our shipping schema is shown in Figure 11.2.

The ship mode dimension identifies the type of shipping company (vessel or truck) and in the case of a vessel identifies the specific vessel. The item di-

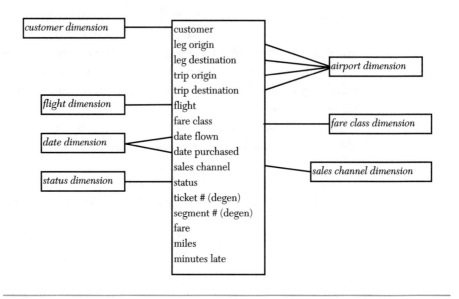

FIGURE 11.1

The airline frequent flyer warehouse.

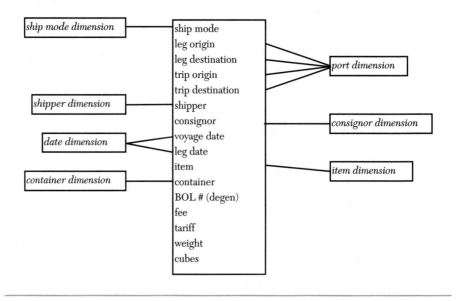

FIGURE 11.2

The shipping data warehouse.

mension contains a description of a particular type of item in a container. The container dimension describes the size of the container and whether it is refrigerated or requires electrical power. The BOL # is the bill of lading number describing the shipment. The grain of the fact table is line item by container on a particular BOL on a particular vessel on a particular leg of a voyage. We assume that the fees and tariffs are applicable to the leg of the voyage.

The shipping warehouse schema looks very much like the frequent flyer schema. Both have a rather large number of dimensions when counting the SYNONYM derived ports and dates as separate.

TRAVEL CREDIT CARD DATA WAREHOUSE

The third example of a voyage schema is a travel-oriented credit card operation that tracks airline flights, hotel stays, and car rentals. We will start with the airline frequent flyer warehouse and add two more similar tables to represent the hotel stays and the car rentals. The hotel stays schema appears in Figure 11.3, and the car rentals schema is shown in Figure 11.4.

The three schemas, frequent flyer, hotel stays, and car rentals can be viewed as a kind of value chain. Drill-across applications can be built that tie these fact tables together on the common dimensions. The common dimensions include

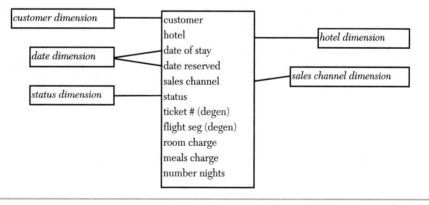

FIGURE 11.3

The hotel stays schema.

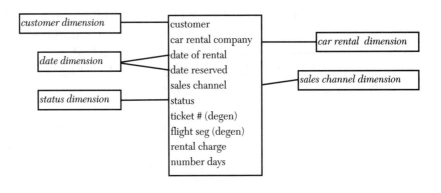

FIGURE 11.4

The car rentals schema.

customer, date, ticket #, and flight segment. The ticket # and flight segment in the two schemas in Figures 11.3 and 11.4 assumes that the hotel stays and the car rentals are part of a trip taken by airplane. These degenerate dimensions allow hotel stays and car rentals to be interleaved into a trip correctly. If the hotel stays and car rentals cannot be linked to an airplane trip, then these degenerate dimensions have null values. For the hotel stays the grain of the fact table is the entire stay. For car rentals the grain of the fact table is the entire car rental episode.

The primary characteristic of a voyage schema is the need to place origin and destination dimensions in the fact table for both the leg and the overall trip.

DATABASE SIZING FOR AIRLINE FREQUENT FLYER FACT TABLE

Please see the discussion at the beginning of chapter 13 for detailed assumptions.

Time dimension: 2 years
Number of frequent flyers: 3,000,000
Average number of flights per year for each frequent flyer: 10

Number of base fact records: 2 × 3,000,000 × 10 = *60 million records*
Number of key fields = 13 (including degenerate); Number of fact fields = 3;
    Total fields = 16
Base fact table size = 60 million × 16 fields × 4 bytes = *3.8 GB*

DATABASE SIZING FOR SHIPPER FACT TABLE

Time dimension: 2 years
Number of vessel voyages per year: 200
Number of containers per vessel voyage: 800
Number of different items per container: 10
Number of legs per voyage: 5
Number of base fact records: 2 × 200 × 800 × 10 × 5 = *16 million records*
Number of key fields = 12 (including degenerate); Number of fact fields = 4;
    Total fields = 16
Base fact table size = 16 million × 16 fields × 4 bytes = *1.0 GB*

DATABASE SIZING FOR HOTEL STAYS FACT TABLE

Time dimension: 2 years
Number of credit card customers tracked: 2,000,000
Number of hotel stays per credit card customer per year: 10
Number of base fact records: 2 × 2,000,000 × 10 = *40 million records*
Number of key fields = 8 (including degenerate); Number of fact fields = 3;
    Total fields = 11
Base fact table size = 40 million × 11 fields × 4 bytes = *1.8 GB*

DATABASE SIZING FOR CAR RENTALS FACT TABLE

Time dimension: 2 years

Number of credit card customers tracked: 2,000,000

Number of car rentals per credit card customer per year: 10

Number of base fact records: $2 \times 2,000,000 \times 10 = 40\ million\ records$

Number of key fields = 8 (including degenerate); Number of fact fields = 2;
   Total fields = 10

Base fact table size = 40 million $\times$ 10 fields $\times$ 4 bytes = *1.6 GB*

12

BUILDING A DIMENSIONAL DATA WAREHOUSE

Building a dimensional data warehouse is a process of matching the needs of the user community to the realities of the available data. There is a set of nine major decision points in the database design that will be driven by the needs of the user community and the realities of the data. This chapter describes a methodology for asking the right questions and eliciting a complete description of the organization's environment so that a satisfactory design for a dimensional data warehouse can be completed. It must be pointed out that this methodology is not a formulaic approach that can mindlessly be applied to an organization. There are significant areas of design judgment that need to be exercised. We always need to ask ourselves whether we are addressing the most important needs of the organization most effectively, and we always need to ask ourselves whether our dimensional data warehouse is simple enough to be usable by the end users and by the software.

THE NINE DECISION POINTS

We start our discussion of the methodology by briefly enumerating the nine decision points of a complete database design. The bulk of this chapter will then be the techniques for gathering the evidence needed to make the nine decisions. At the end of the chapter we will return to the nine decision points to see how the evidence is used to make the decisions. We state the nine decision points as a single design principle:

The nine decision points of a complete database design for a dimensional data warehouse consist of deciding on the following:

1. The processes, and hence the identity of the fact tables
2. The grain of each fact table
3. The dimensions of each fact table
4. The facts, including precalculated facts
5. The dimension attributes with complete descriptions and proper terminology
6. How to track slowly changing dimensions
7. The aggregations, heterogeneous dimensions, minidimensions, query modes and other physical storage decisions
8. The historical duration of the database
9. The urgency with which the data is extracted and loaded into the data warehouse

We recommend that these nine decisions be made in the order given. This methodology is a top-down methodology because it starts by identifying the major processes in the company where data is being collected. Figure 12.1 shows the processes that might be available for a typical retailer. These would represent data extract opportunities in this company. Notice that we start from these data extract opportunities because in most respects it is a waste of time to dream about data sources that don't exist. Our job as data warehouse designers is to start with existing sources of used data.

When the processes are identified, one or more fact tables will be built from each process selected. Before any fact table can be designed in detail, a decision must be made as to what an individual low-level record in that fact table means. This is the grain of the fact table. Typical grains are the individual trans-

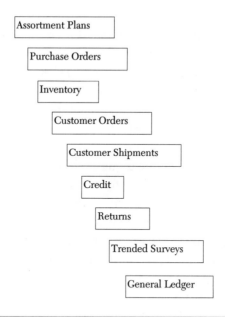

FIGURE 12.1

The available major processes in a retail company (for example).

action, the individual line item, a daily snapshot, or a monthly snapshot. See Figure 12.2 for one of the fact tables, in this case purchase orders (PO).

When the grain of the fact table is known, then the dimensions and their respective grains can be identified. There will be additional dimensions that are not strictly required by the fact table grain decision. In this purchase order line

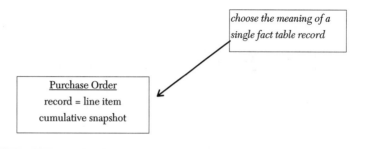

FIGURE 12.2

Choosing the grain of each fact table.

cumulative status fact table, once we identify the time, the product, the vendor, and the degenerate purchase order number dimensions, we can add other helpful descriptive dimensions whose values we know in the context of the purchase order line item. These decision support dimensions include the ship from warehouse, the ship mode, the ship to warehouse, and the manufacturer's deal. The addition of these dimensions does not change the number of records in the fact table, and they are not needed to define a unique key but are very helpful in making this particular fact table more powerful. Each of the dimensions can be thought of as an entry point. See Figure 12.3.

The choice of the dimensions is the key step in the design. We decide on the identity of the dimensions before worrying too much about where we are going to get all the dimensional attributes. Once the dimensions have been chosen, then the next task is to flush out all the measured facts for the fact table (see Figure 12.4), and then finally to complete populating the dimension records.

At this point the main structure of the logical design is complete, and we turn our attention to the top-level physical design issues. These include how to track slowly changing dimensions, and what to do about including aggregations, heterogeneous dimensions, minidimensions, and query modes. We then

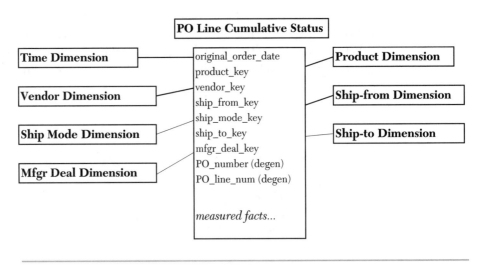

FIGURE 12.3

The fact table with its dimensions identified.

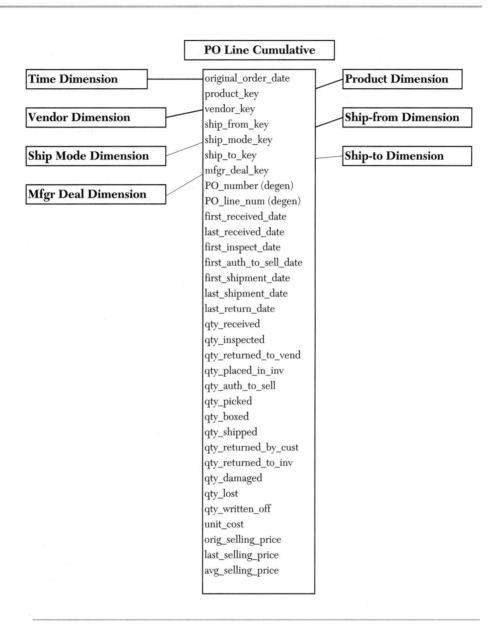

FIGURE 12.4

The fact table with its detailed facts identified.

can plan for the intended duration of the database. In most cases, we leave open the possibility of changing our minds and letting history accumulate for more than, say, the three years we might have initially planned for. Finally, we must decide on the urgency of the data. While we may have decided in the second step that the grain implies daily data capture of all transactions that could affect the cumulative status of the purchase order, we still would have a choice as to updating this snapshot record every day as of the previous day, or perhaps waiting until the end of the week.

Now that we see the nine decision points laid out in logical order, how do we probe the organization to make these decisions?

We cannot make the nine decisions in a vacuum. There is no single answer, even if all the legacy data **copy books** are spread out in front of the designer. The design can only come from a balance of the end user's requirements and the realities of the data. We determine the end user requirements by interviewing the end users and we determine the realities of the data by looking at the copy books and interviewing the **legacy system** DBAs.

INTERVIEWING THE END USERS

Interviewing the end users is the most important first step in designing a data warehouse. The interviews really accomplish two purposes. First, the interviews give the designers insight into the needs and expectations of the user community. All nine of the decision points outlined above will be driven from evidence collected in the interviews. This interviewing is an important step in connecting the data warehouse team to the business. Hopefully this connection has been established long before the data warehouse initiative was begun. If not, this is a great excuse for the data warehouse team to learn what is going on in the business. Knowledge of the business is the "gold coin" for the data warehouse team. The end user interviews must not be left out.

The second purpose of the interviews is to allow the designers to raise the level of awareness of the forthcoming data warehouse with the end users, and to adjust and correct some of the users' expectations. Interviewing the end users is definitely a double-edged sword. The data warehouse team had better be prepared to move ahead with the design of a warehouse shortly after conducting the interviews, because the data warehouse will be on the minds of the end users! An unfortunate syndrome in some organizations is a user community that has become rather testy on the subject of data warehouses because they have been interviewed multiple times, but no data warehouse has been delivered to them.

The actual interviewing process should alternate between end user groups and the legacy system DBAs. As themes begin to emerge from the end user interviews, questions will arise as to whether the underlying data can support the themes. For instance, if the user community has decided that they need to manage the business by the profitability of the various business segments, such as profitability by customer, or profitability by product grouping, then this immediately suggests a whole host of data issues. Profit can be calculated only if both the elements of revenue and the elements of cost are available. Profit can only be subdivided down to customer or product grouping if the elements of cost (especially) make sense at a customer or product-grouping level. For instance, if the stated distribution costs in a company are national averages that are not time dependent, not product dependent, and not warehouse dependent, this raises serious issues about whether the data warehouse can satisfy users' needs to manage their business by profit. The word *profit*, when it emerges as a theme in user interviews, triggers an immediate need to go look at the underlying data sources to see how well they support this theme. Early in the interview process, the data warehouse designers need to explore with the end user groups whether some partial limitations on the data will still be acceptable to them. For instance, the distribution cost data may be product dependent and warehouse dependent, but may be an average cost number set by the manager of logistics every six months for each product and warehouse. This issue needs to be explored during the interviews with the end users to see if that level of cost tracking is acceptable.

The ideal interviews are one-hour sessions where two or three members of the data warehouse design team meet with an area manager and several of his or her subordinates. Really large meetings are a waste of time because one or two vocal people will do all of the talking, and the rest of the people will wish they were back at their desks. One hour is a good target, because it will be easy to fill this time talking about interesting things, and it is much less intimidating to schedule an hour than it is to schedule a half day or a whole day. Normally the design team can get what they need in an hour, and it is a good idea to step back and absorb the main points of the interview before proceeding with the next interview.

In a large organization, one or two examples of every possible constituency must be interviewed, even if they aren't on the first rollout schedule for the data warehouse. It is especially important to get both headquarters and field perspective in the primary interviews. It is also important to get marketing, sales, finance, logistics, and senior management perspectives. A typical schedule of interviews in a large, multi-billion-dollar organization would be one or two weeks of interviews, with 20 to 30 groups. The total number of people affected by the interviews could be 50 to 100 people. It is best not to interview all the marketing teams one after another, and then all of the production teams one after another, and then all the field teams one after another. The designers' understanding of the business will evolve as the interviews progress and it is helpful to return to an early topic late in the interview process. A corollary to this is that by the end of the interview process, the design team should hope to be learning nothing new! The interviews should be quite predictable near the end of the process. If that is the case, then it is likely the interviews have touched all the important themes in the business. If significant new ground is being broken at the end of the interview schedule, then there is the suspicion that the whole picture has not been seen.

Although the ideal user group to interview is an area (first-level) manager and several of his or her subordinates, sometimes the interviews must be with a single person. The design team should be sensitive to not overwhelm an individual contributor by surrounding the hapless individual with a crowd of people asking questions or taking notes. In those cases, the design team should just consist of two people, and the conversation can be relatively low key. The individual contributor, especially if he or she is a young employee, may not be able to answer very strategic questions like "What is the mission of your department?" On the other hand, interviews with executives are often conducted in the executive's office without other subordinates in attendance, and these interviews can be more freewheeling. Again, the design team should limit attendance to two or three people, but the questions should be much more strategic. Any executive worth his or her salt should be able to talk about the mission of his or her department!

THE CONTENT OF THE END USER INTERVIEWS

The secret of the end user interviews is to get the end users to talk about what they do, in their own terms. The interviews should not be "What do you want in a data warehouse?" Designing a data warehouse is IS's responsibility, not the end user's responsibility. The data warehouse designers need to listen to how the end users describe their jobs and accumulate evidence that helps them make the nine decisions. There are a series of questions that can be asked in every interview that normally will stimulate very valuable answers. These questions can be used as a literal checklist. By going through these questions, usually it will be easy to fill up an hour. But be flexible. Occasionally an individual or even a group will answer the questions with a sentence or two and then stop talking. It can feel like pulling teeth. It is all right if those interviews only last 20 or 30 minutes. Rest assured that the next interview will go for an hour and a half and everyone will want to talk! Here are the questions that the author has found to be successful starting points for hundreds of interviews:

- *Will participants briefly introduce themselves?* Carefully note the names and group affiliations of everyone in attendance. This is the time to get spellings of names. When later summarizing the results of the interviews, it is very helpful to list everyone who was interviewed. This lends credibility to the results of the interview process. Get each person to say a sentence or two about his or her responsibilities. This will give the design team some cues about the range of topics that need to be covered before the interview is over. The design team should also introduce themselves. Normally, one person on the design team takes the lead in asking the questions and pursuing various content themes, but it takes the pressure off that person if other designers in attendance keep some questions in reserve to ask at various times in the interviews.

- *What is the mission of your team/group/department/division?* The mission question is a good place to start the interview. It forces the group to step back from what they do and give the design team some perspective. Sometimes it is clear that the group hasn't thought about their mission recently! In this question, and in most of the questions, the design team needs to judge whether the answer is an idealized answer or a real answer. Professional interviewers call these two kinds of responses the normative model of an organization, and the descriptive model of an organization, respectively. Both models are valuable, but listeners should try to decide which one they are getting from the end users. For instance, end users may say "Our job is to watch for *unusual changes* in spending by department from month to month and to determine the reason." This is probably a normative (ideal) description. A good follow-up question is *How do you actu-*

ally do that? Hopefully end users will then give you the descriptive model of what they do. They may say "Well, I know that all of those accounts are updated by the people at the general office, so I call Jane and ask her to look up the underlying detail on her system." Obviously, this is a valuable response, because if the design team hears this more than once, it is likely that "Jane's system" needs to be identified and considered as a legacy source for the data warehouse.

Another question that springs from the original normative response to the mission question is *What do you mean by an unusual change?* This question is an example of following up on the original response. The response to this question will be a direct guide to how the end user tool should be able to handle exception reporting, or how a more sophisticated agent process would comb the data warehouse looking for things to call to a user's attention.

Another follow-up question that springs from the comment about Jane's system is *How would someone know that Jane's department is responsible for those accounts?* The answer to this question probably affects what is stored in the account dimension of this database. Perhaps there needs to be a field called Originating Department. Such a field will not be stored in the general ledger transaction itself, but it is probably known and capturable somewhere.

Continuing with our list of questions we next ask:

- *What is the most significant recent shift in the way you are doing business?* For some reason, there is always a most significant recent shift in the way people are doing business. The most common answer is "We are trying to move to a customer focus." The next most common answer is "We are trying to manage our business by the profitability of each part of the business." These answers have a very significant impact on the design of the data warehouse. In fact, it is likely that the executive who told the organization about this significant shift is expecting the data warehouse to be the primary tool for implementing the new way to manage the business!

  The answer to this question begs for multiple follow-up questions, such as:

- *What do you mean by a customer focus?*
- *How do you think about customers?*

- *How many customers are there?*
- *How do you group customers? Do these groupings change dynamically?*
- *For which parts of the business can you measure profit?*
- *Exactly what are the components of revenue and cost that make up your view of profit?*
- *Are the components of cost accurately measured at the level you expect? Are they activity based?*

These are all example questions that can come from the end users' response. The interviewer needs to use some judgment as to which questions make sense. Some groups will have a narrower focus and issues of customer satisfaction and profitability may not be their primary concern. For example, the warehouse logistics group may be trying to track quality issues with incoming products from various vendors. The interviewer needs to be able to shift gears and ask questions that are appropriate to this area, such as:

- *How do you track quality measures on product deliveries? Is that in a separate system?*
- *Do you maintain a time series of quality measures by vendor?*
- *Do you track the vendors' follow-up back to the original purchase order?*
- *Would it be helpful to have this on-line?*

Another question similar to the significant shift question is:

- *What do your competitors do that you don't?* This can be a good, creative mind-expander kind of question. The danger is that the answer will be a blue-sky answer that is unrealistic in terms of the data resources that are actually available. But the answer may illuminate more clearly some boundaries within the organization about what can be accomplished and what cannot be accomplished. Of course, this can be followed up with:
- *Do you want to do that also?*

This next question is very valuable because it will elicit specific measures that can go into the data warehouse:

- *How do you measure success in your group?* The answers will not only provide candidate fact table measures but will suggest the need for new data sources. Typical answers might be profit, volume (number of units), revenue, share of market, cost containment, number of errors, and the price gap with competitors. Each of these has quite a different impact on a potential data warehouse design. This question is also likely to elicit the mention of special metrics, like **BDI, CDI**, and GMROI. (See the glossary at the end of the book for the definitions.) The design team must track down the exact definition of these metrics and figure out how to represent the additive components within the fact table so that these metrics can be calculated in any query. Many times the users will use the metrics but not be able to supply the exact definition!

The design team should ask about the value chain, if there is one:

- *Does your group look at purchase orders, inventory,* and *shipments?*
- *How much of the value chain are you concerned with?*

In insurance, a similar question can be asked:

- *Do you need to see both premium and loss information?* Obviously, the answers to these questions directly drive the decision to bring up certain fact tables together. These questions are important, because although all the data sources may be available, they may be viewed by management with very different priorities. There are manufacturing companies where distribution and warehouse logistics are simply not very interesting because these areas are viewed correctly as being well managed and not a source of financial risk or opportunity compared with other areas like marketing. Similarly, many insurance companies want to focus first on claims rather than on policy formation. The data warehouse team needs to be very pragmatic and bring up those databases that are of most concern to management first.

The design team needs to ask the grain question directly:

- *Do you need to see the data at a daily grain?* (time dimension)
- *Do you need to distinguish Tuesdays from Saturdays?* (time dimension)
- *Do you need to see how the special promoted items get depleted on a day-to-day basis?* (time dimension)
- *Are monthly snapshots sufficient for what you want to do?* (time dimension)
- *Do you need to track products at the SKU level? at the lot level?* (product dimension)

- *Do you want to track sales at the individual store level? at the customer level?* (store or customer dimension)
- *Do you want to track sales at an individual promotion level in the store on a particular day? How many identifiable promotions are there per year? What is a promotion? What is a special? What is a price zone?* (promotion dimension)

The combination of grains from each of the dimensions yields the grain for the central fact table.

Depending on the database, the design team may need to determine if a table of individual transactions must be maintained, or a cumulative snapshot, or a monthly snapshot, or some combination of these in separate fact tables.

Questions that indicate the need for a transaction-level view, assuming that a transactional view of the data is relevant, include the following:

- *How many transaction types are there? How many of these have associated reason codes? Which ones are interesting to the business? Do you want to break down the activity by transaction type, and further by reason code?*
- *Do you look at counts of particular transaction types?*
- *Do you look at the timings of certain kinds of transactions. or the gaps in between transactions of certain types?* This could include questions relating to loading of telephone service representatives, or the number of impulse pay-per-view calls just prior to a sports event starting on a cable system, or the length of time between an insurance claim opening and the first payment made to the claimant.
- *Would you want to ask how many of the orders were taken on the phone by sales representatives that had less than one month of experience, and what were the number of returns associated with these representatives compared with the average of all other sales representatives?*

These last few questions generally require a transaction-grained fact table to answer. They are hard to answer from a monthly snapshot database because it is difficult to provide enough summary buckets in a monthly snapshot to answer all these varied questions.

On the other hand, there are questions that indicate a specific need for a monthly snapshot fact table:

- *Do you look at the business from a monthly perspective?*
- *Is the calculation of monthly revenue a simple calculation from the transactions during that month or is it a complex calculation depending on a long series of transactions extending back into previous months?* The design team will suspect what the answers are to these questions but they are worth asking. In a straight sales business, the sales transactions are simple debits and credits to the revenue and a special monthly summary database may not be needed unless it is built as an aggregate solely for performance reasons. But in a pay-in-advance business like subscriptions or insurance, the relationship between the transactions and the revenue is very complicated and it is hard to get a swift calculation of monthly revenue. In this case it is almost certain that the business will want a monthly summary fact table as well as a transaction-grained fact table.

A good question to set expectations is:

- *Do you expect this database to tie to the general ledger each month?* The user's answer in most cases is yes. From the end user's point of view this would be the cleanest possible outcome. Unfortunately, most rolling operational databases cannot easily tie to the general ledger. The dimensions of most operational databases are not the same as the accounts in the general ledger, and the general ledger adjustments that occur during the month-end close process cannot be represented in most cases within the dimensionality of the data warehouse. The simple answer to this question is that the only data warehouse fact table that can always tie to the general ledger is the fact table that *is* the general ledger. This point probably should be made with most of the user groups in order to set expectations appropriately.

It is valuable to ask if there are special descriptions of some of the key dimensions that could possibly be added to the data warehouse:

- *Do you maintain a special store profile description, such as floor layouts, or last remodel dates, or department types within the store? How would we get these descriptions in order to add them to the store table?* (store dimension)
- *Do you maintain customer behavior scores or customer credit scores? How can we get these scores in order to add them to the customer table?* (customer dimension)

- *Do you have access to the original credit applications made by the customer? Can we add some of the demographic information from these applications to the customer table?* (customer dimension)
- *Would it make sense to associate demographic data with each of the stores or sales regions? Does someone in marketing already have such demographic data?* (customer dimension or sales team dimension)
- *Do you have a table of ingredients for each of the products? Would it be useful to break down final sales by dependence on ingredients?* (product dimension)

The interviewees will probably like this one. A yes answer to the ingredients question probably means building a special fact table to record the many-to-many relationships between ingredients and products. This, of course, is the same problem as parts and assemblies. In that case, the special fact table is called a *bill of materials*.

It is helpful to ask an interview group who else in the company they think could use the data sources you have been talking about:

- *Who else do you think would be interested in this data? Are they your clients, or vice versa?* The answer to this question may suggest another group that probably should be interviewed. It also tends to build a case for a particular data set to be included in the warehouse if there are multiple groups who would be interested in it.

It is important to ask about how to handle slowly changing dimensions:

- *What happens when you change the organization of your field geography? Do you track the old geography forward, or do you go back in history with the new geography? How long after the reorganization do you no longer care about the old district and region names?* The answers to these questions will drive which of the techniques the design team chooses for tracking these slowly changing dimensions. Remember that the choices are (1) to overwriting the old values, thereby losing the ability to track old values, or (2) creating a new dimension record, thereby perfectly partitioning history by time, but not allowing apples-to-apples comparisons across the change, or (3) adding a Current field in the dimension that allows the change to be tracked forever both forward and backward across the change, but making it awkward to partition history.

- *What happens when you make a minor formulation change to a product? Does production automatically change the SKU number or are you even informed of the change? Do you need to track this difference?* In the sales district example in the previous paragraph, technique #3 was somewhat attractive because it made sense to think of the sales teams in either geography at any point in time. But the product case is different. If the product truly underwent a formulation change, it does not make sense to apply technique #3. Technique #2 is preferable. Hopefully production has already made decision #2 by issuing a new SKU!
- *Do we need to track a full description of the insured party each time they make a claim or a claim is made against them? Which attributes are critical to be tracked?* This kind of question is key in businesses with big customer lists, especially insurance. The answer to this question will determine how to maintain special keys for this slowly changing dimension, and for really big dimensions, how to partition off the critical demographic variables that need to be tracked correctly over time.

A final question concerns urgency:

- *Do you need yesterday's data available today?* Note that this is not the same as the grain question. A group may need to be able to distinguish Tuesdays from Saturdays (grain) but not need yesterday's data today (urgency).
- *How soon after the end of the month do you need the monthly snapshot?*

The answers to these questions will drive the design of the production data extract system.

At the end of the interview, after thanking the users for their time and energy, it is a good time to ask them for sample reports they depend on illustrating some of the issues discussed. Usually by this time they are comfortable that you need access to their most sensitive (e.g., useful) data, and they are glad to hand it over. The goal at the end of the interview process is to have a three- to six-inch stack of management reports.

INTERVIEWING THE DBAS

Although most of the interviews will be with end user groups, it is vital to intersperse these end user interviews with DBA interviews. The DBAs are often the primary experts on the legacy systems that may be used as the sources for the data warehouse. These interviews serve as a reality check on some of the themes that come up in the end user interviews. For instance, as we have discussed, the ability to measure profit by various segments of the business depends critically on what the underlying data is. If profit is the new management technique sweeping the company, then the DBA interview that illuminates the quality of the cost data should take place on the first or second day.

Another area that needs to be looked at closely is any form of call tracking. Often a detailed record of a customer call is logged as a transaction in a call tracking database, but a number of assumptions about that data may not be true. The call tracking database may record the sales representative, but not tie to the specific order. Thus it may be hard to figure out how long the order event lasted or what other transactions took place during the call.

The way to uncover these issues is to crawl through the legacy databases item by item. The DBA must bring the copy books describing the database, and the design team needs to take away copies of the copy books. The questions for the DBA include the following:

- *How do the various production systems relate to each other? Which system feeds which other system? Where does the data start?* Generally, the data warehouse team needs to know where the data originates and how it is transformed from step to step. A classic mistake is for the data warehouse to depend on a data set that is many steps removed from the original data collection. This can become a house of cards that ends up being maintained solely because the data warehouse is relying on a data sample too far down stream. The data warehouse will be less dependent on a series of batch jobs and cobbled-together production applications if the data warehouse taps into the data stream earlier in the process.
- *Who maintains the product master? Who maintains the customer master?* This, of course, directly drives the issue of where the data warehouse gets the masters for some of the key dimensions. The designers should pray that there is a firm answer to these questions. A bad answer is that multiple

groups maintain their own versions of the product master or the customer master. An even worse answer is "We were hoping that you would maintain the product (or customer) master."

- *Please provide me with an English text description of each important table in this database. Please provide me with an English text description of each field in each important table in this database. Please give a row count of every table in the database.* This question should actually be given to the affected DBA or DBAs days or weeks in advance of the interviews so that they can come to the meeting prepared, and with handouts. Even though this may be a fair amount of work, this is a minimum commitment that must be made by the production side of the house in supporting the needs of the data warehouse. This may even be a litmus test for whether IS management is serious about the data warehouse.

- *Which of the fields in the important tables are populated? Which are fully populated? Which are quality assured? Which are required at data input time? Which are validated at data input time? Please give me a printout of the cardinality (i.e., the count of the distinct values) of every field in the important tables. Please print out the first three pages (only) of each important table in the database.* This is a detailed follow-on to the previous question.

- *What do the codes mean? Where are the English text descriptions of the codes? Who can I ask what the codes mean?* A significant responsibility of the data warehouse design team is to provide English equivalents of all the codes. These must be dug up somewhere. It is simply not acceptable in a data warehouse to have unvarnished codes without explanations. The response that "all the marketing people know the codes" is a symptom of how serious the problem is, rather than being an excuse for leaving the descriptions out.

- *How are the keys to these tables administered? How are customer numbers assigned? How are product numbers assigned? Are the keys ever reassigned by production?* These questions have a significant impact on how the data warehouse administers its own keys. As we have seen in previous chapters, the production data extract system has to do a lot of key management, including generalizing production keys for slowly changing dimensions, and creating brand new keys for aggregates. The data warehouse may need to have a cross-reference table between the production keys and its own keys. One hopes that the production keys don't change.

- *What does production do when a customer profile changes? when a product description changes? Is a new production key always generated? Is there a change description available that documents exactly what changed? Are we even notified that anything has changed?* The production database may not know about or care about slowly changing dimensions. Or perhaps they track customers and products very carefully. The ability of the data warehouse to answer certain kinds of questions and the design of the production data extract system will depend significantly on the answers to these questions.

- *Is it possible to directly read the production data files? What systems are available to perform this read step? Are the changed records identified in the production data files? Can we read the original transaction history?* In Chapter 14 we saw that the first step in the production data extract system was reading the legacy data. The second step was isolating what had changed. The transaction history, of course, will be needed if the fact table is at the transaction grain. However, if the transaction grain is not being stored, it may be convenient to get the daily snapshot from the production system directly in one step.

- *Are there any fields in these tables that are used for two or more different purposes, depending on the context?* In a stream of transactions we would expect the Amount field to be used for different purposes, depending on the identity of the transaction. Hopefully in other databases this is not done often because it makes the extraction process much messier.

Again at the conclusion of the interview, after thanking the DBA for all of the copy books and special listings, it may be helpful to ask for any other reports that he or she provides to the user community. The chances are that these have already been provided by the end users, but it doesn't hurt to get multiple copies.

THE NINE DECISIONS REVISITED

With these in-depth interviews as background, it is much easier to imagine making the nine critical design decisions. Again, they consist of deciding on the following:

1. The processes, and hence the identity of the fact tables
2. The grain of each fact table

3. The dimensions of each fact table
4. The facts, including precalculated facts
5. The dimension attributes with complete descriptions and proper terminology
6. How to track slowly changing dimensions
7. Physical storage decisions, including aggregations, heterogeneous dimensions, minidimensions, and query modes
8. The historical duration of the database
9. The urgency with which the data is extracted and loaded into the data warehouse

All of these issues were explicitly woven into the questions in the previous two sections. While the design decisions will be forming as the interviews progress, it is important to defer the design until the interviews are finished. A summary of the interviews should be prepared with 15 to 20 pages of discussion of the business issues raised together with the implications for the design of the data warehouse, and followed by an assessment of whether the data exists within the organization to support the business issue in the data warehouse. The notes taken in the interviews must be combed repeatedly to find the major themes and to coherently organize them. If a significant extract issue exists with the data, this should be pointed out to provide a warning that a particular database may be costly or difficult to bring up. This business findings document should be reviewed by IS management and by key members of the staff who were interviewed, both to get concordance that the findings are accurate and to stimulate feedback on which parts of the data warehouse should be implemented first.

ASSEMBLING THE TEAM

When the path has been cleared to begin the design, the entire data warehouse team should be assembled for two or three days to go through the above nine steps in order. The attendees should be all the people who will have an ongoing responsibility for the data warehouse, including DBAs, system administrators, extract programmers, application developers, and support personnel. End users should not attend this design session because it will be hours or days of crawling through the fact and dimension tables, field by field.

First all the fact tables are identified and their grains chosen. Then the dimension tables are identified by name and their grains are chosen. It generally takes a full day to get this far.

Any E/R diagram for the legacy data is somewhat helpful at this stage but it has little to do with the process of identifying the fact tables or their grains. Rather, the E/R analysis serves to familiarize the staff with the complexities of the data. If an E/R analysis has not yet been performed on the legacy data, it is definitely not worthwhile to stop to perform this step.

FILLING IN THE DETAILS OF THE TABLES

Beginning on the second day, the individual facts are identified, together with their exact legacy sources. When a fact table has been finished, then each of its dimension tables must be flushed out in the same way. The exact legacy source fields are identified for every dimension attribute. This level of the design stops short of developing an exact extract plan or a block diagram of the extract system. That step takes place when the commitment to building the warehouse has been given. The source-field-to-destination-field map that is provided by this step of the design process serves as a detailed specification for the extract system requirements.

THE TOP-LEVEL PHYSICAL DESIGN

After all of the fields in the fact tables and the dimension tables have been identified, most of the attendees at the large design meeting can be excused. A smaller team can then make the initial design decisions surrounding slowly changing dimensions, aggregations, heterogeneous dimensions, minidimensions, and query modes. The tracking of slowly changing dimensions needs to be decided at an early stage because this has a pretty large effect on the storage and administration of the database. In a heterogeneous product environment, the core fact and dimension tables could be brought up first and the custom fact and dimension tables could be added to the database at a later point in time very gracefully without having to alter any of the logic of key administration. Aggregations, minidimensions, and query mode decisions can be made quite late in the game as physical tuning strategies after the database has been brought up.

HOW TO CHOOSE HARDWARE AND SOFTWARE

As the logical and top-level physical design comes into focus, there is an increasingly urgent need to decide on specific hardware and software choices. This is very confusing time for most IS shops, because the systems are expensive, and the decisions are very high profile. The vendors do not help very much because they have different vocabularies, and many times their agenda is to raise doubts about their competitors. What is a customer to think when a vendor claims to have **heteroskedastic forward pipelining** that of course is much better than any of the other vendors? And what about the other vendors who are now all "obsolete"? The author believes that the hardware and software choices boil down to two primary considerations:

1. Does the proposed system actually work?
2. Is this a vendor relationship we want to have for a long time?

Each IS shop will have to evaluate the vendor relationship for itself, but a good way to warm up that vendor relationship is to determine, absolutely, whether the system will work.

If the vendor can supply one or more reference accounts to visit that have already brought up a system much like the one for your organization, then this can be a wonderful way of rapidly calibrating the vendor's claims and determining what it is like to work with that vendor. It may be safe under this circumstance not to conduct a benchmark test.

If there are no available reference sites, then the next best option is to conduct a benchmark on a database that is large enough to be regarded as realistic. First, the vendor should be able to answer the following questions:

- *Can the system query, store, load, index, and alter a billion-row fact table with 12 dimensions?* Perhaps your fact table isn't this large, but the answer to this question should be revealing.
- *Can the system rapidly browse a 100,000 row dimension table?*

If the vendor answers these questions satisfactorily, then a series of three kinds of tests should be planned. The tests include fact table loading, dimension table loading, and multiuser querying. The methodology for the benchmark can be summarized as follows:

Goal: To simulate realistic system loading over an extended period of time in order to subject the target hardware and software platforms to a true test.

Method: *Fact Table Loading*: A large number of records (at least 100,000) are presented to the fact table for bulk loading. The fact table needs to be realistically large (at least 20 percent of design size) so that the indexing costs can be understood. It is assumed that the fact table possesses a single master index on the concatenated key, and perhaps a second index on an anonymous record key. The overall process of loading from start to finish is measured, including dropping any indexes, loading the records, and rebuilding any indexes.

Dimension Table Loading: A small number of records (perhaps 1,000) are added to a large dimension table (such as customer) and a small number of records are updated in place within the dimension table (perhaps 1,000). It is assumed that the dimension table is very heavily indexed for query performance. The performance of these steps is measured (1) by inserting and updating with indexes in place, and (2) by dropping all indexes, performing the insertions and updates, and then rebuilding all indexes. It is acceptable if one of these techniques does not perform well on the target DBMS, since the goal is to find the right administrative scenario for the target DBMS. The result of this test is the smaller of the two numbers.

Querying: Multiple PCs are connected via the network to the target server, each autonomously executing a series of queries. The queries are a realistically balanced set of 80 percent singletable browses and 20 percent multitable joins. Each workstation should run the same query suite in order to be able to measure the total number of query suites processed by the whole user community during the test. The individual queries should be systematically varied so that the test is not unreasonably distorted by caching effects. The number of queries should be great enough (50 or more) so that the database cannot be specially tuned to a particular query set. The clock time for each query, from launch to delivered answer set, must be measured. Test results from this query test include:

1. Average browse query response time
2. Average browse query delay compared with unloaded system
3. Ratio between longest and shortest browse query time
4. Average join query response time
5. Average join query delay compared with unloaded system
6. Ratio between longest and shortest join query time (indicates stability of optimizer)
7. Total number of query suites processed per hour

It is desirable for the browse queries to run very fast since they are related to user interface actions. Although absolute performance for the join queries is not as critical, it is desirable both that the queries execute in a reasonable time and that there not be dramatic variations in runtime between the longest and slowest query. Such variations would indicate a query optimizer that would be unsuitable for information warehouse queries. Note that the browse queries and the join queries must be executed in an intermixed fashion from the same workstations. The browse queries must not be separated into a different job and given a higher priority, since this is not how end user tools function.

Queries: It is not possible to write the detailed SQL for the individual queries because the specific data for the prototype test depends on the detailed database design. However, the queries can be constructed from the following methodology:

Four browse queries are followed by one join query. Each browse query is of the form:

SELECT DISTINCT FIELDNAME

from DIMENSION TABLE
where CONSTRAINT and CONSTRAINT (. . . and CON-
STRAINT)

where the CONSTRAINTs are simple equalities and simple IN lists. This simulates the user browsing pick lists that are constrained from previous picks.

Each join query is of the form:

```
SELECT
    NON-AGGREGATE FIELDNAME1,
    NON-AGGREGATE FIELDNAME2,
    SUM(AGGREGATE FIELDNAME3),
    SUM(AGGREGATE FIELDNAME4),
    SUM(AGGREGATE FIELDNAME5)
FROM
    DIMENSION TABLE1,
    DIMENSION TABLE2,
    DIMENSION TABLE3,
    DIMENSION TABLE4,
    FACT TABLE
WHERE
    JOINCONDITION1
    JOINCONDITION2 and
    JOINCONDITION3 and
    JOINCONDITION4 and
    DIMENSIONCONSTRAINT1 and
    DIMENSIONCONSTRAINT2 and
    DIMENSIONCONSTRAINT3 and
    DIMENSIONCONSTRAINT4 and
    DIMENSIONCONSTRAINT5 and
    DIMENSIONCONSTRAINT6
GROUP BY
    NON-AGGREGATE FIELDNAME1,
    NON-AGGREGATE FIELDNAME2
ORDER BY
    NON-AGGREGATE FIELDNAME1,
    NON-AGGREGATE FIELDNAME2
```

13

AGGREGATES

In the previous chapters we concentrated on the logical design issues for representing a broad range of businesses. We said relatively little about the size of the resulting databases and nothing about performance. It is time to turn our attention to these issues.

DATABASE SIZING

An implicit assumption in all of the designs in Chapters 2 through 11 is that atomic data is good. In nearly every case we chose the grain of the fact table to be the lowest level that was sensible. In most cases the grain was either the production transaction or the control document line item. In each of those chapters we estimated the approximate sizes of the fact tables we designed by making a few simple assumptions. We assumed all the field widths were 4 bytes. This represents a rough balance between fields of different widths in real databases. Small integer keys can be one or two bytes. Date keys are often represented as 4-byte quantities. Long integer keys are usually 4 bytes and can take on 2^{32} = 4 billion values. Other keys may well be very long alphanumeric strings of 12 to 15 bytes, but it is always possible to administer them in the extract process to be anonymous integers. Partly to make the point here that the keys can be quite compact, we have assumed that this kind of administration has taken place and that no key is longer than 4 bytes. A more thoughtful discussion of this decision is given in Chapter 14. We have also assumed that the additive numeric data values are 4 bytes. This assumption is safer than it sounds because later in this chapter we will argue that high-level aggregate records should be in separate derived fact tables, not in the primary fact table. In this way we avoid needing to set the field width for revenue dollars in any of these base-level fact tables to be able to store "the gross national product of the United States in pennies." A 4-byte scaled integer can represent a currency value of more than $40 million to the nearest penny. This is big enough for the line-item-oriented values in most of our examples.

The approximate raw database size for each of the databases we designed in the previous chapters is given at the end of each chapter. These sizes represent the total row size of base-level data, without indexes or aggregations (summaries). For the narrower fact tables, with four or fewer fact fields, the size of the master index on the composite key of the fact table will be in the range of 60 percent to 80 percent of the base fact table size. For wide fact tables, with 15 or 20 fact fields, the proportion of the master index size to the base table size will be smaller, potentially declining to the 30 percent to 50 percent range. In all these cases the size of the dimension tables and their associated indexes will be very much smaller than the fact tables and their indexes. The only dimension tables that are bigger than a small percentage of the fact table size are the individual customer dimensions in the financial services examples and the individual covered item dimensions in the insurance examples. Even a large customer dimension with 10 million records is not likely to be much larger than 5 or 6 GB with an elaborate set of indexes. We will visit the detailed issues of indexing dimension tables in the next chapter.

All of the fact tables developed in this book range from less than 1 GB to a high of 52 GB for just the base data, excluding indexes and aggregations. In most cases we have chosen as fine a grain of data as is practical, considering the definition of a transaction on the legacy system, and considering the limitations on the available information. For instance, we chose not to represent the grocery store at the individual ticket line item level because in most grocery stores we cannot identify the customer, and hence the purchase/repurchase behavior in the customer data cannot be readily analyzed. All of these databases fall into an eminently practical range for today's (1995) technology. Roughly speaking, fact tables of less than 1 billion rows and smaller than 100 GB can be loaded, indexed, and queried efficiently using the techniques described in this book.

Stepping back from these databases, however, it is clear that there is yet another wave of even larger databases that will need analysis in the next few years as technology is capable of storing and indexing much larger data sets. Examples of these larger data sets include mass merchandiser line item detail, telephone company call tracking, and credit card purchase tracking. We can estimate the sizes of these databases using the same logic as before:

Mass Merchandiser Line Item Detail

Time dimension: 3 years
Total annual merchandiser revenue: $80 billion
Average size of line item on an individual customer ticket: $5
Number of line items per year for total business: $80 billion / $5 = 16 billion
Number of base fact records: 16 billion × 3 = *48 billion records*
Number of key fields = 4; Number of fact fields = 4; Total fields = 8
Base fact table size = 48 billion × 8 fields × 4 bytes = *1.54 TB = 1540 GB*

Telephone Call Tracking

Time dimension: 3 years => 1095 days
Number of tracked calls per day: 100 million
Number of base fact records: 1095 × 100,000,000 = *109 billion records*
Number of key fields = 5; Number of fact fields = 3; Total fields = 8
Base fact table size = 109 billion × 8 fields × 4 bytes = *3.49 TB = 3490 GB*

Credit Card Purchase Tracking

Time dimension: 3 years => 36 months
Number of credit card accounts: 50 million
Average number of purchases per month per account: 30
Number of base fact records: 36 × 50,000,000 × 30 = *54 billion records*
Number of key fields = 5; Number of fact fields = 3; Total fields = 8
Base fact table size = 54 billion × 8 fields × 4 bytes = *1.73 TB = 1730 GB*

Although these large databases are above the current (1995) comfort zone of one billion fact table records and 100 GB of base data size, nevertheless they are within reach. It seems likely that by the turn of the century, hardware and software technology will comfortably embrace these large data sets.

ADVANTAGES OF AGGREGATES

A major point of the analysis done in the previous section is to show that the foundation layers of all these dimensional data warehouses have a huge number of records. As we have mentioned, this large number of detailed records is needed, not because an analyst is going to need a single record at this level, but because the analyst must be able to make very precise cuts between records. If we don't track the individual account, we can't group accounts into the most interesting clumps. If we don't track the lowest-level product subdivision, then we can't pull out all the groups of products we might want to track.

Even though many queries will opportunistically need to retrieve clumps of base-level data, most queries will relax the constraints on one or more of the dimensions. If all we have is base-level data, then relaxing constraints on one or more dimensions means that we let a vast number of records into our query. Consider the following business questions for a large retail company:

- How much total business did my newly remodeled stores do compared with the chain average?
- How did leather goods items costing less than $5 do with my most frequent shoppers?
- What was the ratio of nonholiday weekend days total revenue to holiday weekend days?

In all three cases, we need very detailed data from one of the major dimensions, but we are either summarizing or omitting detail from some of the other dimensions. In the first question, we need specific stores but we are summarizing over all products. In the second, we need specific products but we are summarizing across all stores. In the third, we need specific days on the calendar but we are summarizing across both product and store. All of these questions will be expensive to process if we have only base-level data. What is needed here is a set of several different precomputed aggregates that will accelerate each of these queries. The effect on performance is not small. It is typical to expect anywhere from a tenfold to a thousandfold improvement in runtime by having the right aggregates available. We state this as a design principle:

The use of prestored summaries (aggregates) is the single most effective tool the data warehouse designer has to control performance.

This principle assumes that the database is set up according to the techniques described in this book, namely as a dimensional data model, and that the designer is not fighting the DBMS optimizer. As we described in Chapter 2, the DBMS should always evaluate the dimension tables first, and then present the composite key candidates to the fact table for lookup. This deterministic evaluation approach means that the DBA should not be wasting his or her time trying to get the optimizer back on track. Rather, the DBA should be spending time watching what the users are doing and deciding whether to build more aggregates.

Another benefit of aggregates is that they can be guaranteed to be correct. The definition of *established products* may be obvious to most marketing managers in a company, but it is risky to have every user build this group every time an analysis is done.

HOW TO STORE AGGREGATES

An aggregate is a fact table record representing a summarization of base-level fact table records. An aggregate fact table record is always associated with one or more aggregate dimension table records. For example, in a base-level fact table dimensioned by UPC level products, individual stores, and individual days, we can imagine the following aggregate records:

- Category-level product aggregates by store by day (a one-way aggregate)
- District-level store aggregates by product by day (a one-way aggregate)
- Monthly sales aggregates by product by store (a one-way aggregate)
- Category-level product aggregates by store district by day (a two-way aggregate)
- Category-level product aggregates by store district by month (a three-way aggregate)

Not only do we have these new fact table records, but we must have aggregate dimension table entries describing category level products, store districts, and months. Where do we put these new fact table records and dimension table records, and how do we administer them?

There are two main approaches to storing the additional fact and dimension table records needed for aggregates. The techniques can be described as *new fact tables* and *new Level fields*. The two techniques have nearly identical impacts on overall data storage and on the administration of keys, but they have very different impact on applications and data loading. We will describe the two approaches in detail.

New Fact Tables for Aggregates

Suppose in our grocery store retail database that we wish to create aggregate records for category totals in the product dimension, aggregate records for district totals in the store dimension, and aggregate records for monthly totals in the time dimension. This actually implies seven different kinds of aggregate records:

1. One-way aggregate: category totals by store by day
2. One-way aggregate: district totals by product by day
3. One-way aggregate: monthly totals by product by store
4. Two-way aggregate: category totals by district totals by day
5. Two-way aggregate: category totals by month totals by store
6. Two-way aggregate: district totals by month totals by product
7. Three-way aggregate: category totals by district totals by month totals

Each of these aggregate types occupies its own fact table. These fact tables can be thought of as *derivative* fact tables since they are derived from the main base-level fact table. Each fact table must be joined to one or more derivative dimension tables. For example, the first one-way aggregate fact table listed above must be joined to a derivative product dimension table consisting only of category entries. The schema appears in Figure 13.1.

The category dimension table is a drastically reduced version of the original product dimension table shown in Figure 3.7. The only attributes from Figure 3.7 that make sense at the category level are category description and department description. All the other attributes must be suppressed because they describe individual products. The category keys are entirely new artificial keys that did not exist in the base-level product table. It is usually the responsibility of the data warehouse team to build these keys during the nightly extract process when the base-level data comes in from the stores. This procedure is described in detail in the next chapter. The other dimensions are unaffected in this category aggregate sales fact table in this case because we are leaving

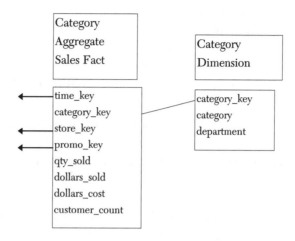

FIGURE 13.1

The category aggregate sales fact table.

all the other dimensions at their original base-level granularity. This leads to a design principle:

The creation of aggregate fact table records always requires the creation of artificial keys in each of the dimensions being aggregated.

The category aggregate sales fact table is populated entirely by records that did not exist in the base-level sales fact table because every record is a category total. The records have the same structure as the records in the base-level sales fact table, because all the keys make sense at the category level, and all the facts can be summarized to the category level. The first three facts (quantity sold, dollars sold, and dollar cost) are fully additive along all the dimensions, and there is no controversy in computing the aggregate entries for each category total. The last fact, customer count, however, cannot be derived from the base-level fact table records. The category customer count must be calculated when the original transactions are being processed. Thus when an individual customer ticket is encountered that has several paper category purchases on it, the cumulative customer count for the paper category in that store on that day is incremented by exactly one. This semiadditive fact is useful at any aggregate level, but the data warehouse team needs to plan for this fact being part of the aggregations from the beginning because it is hard to add this one into the database at a later time. To populate this field after the fact would require digging out all the old transaction records to do the computation correctly.

It is not always the case that all the dimensions make sense at an aggregate level. For instance, in the insurance company databases, line of business aggregates calculated by aggregating in the product dimension would normally suppress dimensions like the individual insured party, the individual covered item, and the employee responsible for the transaction. If these dimensions were not suppressed, the line of business aggregates would be meaningless because the fact table would still be at the grain of individual insured party and individual covered item.

The same design technique is used for all the other aggregate fact tables listed above. Only three aggregate dimension tables are needed to support all the aggregate fact tables:

1. Category dimension
2. District dimension
3. Month dimension

These three aggregate dimension tables are used in the obvious combinations to drive the seven aggregate fact tables previously listed.

Notice in our category aggregate sales fact table that not only can we accelerate category totals but we can accelerate department totals that roll up from category. We may well decide not to build a separate department aggregate table because we get quite good performance on department totals by using the category aggregate fact table. Another way to say this is that any dimension attribute that survives in the aggregate dimension table can be used more efficiently in the aggregate schema than in the base-level schema because it is guaranteed to make sense at the aggregated level.

We will talk in Chapter 14 about monitoring user queries as the basis for deciding which aggregates to build, but it is safe to say that in a mature data warehouse environment, there may be more than one kind of aggregate in some of the dimensions. For example, we might decide to build the following complete set of aggregates in each dimension:

- Product: category, all merchandise total
- Store: district, division, all store total
- Time: month, year

If we separate each kind of kind of aggregate into its own fact table and build aggregate dimension tables everywhere needed, we end up with a large number of tables. We would need seven aggregate dimension tables, although the dimension tables for all merchandise, all stores, and years would be tiny tables possessing one record, one record, and three records respectively. We would also need 35 aggregate fact tables:

1. One-way: category by store by day
2. One-way: all merchandise by store by day
3. One-way: district by product by day
4. One-way: division by product by day
5. One-way: all stores by product by day
6. One-way: month by product by store
7. One-way: year by product by store
8. Two-way: category by district by day
9. Two-way: category by division by day
10. Two-way: category by all stores by day
11. Two-way: category by month by store
12. Two-way: category by year by store
13. Two-way: all merchandise by district by day
14. Two-way: all merchandise by division by day
15. Two-way: all merchandise by all stores by day
16. Two-way: all merchandise by month by store
17. Two-way: all merchandise by year by store
18. Two-way: district by month by product
19. Two-way: district by year by product
20. Two-way: division by month by product
21. Two-way: division by year by product
22. Two-way: all stores by month by product
23. Two-way: all stores by year by product
24. Three-way: category by district by month
25. Three-way: all merchandise by district by month
26. Three-way: category by division by month

27. Three-way: all merchandise by division by month
28. Three-way: category by all stores by month
29. Three-way: all merchandise by all stores by month
30. Three-way: category by district by year
31. Three-way: all merchandise by district by year
32. Three-way: category by division by year
33. Three-way: all merchandise by division by year
34. Three-way: category by all stores by year
35. Three-way: all merchandise by all stores by year

Although this is a large number of combinations, there is no escaping the possibility of building all these aggregate types if we think that the various aggregation levels in these three dimensions are necessary. Although 35 fact tables are a little overwhelming, it is still a good idea to break out the aggregates as separate tables for the following important reasons:

- Any application using one of the tables cannot possibly double count. We will see in the next section that it is possible to double count when using the other main technique of new Level fields instead of new fact tables.
- In a correctly designed data warehouse, *end users and application developers will never see any of these aggregate tables*. The aggregate tables are known only to the "aggregate navigator" and the DBA. The aggregate navigator is a layer of software that chooses the appropriate aggregate table at query time, thereby relieving the application developer and the end user from having to be aware that the aggregate tables even exist. Aggregate navigators are discussed in detail later in this chapter.
- The separate aggregate types can be created, dropped, loaded and indexed separately when they are in separate tables. Since they will probably be introduced into the database environment at different times, the separate tables approach allows a more incremental style of management.
- Using separate tables does not create more categories of aggregates. As we will see in the next section, using Level fields (the alternate approach) requires exactly the same number of aggregate records, aggregate types, and new aggregate keys. In this sense, there is no difference between the two approaches.
- Using separate aggregate tables allows the metatables describing the aggregates to be simpler than the approach of using Level fields. The aggre-

gate tables can be chosen by the aggregate navigator simply by looking at the available dimension fields in the DBMS system tables, rather than having to describe the aggregate types in detail in metatables. This architecture is described later in this chapter.

- The choice of aggregate dimension keys is a little simpler in the separate fact table approach, because the aggregate dimension keys do not have to live in the same space as the base-level dimension keys. For instance, in the product dimension, the base-level keys could be the full 11-digit UPC code perhaps with a couple of version number digits to allow local tracking of slowly changing dimensions where the UPC code has not been changed. In the separate fact table approach, the keys for the aggregates such as category do not need to be 13-digit items as they would using the Level field approach. See the next section to see why this is the case.

- The maximum field width for numbers is more manageable in the case of separate fact tables. Notice that the last fact table in the long list presented above is the all merchandise by all stores by year table. The few dollar facts in this table will be in the billions of dollars. In a DBMS with fixed-width field declarations, a lot of space may be wasted because of these few very large values. In the separate fact table approach, the base-level fact table would never contain a number this large.

New Level Fields for Aggregates

The other approach to storing aggregates is by using Level fields in the affected dimension tables, and thereby allowing the aggregate fact records to reside in the original fact table. This approach creates exactly as many aggregate records as the first approach, and requires the generation of exactly the same aggregate keys in both the dimension tables and the fact table. The only difference is where the aggregate dimension records and the aggregate fact records are stored. In the approach using Level fields all the new aggregate records are stored in the original dimension and fact tables.

The approach of using Level fields to identify the aggregate dimension records is widely used by commercial data suppliers of grocery store and drug-store data such as A.C. Nielsen and IRI.

The grocery store aggregate example with category totals that we developed on page 193 looks like Figure 13.2 when we use Level fields. The original

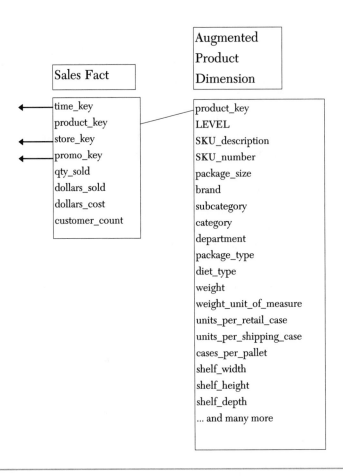

FIGURE 13.2

The category aggregate sales fact schema using level fields.

product dimension table is used with all of its fields, augmented by the addition of a Level field (in position #2 in Figure 13.2). The Level field describes the aggregation level of every record in the dimension table. All of the original base-level records are encoded with Level = Base. The new category total records are encoded with Level = Category. These category aggregate product records need to have keys that are compatible with and do not conflict with the original base-level keys in the product dimension table.

The Category and Department fields in the product dimension table will be well defined for the category-level records as we saw in the separate fact tables approach. However, all the rest of the fields have no valid meaning, and have to take on null or "NA" or "Total" values.

The most serious applications problem with the Level field approach, however, is that it is possible to double count. This happens if the requesting application fails to constrain on a single value for the Level field. For instance, if the only product table constraint is Category = Paper, then both the base-level records and category-level records will be retrieved. Another way to say this is in the following design principle:

> **If aggregates are represented in the original dimension and fact tables by means of the Level field construct, then every query ever presented to that schema must constrain the Level field to a single value or double counting will occur.**

If Level fields are used in more than one dimension, then the above principle holds for each such dimension. For this reason especially, and for the full list of reasons given at the end of the last section, we recommend that each aggregate type be broken out into a separate fact table, with the proper derived dimension tables supporting the separate fact table. We summarize this as another design principle:

> **Each type (grain) of aggregate should occupy its own fact table, and should be supported by the proper set of dimension tables containing only those dimensional attributes that are defined for that grain of aggregate.**

SPARSITY FAILURE AND THE EXPLOSION OF AGGREGATES

The planning of aggregate table sizes can be tricky because of a phenomenon known as *sparsity failure*. We have seen in the base-level fact table that the table is usually quite sparse in the residency of the keys. For example, in the grocery store item movement database, only about 10 percent of the products in the store are actually sold in a given store on a given day. Even disregarding the promotion dimension, the database is only occupied 10 percent in the three primary keys of product, store, and time. However, when we build aggregates, the occupancy rate shoots up dramatically. To see how this can affect aggregate planning, consider the case where we have a base-level fact table of grocery store item movement, as described in Chapter 3. Suppose we have the following:

- Ten thousand products with 2,000 proposed aggregates
- One thousand stores with 100 proposed aggregates
- One hundred time periods with 30 proposed aggregates

The product aggregates could be brands, and the store aggregates could be districts, and the time aggregate could be months, assuming the base times are weeks. Looking at this list of proposed aggregates, we see that the product dimension is being augmented by 20 percent, the store dimension is being augmented by 10 percent, and the time dimension is being augmented by 30 percent. Although we suspect that there may be a multiplicative effect between dimensions, we still hope that the combined effect of adding aggregates in all three of these dimensions will be no worse than, say, 50 percent. Unfortunately, because of sparsity failure, the situation is far worse. This set of aggregates will actually grow the database by almost an additional 400 percent!

To see how this aggregate explosion occurs, consider the seven kinds of aggregates we already know (from earlier in this chapter) that we must build. These include the following:

1. One-way aggregate: brand totals by store by day
2. One-way aggregate: district totals by product by day
3. One-way aggregate: monthly totals by product by store
4. Two-way aggregate: brand totals by district totals by day
5. Two-way aggregate: brand totals by month totals by store
6. Two-way aggregate: district totals by month totals by product
7. Three-way aggregate: brand totals by district totals by month totals

For the first aggregate, brand totals by store by day, although only 10 percent of the base-level (UPC) products are sold in a given store on a given day, the representation at the brand level in a store on a day will be much higher. Consider that only one of the various sizes and package types for the brand needs to be sold in order for the brand to appear in the daily data. We could easily see 50 percent of the brands in the daily store data as opposed to only 10 percent of the individual products. This growth by a factor of 5 in sparsity exactly makes up for the reduction by a factor of 5 in the product dimension by going to the brand level. The aggregate records alone in this first aggregate fact table total 100 million records, equal to the original fact table size. This is not a mistake, nor are the records meaningless. All of the aggregate records in this table are true summaries!

A similar argument holds for the other one-way aggregates. Although only 10 percent of the base-level products sell in a given store on a given day, probably 50 percent of the base-level products will appear somewhere in each district of stores on a given day. Continuing in the same theme, we can expect to see 50 percent of the base-level products selling over the course of an entire month in a given store.

The sparsity failure is of course even more dramatic for the two-way aggregates. We can expect to see 80 percent of the brands selling at a district level each day, as well as 80 percent of the brands selling over the course of a month on a given store. We will see 80 percent of the base-level products selling in an entire district if we wait for a month.

Finally, for the three-way aggregate, we will see 100 percent of the brands selling at the district level if we wait for a month. All of this can be summarized in the following table:

TABLE	PRODUCT	STORE	TIME	SPARSITY	# RECORDS
Base: product by store by week	10,000	1,000	100	10%	100 million
One-way: brand by store by week	2,000	1,000	100	50%	100 million
One-way: product by district by week	10,000	100	100	50%	50 million
One-way: product by store by month	10,000	1,000	30	50%	150 million
Two-way: brand by district by day	2,000	100	100	80%	16 million
Two-way: brand by store by month	2,000	1,000	30	80%	48 million
Two-way: product by district by month	10,000	100	30	80%	24 million
Three-way: brand by district by month	2,000	100	30	100%	6 million
				GRAND TOTAL:	494 million

Our original fact database has grown from 100 million base records to 494 million total records with aggregates! The database has grown by 394 percent even though no single dimension grew by more than 30 percent. Sparsity failure may be difficult to predict accurately but it is guaranteed to happen to some degree whenever aggregates are built. The obvious solution is to judiciously build aggregates. The most dramatic way to cut down on aggregates while still benefiting from their value is to make sure that the average aggregate in each dimension summarizes at least 10 and preferably 20 or more records. In our example, insufficient bottlenecking was probably the reason for the large number of aggregates. Our product dimension only summarized five lower-level products on the average, and the time dimension only summarized three time periods on the average. The one-way aggregates on product and time contributed 260 million of the 394 million aggregate records. If both these aggregates had instead summarized 20 lower-level items, these one-way aggregate tables would only have had 70 million total records, even if the sparsity had crept up to 70 percent. We summarize this section with a design principle:

> **The single most effective way to control an aggregation explosion, but still benefit from the value of aggregates, is to make sure that each aggregate summarizes at least 10 and preferably 20 or more lower-level items.**

INDEXING ISSUES

Aggregates interact with indexes in a very interesting way. By judiciously choosing aggregates, the DBA can greatly reduce the pressure to build indexes on the fact table. Consider the case where we have a retail item movement fact table with the primary dimensions of time, product, and store. We decide to build a master composite index on this fact table using the keys in the above order, namely, time by product by store. In Chapter 14 we will discuss the implications of choosing this particular order, but for the moment the important concern is that we have built a composite index on all three primary dimensions. Virtually all DBMSs will use as many leading terms of this index as they can. Ideally, time, product, and store are all constrained, and the index can be descended all the way to its leaf nodes. However, if only time and product are constrained, most DBMSs will still use the first two levels of the index to beneficial effect. A classic conflict arises if there are queries that don't constrain product, or even worse, don't constrain time. Using the time by product by store index, a query that doesn't constrain product will only be able to use the first level of the index. It may be faster in this case to perform a full table scan.

Usually in this case, the DBA will decide to build a second master index on time, store, and product. The problem with this decision is that in a dimensional data warehouse, the composite indexes on the fact tables are extremely expensive. A typical composite index on a narrow fact table with four or fewer facts may be 80 percent the size of the fact table itself. A second composite index will cost another 80 percent, not to mention the administrative overhead to build and maintain such an index.

Fortunately, aggregates come to our rescue. Note that a query that doesn't constrain the product dimension actually is a query that is summarizing across the entire product dimension. Remember that virtually every fact table query in a dimensional data warehouse is a Sum, Count, Min, Max, or Avg. If we are summarizing across the product dimension then we should be using an aggregate! If we have a derivative fact table available with only the dimensions of time and store, then we jump to that table where our remaining constraints are capable of traversing the entire composite index. This is actually worth two design principles:

A loose constraint, or no constraint, in a base-level fact table is actually a tight constraint in an aggregate fact table.

Only one sort order on the master composite index on the fact table needs to be built, since other sort orders based on missing dimensional constraints should be handled by separate aggregate tables instead.

ADMINISTRATION ISSUES

The creation of aggregates requires a significant administrative effort by the owners of the data warehouse. Unlike the base-level records, where the production system may provide a framework for administering keys, usually the data warehouse team is on its own for creating and maintaining the aggregate keys.

Aggregate keys need to be created only for the new dimensional entries like product brands, store districts, or time months. The fact table, of course, simply uses these keys, and base-level keys, in various combinations, since the fact table by definition is the home of foreign keys.

In a given dimension like product the keys should probably be sequentially generated, by type. Thus all the brand keys might fall in the numeric range of 10,000 to 19,999, while the category keys might fall in the range of 20,000 to 29,999, and so on. Keys should be assigned sequentially from this key space, and never reused. This would allow the lists of brand keys and category keys to be administered separately. They should not be jumbled together. Brand keys and category keys will be used in different tables, since category is a different aggregation level from brand. We would have to use the Level field approach if brand and category aggregates were to be stored in the same table.

As we stated earlier, if each of the fact aggregate types are stored in a different fact table, then key administration is simplified. Even if the base-level product keys are complex derived keys based on the 11-character UPC code, the aggregate product keys can be nice clean integers because they don't have to reside in the same dimension tables or fact tables as the base-level keys.

APPLICATION ISSUES

Until recently, the presence of aggregate records in the data warehouse caused the application designer and DBA a giant headache. Although there was no question that queries were dramatically sped up by the presence of aggregates, the SQL in the requesting application had to know that the aggregate was there and had to specifically request it. Even for the same request, the SQL had to be different depending on whether the aggregate was present. For example, the base-level SQL for a simple query might look like this:

```
select category_description, sum(sales_dollars)
from base_sales_fact, product, store, time
where base_sales_fact.product_key = product.product_key
and base_sales_fact.store_key = store.store_key
and base_sales_fact.time_key = time.time_key
and store.city = 'Cincinnati'
and time.day = 'January 1, 1996'
group by category_description.
```

This query would show total sales by category in Cincinnati stores on New Year's Day, 1996. This query would touch every product record for Cincinnati stores on that day because it is going against the base-level fact table. If there was an aggregate fact table with category totals, the query would look like this:

```
select category_description, sum(sales—dollars)
from category_sales_fact, category_product, store, time
where category_sales_fact.product_key = category_product.product_
    key
and category_sales_fact.store_key = store.store_key
and category_sales_fact.time_key = time.time_key
and store.city = 'Cincinnati'
and time.day = 'January 1, 1996'
group by category_description.
```

The six boldface items in the above query are the items that are different between the base-level query and the category-aggregate-level query. Upon close inspection, we see that all we have done is substitute the aggregate fact table name for the base fact table name, and substitute the aggregate dimension table name for the base dimension table name. The category-aggregate-level query, of course, will probably run 100 times as fast as the base-level query.

Until recently, this difference in the SQL, which affects both the from clause and where clause, caused an *applications discontinuity*. The end user's query tool, report tool, or application simply had to be coded differently, depending on whether an aggregate was available. Even worse, once an application was written and running, if the profile of available aggregations changed, there was no choice but to roll over all the end user's query tools, report writers, and applications. To forestall this disaster, the DBA was tempted to over build the portfolio of aggregates for a rainy day. This has been one of the causes of aggregate explosions in early data warehouse environments.

AGGREGATE NAVIGATION

The applications discontinuity and aggregate explosion have been directly addressed by a new layer of software between the end user application and the DBMS. This new layer of software is called the *aggregate navigator*.

The role of the aggregate navigator is to intercept the end user's SQL and transform it so as to use the best available aggregate. The end user's query tools, report writers, and applications all speak nothing but base-level SQL. Even the advanced applications developer does not worry about the identity of aggregate tables. Everything is permanently coded in base-level SQL. The architecture for the aggregate navigator looks like Figure 13.3.

All of the end user clients direct their communications to the aggregate navigator. From the end user's point of view, the aggregate navigator is the network server. End users are never allowed to look directly at the real DBMS. All end user applications speak base-level SQL exclusively. The aggregate navigator maintains special metadata describing the current profile of aggregation tables stored on the DBMS. The aggregate navigator also maintains statistics on the end user queries, showing which aggregates are being used and which aggregates should be built to help slow running queries.

The function of the aggregate navigator is to transform the user's base-level SQL into *aggregate aware* SQL. The aggregate navigator then communicates with the real DBMS. The real DBMS returns the answer set to the ag-

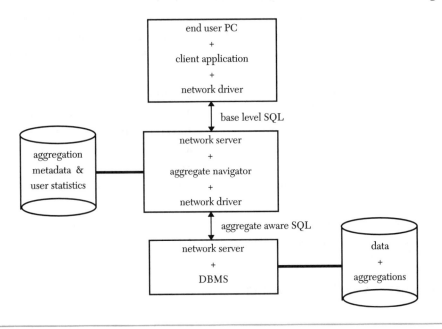

FIGURE 13.3

Aggregate navigator architecture.

gregate navigator, which in turn passes the answer set back to the original end user.

Logically the aggregate navigator is a separate layer that should reside on the network outside the end user's PC. The aggregate navigator is a true network resource. It would make sense for the aggregate navigator to be a separate network node or to reside on the same machine as the DBMS. It seems likely that DBMS vendors will decide to offer aggregate navigators as part of their bundle of software modules, and thus aggregate navigators will probably end up on the same machine as the DBMS.

It is important that aggregate navigation not be done on the end user's PC. The maintenance of the crucial metatables is a network and DBA responsibility and every SQL query tool, report tool, and application should transparently benefit from aggregate navigation. Although a few query tool vendors are currently offering aggregate navigation, this is the wrong architecture, and these query tool capabilities should become irrelevant as the proper network architecture is established. We summarize this section with a design principle:

> An aggregate navigator is an essential component of a data warehouse because it insulates end user applications from the changing portfolio of aggregations, and allows the DBA to dynamically adjust the aggregations without having to roll over the applications base.

INCREMENTAL ROLLOUT OF AGGREGATIONS

The presence of an aggregate navigator allows the DBA to adopt an incremental approach to rolling out aggregations. Each week, by studying the query statistics maintained by the aggregate navigator, the DBA can choose to adjust the portfolio of aggregations. Aggregations can be added or subtracted. Note that the grain of the decision is at the level of whether an attribute is fully represented or not represented at all in an aggregate dimension table. In other words, the decision to build category-level aggregates means that an explicit aggregate must be built for each and every category. It is not allowed, in the architecture described here, to build only some of the category aggregates and leave others out. The aggregate navigator will determine whether an aggregate table can be used solely by the presence of the attribute *category* in the aggregate dimension table. If category is there, it is assumed that the aggregate dimension table and the fact table it is associated with will support any query on category values.

THE AGGREGATE NAVIGATION STRATEGY

We saw in the SQL example above that the modifications required to convert an SQL query from base-level SQL to aggregate-aware SQL consist entirely of replacing the base-level fact and dimension table names with aggregate fact and dimension table names. We can choose the best aggregate fact and dimension tables with the following simple algorithm:

1. Rank order all the aggregate fact tables from the smallest to the largest.
2. For the smallest aggregate fact table, look in its associated dimension tables to verify that all of the dimensional attributes in the current query can be found. If they are all found, then we are done. Replace the base-level fact and dimension table names with the aggregate fact and aggregate dimension table names.
3. If step 2 fails, find the next smallest aggregate fact table and try step 2 again. If we have run out of aggregate fact tables, then we must use the base tables.

The charm of this algorithm is that it doesn't require very complicated metadata to describe the aggregates themselves. All that is needed is a sorted list of the aggregate fact tables in descending order of size, together with the name mapping of table names and key field names so that the substitutions can be performed. A complete listing of all the field names in the dimension tables is not required since that listing can be found in the system dictionary, and there is no point in duplicating the system dictionary.

This algorithm is simple enough that a competent IS shop with C programming skills could probably implement its own navigator in a few days of programming. Commercial-grade versions of an aggregate navigator should include good statistics tools as well as aids for building the aggregates.

This algorithm could be modified to handle aggregates represented in tables using Level fields but the processing is messier. We would need to know a preferred order of levels to descend, and then we would need to look within the values of the requested fields in the dimension tables to see if they were represented by real values or with the default Total values. If a requested field had a Total value, that would mean we were at too high a level of aggregation. The only way to avoid this kind of messy search in the dimension table would be to maintain a very much more elaborate set of metatables containing this information. In a wide product table, or a wide customer table, with 150 attributes, all 150 attributes would need to be represented. This structure would need to be updated by the DBA or by a smart application. This is another reason for favoring the separate fact tables approach for handling aggregations. With separate fact tables, the required searching is done directly in the system tables and all we are looking for is existence or nonexistence of a field, not its values.

AGGREGATIONS PROVIDE A HOME FOR PLANNING DATA

As our final comment on the subject of aggregations, we note that the presence of aggregation tables often provides a happy home for planning data. Usually aggregations are built from the base layer upward, culminating in high-level product category and high-level customer totals. Coincidentally there is often a planning process in place that creates plans or forecasts at these very same levels. A good marriage of these two kinds of data can take place by recognizing when aggregate "actuals" and planning or forecast numbers coexist. The aggregate fact tables can easily be extended with planning and forecast facts, and applications that need to compare actual with plan or actual with forecast must know to use these tables. Actually, the aggregate navigation algorithm can be used to find the proper actual/plan tables by generalizing step 2 in the algorithm to look at the fact fields as well as the dimension fields. The alert reader will have already noticed that this was required anyway, because there may be facts used in a query that are not present in the aggregation tables.

THE BACK ROOM

In this chapter and the next we will describe what it is like to own and manage a dimensional data warehouse. We will separate the responsibilities into back room and front room responsibilities. Sometimes we say that the back room is where the DBAs hang out, and the front room is where the **MBAs** hang out. Both of these categories of IS personnel are essential to making the data warehouse function effectively. In this chapter we will describe the back room responsibilities of building and using the production data extract system, building and using aggregates, performing daily data quality assurance, monitoring and tuning the performance of the system, backing up and recovering the data warehouse, and communicating to the user community from the back room. In the next chapter we will describe the front room responsibilities, which include building reusable application templates, training the users on both the applications and the data, and keeping the network running efficiently.

THE DAILY RHYTHMS: QUERYING AND LOADING

A data warehouse has very bimodal usage. Most data warehouses are on-line 16 to 22 hours per day in a read-only mode or nearly complete read-only mode. The data warehouse then goes off-line for 2 to 8 hours, usually in the wee hours of the morning for data loading, data indexing, data quality assurance, and data release. Although both of these daily phases typically consume very significant computer resources, the query phase can be thought of as highly variable and somewhat soft in its insistence on response time, and the loading phase can be thought of as highly predictable and extremely demanding in its insistence on response time. The query phase is like running a restaurant, while the loading phase is like conducting a fire drill.

THE QUERY PHASE

The entire user community is connected via query tools to the relational DBMS. In this chapter, when we say "query tool" we mean any client application that maintains a network connection to the DBMS for the purpose of sending SQL and receiving answer sets. This would include so-called ad hoc query tools, as well as report writers, and other monolithic applications on the user's desktop. The ideal architecture for a query tool involves sending relatively small SQL messages to the DBMS (all data warehouse queries qualify as "small") and receiving back relatively small answer sets of a few hundred to a few thousand rows of data. In spite of this nice bottleneck architecture, the effect of an individual query on the DBMS is wildly varying. Even when two users each request 100 rows in their answer set, the first user may need to touch only 100 rows in the underlying data, while the second user may need to touch one million rows in the underlying data. This makes predicting the load on the DBMS at any given moment nearly impossible. Even a careful analysis of the individual query syntax is not a very good guide to predicting query performance because the runtime will depend on the sparsity of the data across the dimension keys requested in the query. As relational database vendors focus more effectively on the **data cube** aspects of dimensional data warehouses, they should be able to assess the sparsity of a query before it is run, and thereby more accurately predict the runtime. As of 1995, however, these kinds of accurate predictions are a pipe dream.

In a large user environment, with a hundred or more users eligible to access the DBMS, the processor demands will be fairly predictable for the community as a whole. Demand will peak in the same way that time-shared mainframe demand peaks, namely at 10 A.M. and 3 P.M. Query demand will drop to 10 percent of the peak values after 6 P.M. but will remain at a steady low level during the night as long as the system is up. For a user community with 100 eligible end users with modern client tools and properly balanced networks, the

DBMS will see at least 3,000 queries per day. Virtually all of the queries will be SELECT statements. Eighty percent of these queries will be browses, which are single table SELECTs, and 20 percent will be multitable joins. If the DBMS is only doing 100 queries per day for this size user community, this is a sure sign of a sick system. Almost certainly the culprit is an overly complex, hard to understand, E/R-based data warehouse schema. As user communities become more sophisticated and as the tools improve, these query loads will increase to 8,000 or more queries per day per 100 users. At these high levels, 90 percent of the queries will be single table SELECTs (browses), and 10 percent will be multitable joins. These query load levels have been measured directly by the author in real-life environments.

BROWSE QUERIES

Browse queries and multitable join queries present very different processing demands on the DBMS server. Browse queries usually touch a single attribute in a dimension table or a system table through an index. Even in a multiprocessor system, a browse query is often serviced by a single processor. Many browse queries are unconstrained SELECT DISTINCTs, like this:

SELECT DISTINCT BRAND FROM PRODUCT

This would be a flick of the wrist for an end user who is trying to see which brand to select from a pull down menu in a windows-based reporting tool.

Those systems that can resolve an unconstrained SELECT DISTINCT by consulting only the index and not touching the underlying data will give dramatically better performance on these kinds of browse queries compared to systems that have to touch all of the dimension records. In the future, through the use of bit-vector indexes, even constrained SELECT DISTINCTs should perform well on large dimension tables. A constrained SELECT DISTINCT would look like this:

SELECT DISTINCT BRAND FROM PRODUCT WHERE CATE-GORY = 'PAPER'

This would be the second query in a "progressive browse." The first query enumerated the categories, and the user selected Paper. In this second query the user only wants to see the paper brands. This progression may well continue, with third and fourth queries continually narrowing a search. The final result is probably a constraint on the product dimension that will be part of a multitable join query.

MULTITABLE JOIN QUERIES

Multitable join queries, as their description implies, involve the fact table and several dimension tables. In this book we recommend not trying to combine two or more fact tables in a single SELECT statement. All existing DBMSs show very degraded performance when trying to combine multiple fact tables in a single SELECT statement. In Chapter 16, we will show that comparison queries and drill-across queries that need multiple fact tables can be handled efficiently by fetching answer sets from the fact tables one at a time and combining these answer sets in the client application.

Multitable join queries in a dimensional data warehouse can be evaluated via a deterministic join strategy, as described earlier in this book. First, the dimensional tables are all evaluated and a list of primary key values from each of the tables is generated. It is possible that rather than an actual, explicit list of keys, a key fetching stream is established that can produce the dimension keys on demand from a requesting process. In any case, the separate dimensions combine to generate a real, or virtual, set of composite keys in sorted order that is presented to the fact table's composite key index. More abstractly, the end result of the dimensional constraint process produces a sorted list of composite keys, and the fact table itself is a sorted list of composite keys. Fetching facts from the fact table consists of finding the matches between these two ordered sets of composite keys in the fastest possible time. This process is highly susceptible to parallelization and to the implementation of clever algorithms. Generally, multitable join queries are far more likely to involve multiple processors and consume more CPU and disk resources than browse queries.

THE LOADING PHASE

In the loading phase, all or part of the data warehouse is taken off-line while new data is loaded. The new data is virtually always an extract from one or more production systems. This data is delivered via the production data extract system that must be built by the data warehouse team. Building the production data extract system is the one step in the implementation of a data warehouse that is the most fraught with delays and underestimates. Typically a prediction that the production data extract system can be built in three months turns into a six- to nine-month job. In the next few sections we will describe in detail what the production data extract system must do for a dimensional data warehouse.

The data warehouse team should configure the overall system to minimize downtime due to data loading. One way to do this is to mirror the data warehouse as shown in Figure 14.1. There are a number of benefits to this configuration for data warehousing, even though mirroring is often associated with transaction processing. During the day, while querying is going on, the mirrored configuration provides high reliability in the event of an isolated disk drive failure. Additionally, in many operating systems, the mirrored configuration performs nearly all disk-intensive operations close to twice as fast as a nonmirrored configuration because the operating system can choose which of the two mirrors is able to return the data first. This capability is at the low level of the operating system and the file system and is not part of the DBMS or application logic.

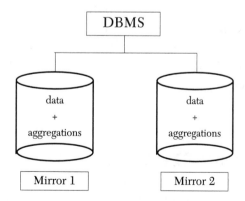

FIGURE 14.1
A mirrored data warehouse.

During the night, when loading is going on, the mirror is deliberately broken. If the DBMS machine is a multiprocessing machine (either **SMP** or MPP), some fraction of the processors can be devoted to continuing queries on one of the mirrors whose data remains unchanged, while the remainder of the processors begin the night's load on data that will be changed. This allows the machine to remain up for querying for very close to 24 hours per day, while also allowing a lengthy and complex load and index cycle to be completed.

At the end of the loading phase, a quality assurance check is made on the data in the mirror that has been changed. If the quality assurance check is successful, then the first mirror is taken off-line, and an *all-disk-to-all-disk* data transfer takes place. Even on a very large system, this can usually be done in less than an hour. When this transfer is complete, the mirror is reestablished and the entire system is brought back on-line.

If the quality assurance check fails, and the data is corrupted, the all-disk-to-all-disk transfer can take place in the opposite direction, thereby restoring the previous day's exact configuration.

A further refinement of this technique involves three mirrors. Two of the mirrors remain on-line during the night, providing both availability and data redundancy. Only the third mirror is updated during the loading phase.

Another desirable characteristic to support loading of very large tables is the segmentable fact table index. Since the majority of nightly (or weekly or monthly) loads append data at the end of a time series, it is extremely helpful if the master index on the fact table can be dropped only for the most recent time period, rather than for the whole table. This allows the loads into the most recent time bucket to be performed much faster than if the index remains in place, and allows the portion of the index that is dropped to be rebuilt quickly once the loading is complete. A number of DBMS systems have segmentable indexes.

THE PRODUCTION DATA EXTRACT SYSTEM

Every time data is extracted from a production database to be delivered to the data warehouse, most or all of the following eleven steps are required. The data warehouse team must build a software and administrative system to accomplish these eleven steps. This system is called the production data extract system.

The eleven steps in the daily production extract are as follows:

1. Primary extraction (read the legacy format)
2. Identifying the changed records
3. Generalizing keys for changing dimensions
4. Transforming into load record images
5. Migration from the legacy system to DDW system
6. Sorting and building aggregates
7. Generalizing keys for aggregates
8. Loading
9. Processing exceptions
10. Quality assurance
11. Publishing

Primary Extraction

The first challenge is to read the legacy data. This varies from being easy to being very difficult. If the production data is maintained by a transaction-oriented relational database system, then reading the data is easy. Any number of tools and applications can use SQL to extract data in a wide variety of formats to the next step in the process. Data can be fetched to a file or streamed one record at a time to a requesting application. However, if the production data is stored in a proprietary system, such as a third-party vendor's order entry package, the file formats may not be publicly known. It may not be possible to read the production data directly. The data warehouse team may be reduced to running a report or creating a utility dump file of the data from the production system. Many of the third-party data extract tools add significant value in this primary extraction step. It is worthwhile to carefully catalogue all the production sources that need to be extracted into the data warehouse and then to review the available data extract tools to see how much coverage they provide. The data extract tools are expensive and it does not make sense to buy them until the extract and transformation requirements are well understood.

Identifying the Changed Records for a Snapshot Fact Table

Extracting data into a daily, weekly, or monthly snapshot fact table involves determining what has changed since the last time a snapshot was built. There are two main ways to attack this problem. Either the original production transactions are available and can be processed by the data warehouse to build up the new snapshot, or the production transactions are not practical to process and the data warehouse will have to determine what has changed in the production system since the last snapshot by looking at the underlying files maintained by the production system. It is worth remembering that many production systems are not transaction based. They are simply "changed" through terminal interfaces.

If the data warehouse team starts with the production transactions, then a relatively complex application will have to be built to mimic the transaction processing system itself. This is rarely a good idea if the only goal is to build a monthly snapshot fact table. It would be better in this case to extract the current balances of all the accounts at month end and see what has changed. However if the data warehouse consists of both a transaction-oriented fact table as well as a monthly snapshot fact table such as we designed in both the subscriptions business (Chapter 8) and insurance business (Chapter 9), then it may make sense to process all the transactions during the extract, since they need to be loaded one by one into the transaction fact table anyway.

In many cases the data warehouse team must examine the production files to see what has changed. The identification of the changed records in the production files is intimately involved with primary extraction. Ideally, the data warehouse team would like to see only what has changed from the last time a successful extract was performed. Then only this changed data is actually extracted. Real life is rarely this simple. If the production data is well organized into accessible tables, where each production record is time stamped whenever any change has taken place, and if this changed data can be isolated and fetched, then these first two steps are fairly simple to plan. If the changed records are not time stamped, then each production table may have to be compared against a data warehouse copy built during the previous extract. The changes that are discovered can then be "transactionalized" as if they were original transactions. These **pseudo transactions** could be fairly useful if they were pulled out of the production system on a daily basis because they could be time stamped with the day, and daily pseudotransaction counts could be measured.

The maintenance of comparison copies of production files is a significant application burden that is uniquely the responsibility of the data warehouse team. These production file copies should probably be maintained on the legacy system because it is desirable to transfer as small an amount of data as possible between the legacy system and the data warehouse system. Also, the various comparison and transformation steps are easier to handle in the native environment of the production data than in a downstream environment that probably is using a different operating system and different file formats from those used by the production legacy system.

Generalizing Keys for Changing Dimensions

In Chapter 7 we discussed slowly changing dimensions, such as the product dimension or the customer dimension. For medium-sized versions of these dimensions, especially 100,000 dimension records or less, it made sense in Chapter 6 to track the slow changes by issuing a new product key or customer key each time the description of the product or customer changed. We did this only when we wished to keep each separate description of product or customer, and we wished to very accurately segment history by each of the different product or customer profiles.

To have a slowly changing dimension, the data warehouse team must create an administrative process for issuing new dimension keys each time a trackable change occurs. There are two main alternatives for administering keys this way:

1. Derived keys
2. Sequentially assigned integer keys

A derived key is often a concatenation of the production key with some version digits. For example, if the production product key is a 12-character SKU number, then the generalized key for the data warehouse could be the 12-character SKU number plus two version digits. Presumably the first version of the product would have a data warehouse key of SKU# + 01, and the second would be SKU # + 02, and so on. Obviously this kind of administration is needed only if all three of these conditions are true:

1. The production system changes the product description.
2. The production system does not change the SKU number.

3. The data warehouse team thinks the change is important enough to track separately, that is, not overwrite.

The data warehouse team will have to maintain version number counts on all SKUs in order to know what version number to assign next. The advantage of this approach is that it is relatively simple to administer. The disadvantage is that the keys may get very long and unwieldy. One wonders if a 14-character or even longer key would slow down the DBMS's join processing noticeably. Remember also that it is not desirable to have a user application navigating the derived key to pluck out the SKU number for constraining or reporting. In this case, the SKU number should additionally be stored in the product table as if it were a normal dimensional attribute. The fact that the SKU number is used administratively in the construction of the key should never be taken into account by an application.

The alternative to the derived key is the sequentially assigned integer key. In this case, the data warehouse team assigns all product keys from a simple sequential list of integers. Such keys are anonymous, and convey no information by themselves. The advantage of using a sequentially assigned integer key is that the keys are very much smaller and the performance of the database may possibly be improved. A 4-byte integer should be enough for any conceivable application with medium-sized dimension tables. The disadvantage of the sequentially assigned integer key is that every extract operation will have to consult a cross-reference table maintained by the data warehouse team to assign the correct dimension key, although such a cross-reference table is probably not much more administrative overhead than the version number tracking that is required for the derived keys.

Metadata

The last two steps almost certainly require considerable "state," or metadata, to be maintained by the production data extract system. If a comparison copy of the legacy system must be maintained in order to discover the differences since the last data extraction, then this is a large and unwieldy example of metadata. When processing slowly changing dimensions, there is a need to store the current snapshot status of each affected dimension record, as well as the next available dimension key value. This is a more modest form of metadata. Later in the extract process we have a similar need to keep track of generalized keys for aggregations. This is yet another example of metadata, probably stored on a different machine than the first examples.

Metadata is a loose term for any form of auxiliary data that is maintained by an application. We also have metadata kept by the aggragate navigator and the myriad front end query tools. There is no standard for metadata and there never will be because both front end and back end tool vendors create metadata without regard for standards or centralized administration. The best that a data warehouse team can do is carefully document all the forms of metadata so that they will know which files are owned by which applications. The data warehouse team can also judge a tool by the metadata administration requirements it imposes. For instance, some aggregate navigators can require 40 or more tables to be maintained to describe a data warehouse's aggregates. This certainly seems questionable, and is a burden that the data warehouse team should think twice about before assuming.

Transforming into Load Record Images and Migrating to the Data Warehouse

Once the production data has been extracted, and changed records isolated, and dimension key assignments made, it is time to create the load record images of the records. This simply means arranging the production data in the proper rows and columns for direct and immediate loading into the data warehouse. Notice that we are placing this step in front of the migration step from the legacy system to the data warehouse system. This is because the integer, floating point, and date format conversions that may be required can probably be accomplished more easily in the legacy environment than in the destination data warehouse environment. Rather than mincing words here, what we are trying to avoid is being handed an IBM format tape with unusual packed decimals and unusual date formats, and trying to decipher these formats on a UNIX system.

In general, it is to the advantage of the data warehouse team to have as many of the extraction steps handled on the legacy system as possible, especially those early steps that result in a large amount of data being compressed into a small amount of data. The biggest reduction in data size occurs when the changed records are identified and isolated. When this is done on the legacy system, it not only cuts the data size down, but the comparison copies of the production system must then reside on the legacy system as well.

Sorting and Building Aggregates

Chapter 13 described the architecture of aggregates in detail. The production data extract system must include the building or updating of aggregates as part of the daily processing. In general, the aggregate records should be built outside the DBMS and then loaded with the bulk loading facility just like any other records. We recommend building the aggregates outside the DBMS because the massive sorting and summarizing operations required to build aggregates can be handled much more efficiently with a dedicated sorting package like Syncsort on either an IBM or a UNIX machine than by using the sorting capabilities of the relational DBMS.

An aggregate can be viewed as a break row in a simple sorted report. This is how the aggregates should be built in the extract process. If product sales records are sorted by high-level category, then whenever the category value breaks, an aggregate record can be created. Each level of aggregate created will require a separate sorting pass.

When the aggregate fact record is created, one or more generalized dimension keys must be supplied. Recall from the architecture of aggregates discussion in Chapter 13, that the aggregates themselves are identified by special dimension records, for example, the brand aggregate or the category aggregate in a product dimension table. The fact records corresponding to these aggregates then use the special dimension keys in each of the dimensions where an aggregate is called for. Thus, as in the slowly changing dimension administration discussed a few paragraphs earlier, the creation of the new keys for aggregates takes place when administering the dimensions. During a given load, newly minted dimension keys may not be required. If the category aggregate is already in use, then that key can simply be used. If a new category or a new brand or a new time period aggregate is being created, then an administrative process will have to supply the new key value. In all probability, such aggregate keys must be anonymous, since there is no easy way to generalize such things as the SKU numbers within a large collection of products in an automated way. It will be simpler just to assign a new sequential integer each time a new brand or category is encountered.

The assignment of key values to time aggregates is a little peculiar. In many data warehouses, the key value for a time aggregate like week, month, or quarter is a date-valued key representing the first day or the last day of the period. Keeping an explicit date-valued key for time aggregates is probably only marginally helpful. In virtually every interesting data warehouse, this time key is not used naked by the requesting applications, but is joined to an explicit time dimension table. The time dimension table contains a number of useful attributes that are hard or impossible to get from an SQL date-valued object. These attributes include the designations of fiscal periods; the names of marketing seasons or calendar seasons; and cumulative counts, such as the week number within the year, or absolute week numbers in an epoch. If such an explicit time dimension table is important, then the actual value of the time key does not matter, and it does not need to be a date-valued field.

Loading, Indexing, and Exception Processing

Loading data into a fact table should be done as a bulk loading operation with the master index turned off. As mentioned earlier, it is desirable if the master index can be segmented so that the portion of the index for the most recent time period can be dropped and then rebuilt when the data has been loaded. It will be much faster to perform a bulk load rather than process the records one at a time with SQL INSERT or UPDATE. A bulk data loader should allow the following for fact table loads:

- The parallelization of the bulk data load across a number of processors in either an SMP or **MPP** hardware environment. Be on guard for DBMs that only allow parallel loads of empty tables.
- Selectively turning off or disabling a small portion of the master index during the bulk load, and then selectively turning on or enabling the portion of the master index following the bulk load
- Insertion and update modes selectable by the DBA, including insert only, overwrite only, insert or overwrite, and insert or add to values
- Referential integrity handling options, including ignore referential integrity (not recommended), halt load on referential integrity violation (not very practical), send referential integrity violations to load suspense file for hand processing, and load referential integrity violations with specially created dimensional records

Loading and indexing should be able to gain enormous benefits from parallelization. This is one of the most attractive uses of SMP or MPP hardware in a data warehouse environment. The ability during a bulk data load to insert or overwrite, and the ability to insert or add to values simplifies the logic of data loading considerably. Adding to values is especially useful where a bucket is being accumulated during a time period. In cases where product sales are being loaded on a daily basis, during the early days of a reporting period, most of the activity will be the creation of new buckets. Toward the end of the reporting period, much of the activity will be the updating of the totals in existing buckets. If the bulk loader can gracefully straddle these two cases without having to program explicit tests and INSERT or UPDATE statements, the logic and the speed of loading will be greatly simplified.

Loading referential integrity violations with specially created dimension records is an attractive alternative in some cases. In this way the referential integrity violations can be processed within the database rather than outside of the database. The template dimension records can have special values for some of the attributes, like Brand = INTEGRITY CHECK, that would make it easy to find them after the load is complete. If the product key is previously unknown but legitimate, then the template dimension record simply needs to be filled out correctly. If the product key is bogus, then after the correct product key is identified, the fact records with the bogus keys are modified, and the bogus product dimension record is dropped.

Loading data into a dimension table is quite different from loading data into a fact table. The fact table typically has one or at the most two large indexes built on a combination of dimension keys. A dimension table, however, typically has many keys built on its textual attributes. Every dimension table attribute that is likely to be used as the source of constraints is a candidate for a separate index. Only those dimension attributes that have low cardinality or are not frequently constrained may avoid having an index. Even the low cardinality attributes may want to have an index if it interacts favorably with the browsing user interface. For instance, if a dimension attribute has a cardinality of only four, it may be attractive to index it to be able to display the four values quickly if the values can be derived from the index rather than by looking at all the underlying records. It would be even more attractive to have the index if it can be used with constraints on other attributes in the manner described at the beginning of this chapter. Because of these issues, it seems likely that indexes will be built on many, if not all, of the attributes in each dimension table.

The large number of indexes on a typical dimension table raises some administrative issues. The total disk space required for a dimension table in many cases will be three to four times the disk space required for the raw data. Of course, this will still pale by comparison with the disk space needed for the fact table. Adding a record or updating a record in a dimension table is likely to be a slow process, especially compared with adding a record to a fact table. Again, it would be very desirable if the updating of indexes could be deferred until all the dimension records have been added or updated, and it would be desirable to have the indexes on a dimension table be updatable in parallel on an SMP or MPP machine.

Quality Assurance

When all the base and aggregate records have been loaded, and all the referential integrity violations dealt with, the data quality assurance manager needs to make a global assessment of the status of the load. If daily shipments data has been uploaded from the production shipments system, it may be possible to compare the **flash total** for the previous day with the same flash total generated by the production system. This is a quick and powerful check of the integrity of the load if it can be performed. If the data warehouse flash total matches the production flash total, it is likely that all the base-level records were correctly loaded. Furthermore, each of the aggregate levels in all the dimensions except time can be matched against the same flash total. If everything matches, the load is probably perfect.

If no flash totals are available for comparison, then completeness checks and reasonableness checks must be performed. A completeness check counts the number of reporting units, such as stores, and sees whether they all reported in the day before. A reasonableness check adds up a key additive fact and sees if the number falls within reasonable bounds and sees whether the number is a reasonable extrapolation of previous history.

In a complex distributed environment like a major retailer, it is not reasonable to expect 100 percent of the reporting units to report every day. A given store may not close its books on time, due to human or equipment problems. The store may be unable to report its results because of communications difficulties. The data quality assurance manager needs to assess the quality of the previous day's load and judge whether the omission of a few stores threatens the integrity of entire load. Often in these cases, the recalcitrant stores will report their sales later in the day or possibly the following day. Care must be taken if the store reports in very late that the separate days' sales are eventually identified accurately and not lumped together. This is not hard if the store uploads all transactions to headquarters but it may be difficult if the store POS system simply collects item movement endlessly until the books are closed. In extreme cases where the load process is incomplete or there is corrupted data, the entire load may need to be backed out, and reattempted the following day. This can work fairly smoothly if the system is mirrored in the way described earlier in this chapter. It often does not make sense to treat the data warehouse load as an ordered series of transactions that can be rolled forward and rolled back. It is better to think of the load process as one giant transaction. If the load gets corrupted, it usually makes more sense to back off, erase the partial load, wait for the next load window, and try again.

Publishing

The final step in the daily production load process is to alert the user community to the state of affairs. This should be a regular routine that the users grow to rely on. Every user should be alerted to the data quality assurance manager's assessment of last night's load. The completeness of the load, the final completeness of the previous day's load, and the areas to use or avoid should be spelled out in the daily message.

In Chapter 17, we will also comment on the ability of query tools to provide an assessment of the data that has gone into a query.

CONFORMING DIMENSIONS

Frequently when loading data from multiple sources a conflict arises because the data arrives with incompatible granularity. For instance, syndicated data may be purchased that does not match internal data very well. The time periods may be different, the product dimension may be slightly different, and the market dimension provided by the syndicated data source may not match to the company's sales geography. This is a very serious issue.

In order to use multiple data sources together, the data warehouse team has no choice but to conform the dimensions. Conforming the dimensions means forcing the two data sources to share identical dimensions. It is generally all right if one of the data sources possesses a dimension completely missing from the other data source, but if the two data sources have the same dimension, such as time, product, or market, then each of these dimensions much match exactly between the two sources. It is not all right if the dimensions are merely similar. A constraint such as Brand = Ajax must mean precisely the same set of SKU-level products in both data sources or wrong results will be reported. Furthermore, even when the constraint means the same thing, it must be spelled exactly the same in both data sources. The only way to accomplish this is to have the two data sources share the same dimensional keys, exactly.

Conforming two data sources usually means expressing both data sources at the lowest level of granularity that is common to both sources. For instance, if one data source is based on weeks and the other is based on months, there is usually no effective recourse except to reextract both sources at a daily level. Weeks just don't roll up to months.

If sales data is expressed geographically, conformation may be possible if the original store location can be found in both data sources. Points in space can roll up to any geographic clustering. Areas such as counties are very hard to conform to other incompatible areas such as sales districts, unless the sales districts happen to be made up along county boundaries precisely.

Syndicated data such as Nielsen or IRI data is often made available to the data warehouse, and a request is made to present this data together with internal shipments data. Unfortunately, the Nielsen or IRI data was probably purchased by the marketing department and was not purchased so as to allow the dimensions to be conformed to the other internal corporate data sources. Such data cannot be used effectively with internal data unless the data acquisition contract is redrawn with the syndicated data supplier, and the various dimensions are conformed to the internal dimensions in use by all the other databases. Usually this means conforming the time dimension and the market dimension to the internal standards. Another issue that usually comes up when Nielsen data or IRI data is brought into the data warehouse is that very few of the facts are additive. Traditionally the data supplied to the marketing departments by these suppliers has been not much more than electronic images of paper reports. These data sets are riddled with nonadditive ratios, market shares, and cumulative facts. Usually the additive components required to construct a dimensional view of the data cannot be derived from what is handed across by the syndicator. The most critical fact usually missing from these databases is the All Commodity Volume that serves as the unweighting factor required to convert nonadditive distribution percentages into additive sales volumes. To their credit, Nielsen and IRI have a very clear view of dimensional databases and in general are quite happy to supply a beautiful additive dimensional database, if requested. The problem is that the current contract with the marketing department may well be for old-style database that is not suitable for immediate incorporation into the data warehouse.

NEW IS BACK ROOM ROLES

The complex set of tasks required to build a production data extract system and keep it running imply a set of new roles for IS. In nearly all of these cases, the roles are familiar extensions or modifications of traditional IS roles. New back room roles include the following:

- *Extract analyst*—responsible for designing and creating functional specifications and performing requirements analysis.
- *Extract programmer*—responsible for programming production data extracts, identifying changed records, assigning new keys, and preparing load record images ready for migration to the data warehouse.
- *Extract liaison manager*—responsible for overseeing the daily extract, for judging which changes to dimension attributes are worth tracking with slowly changing dimension keys, and negotiating with the production system managers for timely delivery of data and notification of changed data and changed formats.
- *Master dimension table manager*—responsible for maintaining the corporate product master, the corporate customer master, the corporate promotions master, the corporate sales team master, and other similar central dimensions. Responsible for key creation and assignment, including handling slowly changing dimension keys and aggregate keys.
- *Dimension table quality assurance programmer*—responsible for the completion of textual attributes in dimension tables, removal of mistakes and slightly different variations.
- *Aggregate monitoring manager*—responsible for monitoring the statistics from the aggregate navigator, and for building new aggregates. Responsible for informing the user community when new aggregates are built to encourage them to try previously long-running queries.
- *Data load quality assurance manager*—responsible for overseeing the daily data warehouse load and passing judgment on whether to release the newly

loaded data to the user community. Responsible for communicating to the user community the status of the data warehouse.

- *Data warehouse backup and recovery manager*—responsible for backing up and recovering the one transaction per day (containing millions of records).
- *Data warehouse metadata manager*—responsible for providing space for and supporting all forms of metadata associated with the production data load, the aggregate navigator, and query and reporting tools. This includes comparison tables for finding changed records in the production systems, as well as current key status to allow the formulation of new dimension keys.

15

THE FRONT ROOM

In this chapter we will continue our description of what it is like to own a dimensional data warehouse. In Chapter 14 we described the back room, or DBA, activities of building and using the production data extract system, building and using aggregates, performing daily data quality assurance, monitoring and tuning the performance of the system, backing up and recovering the data warehouse, and communicating to the user community from the back room. In this chapter we describe the front room responsibilities, which include building reusable application templates, designing usable graphical user interfaces, training the users on both the applications and the data, and keeping the network running efficiently.

QUERY TOOLS AS CLIENTS

In this book we will refer to *query tools* as any client software package that maintains a connection with a server-based relational DBMS, and that performs two characteristic functions:

1. The query tool controls the DBMS by sending SQL requests to the DBMS. These requests are naturally quite small, generally less than a few thousand characters.
2. The query tool waits to receive answer sets back from the DBMS. An an-

swer set consists of a set of column labels corresponding to the select list in the SQL statement, together with a relatively small number of data rows. Most answer sets delivered back to a query tool range from a few rows to a few thousand rows.

The bottleneck described here is extremely important. The function of the DBMS is to manage very large amounts of data and service SQL requests. Most users of data warehouses are remote from the DBMS and are using powerful PCs connected to local area networks. Even with a high-speed network connection, it is important to send and receive relatively small amounts of data. The "query tool architecture" is an ideal usage of the client/server approach. It also means that query tools are quite portable, in that they can be taken to a more remote location and still function usefully over a low bandwidth connection to the DBMS.

A query tool as described in this book can be a standalone software package more or less limited to building SQL statements and displaying answer sets, or it can be a standard spreadsheet with embedded SQL statements, or it can be a report writer with facilities for displaying and formatting reports in both textual or graphical modes, or it can be a monolithic decision support application with a custom user interface perhaps programmed in Visual Basic or Power Builder.

The owner of a dimensional data warehouse needs to qualify and select a number of query tools for different purposes in the organization. It is unrealistic to expect to have only one query tool in a large organization, any more than one could expect to have one spreadsheet or one personal time manager. However, it is very important that all query tools obey the same architecture, or the data warehouse will be very hard to support. The components of the architecture that should be adhered to by all query tools include the following:

- The usage of SQL as the medium for requesting data from the DBMS. Although the SQL language is not perfect, and in this book we recommend a number of useful extensions to the language, nevertheless it is overwhelmingly the standard of communication with DBMSs. Using SQL means that as the data warehouse owner, you have a fighting chance of replacing a front end query tool with another one, or replacing a back end DBMS with another one, without completely losing the investment made in applications building, extract programming, and administration.

- The usage of a database independent connectivity interface, such as ODBC or EDASQL. The configuration of network drivers for these interfaces in client PCs is administratively complex, especially if the user tries to load more than one of these drivers.

- The reliance on a network-based aggregate navigator, as described in Chapter 13, to convert base-level SQL into aggregate aware SQL. The aggregate navigator breaks the link between the user's query tools and the complex portfolio of aggregates maintained by the DBA. When the DBA adds or subtracts an aggregate table from the dimensional data warehouse environment, all the query tools in the organization will immediately adapt to and benefit from the change if the organization is using a network-based aggregate navigator. Both the end user and the application developer can go about their business without thinking about the presence of aggregates. Aggregate navigators embedded in proprietary query tools are undesirable because they don't let all clients benefit from aggregate navigation, and they impose their own separate administration on the DBA.

- The reliance on the bottleneck style of communication with the DBMS, with relatively small SQL messages being sent to the DBMS and relatively small answer sets being received from the DBMS. What is excluded here is the occasional download of many megabytes of data to the client PC for fast local navigation. The problem with this approach is that the demand on a dimensional data warehouse even from a single user is much too robust to occasionally download a large subset of the data. The user may start by asking how a particular product is selling (download #1), but the next question is "How did that compare to last year?" (download #2), and then "What fraction of the surrounding category is that particular product?" (download #3 at a different grain, requiring two downloads in the client), and finally, "How much of the product is still in finished goods inventory?" (download #4 from another fact table). Then the same user will sit down that afternoon and do a promotions analysis or look at distribution logistics. All of this argues that with such wide-ranging and unpredictable demands on the dimensional data warehouse, it is unrealistic to perform a large and expensive download from the DBMS to the client many times per day. This architecture also breaks if the connection is of low bandwidth. With the DBMS vendors making dramatic progress on the performance of queries on the large centralized data warehouses, the need to download databases to a client OLAP tool will not be urgent.

QUERY LOADS IN DIMENSIONAL DATA WAREHOUSE ENVIRONMENTS

In a typical data warehouse environment in a large organization where the overall system has been well designed and is fully operational, for every 100 users who from time to time may be connected, the system can expect to experience an average of at least 3,000 end user queries per day, of which 80 percent are single-table browse queries and 20 percent are multitable joins. A query is an SQL SELECT statement. The browse queries will be made against the dimension tables as well as small metatables that support the query tool's use of the data warehouse. The browse queries made against the dimension tables will mostly be SELECT DISTINCT queries or SELECT COUNT DISTINCT queries, where the user is glued to the screen of the PC and is waiting for a pull down menu to be displayed or a list of values to be presented as alternatives. Any unnecessary delay at this stage is fatal. The tiniest browse queries must go round trip from the user's PC to the DBMS and back in less than a second. The texture of these browse queries was described in the last chapter.

Multitable join queries account for about 20 percent of the total number of SELECTs seen by the DBMS but account for the majority of the resources used by the user community. A large multitable join query may demand all the processors and all the disks to satisfy the query. Although the template for a multitable join is nearly identical from query to query, the demands on the DBMS are wildly variable. The change of just one constraint in a large multitable join from PRODUCT.PACKAGE_TYPE = 'Squeezable Small Bottle' to PRODUCT.PACKAGE_TYPE = 'Standard Box' could result in 100 or even 1,000 times as much data being fetched from the base-level sales table.

The total daily demand of 3,000 queries for a typical 100-person community is somewhat conservative. This level has been measured in many environments by the author, as far back as ten years ago. As tools improve, and as more interesting data becomes available, the total number of SELECTs being processed will significantly rise. The author has measured one leading-edge data warehouse environment recently where the 100-person community is creating 8,000 SQL SELECT statements per day. Because of the use of modern user-interface-intensive tools with a lot of interactive pull down menus and other dynamic user aids, the proportion of browse queries has risen from the standard 80 percent to about 90 percent at this site. Hopefully what this trend shows is that the number of natural business questions (multitable joins) is staying relatively constant at 6 to 8 per user per day, but the better user interfaces are increasingly peppering the database with helpful small queries to aid the user's navigation. Remember that this load is measured for 100 potential users, not 100 actual users. If only about half the users are logged in on a given day, then this means that on a typical day when a user is on the system that actual user is issuing somewhere between 12 and 16 multitable join queries, and between 48 and 144 browse queries.

In Chapter 16, we will argue for an applications architecture that emphasizes a larger number of simpler multitable joins, rather than a smaller number of more complex multitable joins. We will argue that the query tool should issue several simple multitable join queries to populate a complex report and then combine the separate results in a sort merge process within the query tool. The reason for this approach is that single SQL statements that attempt to return all the data for a complex report are so complicated that no query tool is prepared to generate the massive single SQL statement, and no DBMS could then figure out how to evaluate it. The effect of this applications architecture will be to increase the number of multitable join queries seen by the server, but hopefully also to lower the overall processing demand in the server, because each request will be simple and easily executable.

COMPLETING THE APPLICATION

Earlier in the book we stated that a great data design and a great DBMS implementation are still only 60 percent of the data warehouse solution. The remaining 40 percent is the client delivery of the data to the screen or to the paper. Although we will discuss the techniques for processing the data in detail in Chapter 16, in this chapter we must take a data warehouse manager's perspective and identify the key, expensive activities.

End users rarely just bring back data to the screen. There are three main kinds of more fundamental activities users do as a result of bringing data to the screen:

1. Comparing
2. Presenting
3. Asking why

As owners of the data warehouse we are responsible for providing tools that make these activities as easy as possible. The end user needs for comparing, presenting, and asking why are a complex set of responsibilities that the data warehouse manager must continually be reviewing and responding to. End users' main goal is to get their jobs done with a minimum of distraction and hassle. The data warehouse manager must actively help end users achieve this. The main dilemma facing the data warehouse manager is choosing a set of tools that somehow balances power and ease of use for comparing, presenting, and asking why. Although we will make this point in much more detail in Chapter 16, it is appropriate to state two important design principles in the choice of query tools:

In the tradeoff between power and ease of use, ease of use must always come first. End users will not use a tool that seems too complicated. If the tool is perceived as complicated, either IS will have to use the tool on the end user's behalf, or the tool will not be used.

Simplicity is mostly a function of whether the user can get to the desired result in "one button click," where that button click is obvious from the user interface. If the user believes that the query tool is simple by this definition, then the query tool will probably be spontaneously and repeatedly used.

These principles have powerful consequences. They imply that the average user community cannot be given an ad hoc query tool and told to "go at the database." IS shops are often attracted to powerful query tools with lots of features and lots of windows. The large number of features and windows appeal only to dedicated computer professionals. Complicated, nonobvious screens are threatening to end users. If an end user is alone in the office and cannot figure out how to proceed with the query tool and cannot get a result on the screen, it is very likely that the tool will never get another chance by that user.

A valuable measure of complexity is the number of button clicks or context switches required to perform a task. A button click or a context switch is a distraction from expressing the primary intent of a command to the computer. Button clicks and context switches are distractions comparable to the phone ringing. More than one or two such distractions during a command to the computer to do something and the end user will be weary, frustrated, and unable to clearly concentrate on the original task.

The query tool should be matched to the user's task. A major mistake is to give end users a tool that lets them see the underlying physical tables in the database and lets them draw in the join paths. Not only is the act of choosing joins dangerous, but it isn't the task the user signed up for.

Press the Button, See the Report

For these reasons, the data warehouse manager must very carefully qualify query tools to the task at hand. An ideal query tool, whether it is standalone SQL generator, a report writer, or a monolithic application, should take the form of a precanned, parameterized report. In other words, it should be a template that can be changed easily. This template should work immediately on the user's desktop with one button click: "Press the button. See the Report." If we want to change the report, a set of usable alternatives should be one button click away. For instance, browsing a list of market names to constrain should be one button click away. Once this happens, then again, Press the button, See the Report. If users are emotionally certain that the tool is this simple, then they will return to it again. Eventually users will learn more complex behavior, but only if they use the system regularly over a period of time.

In a large organization with a significant dimensional data warehouse, there will be a number of very different kinds of analysis possible on the underlying data. An analysis of the types of insurance claims by insured party is very different from an analysis of the mean time between the onset of the claim and the first payment. Yet we may use the same data warehouse to support both analyses. In this case the data warehouse team should build two different templates, one for Claim Type Analysis, and one for First Payment Latency Analysis. Each would be set up with different user prompts and different pull down menu alternatives. Each would run on the user's desktop immediately and produce an appropriate starter report. The key insight here is that the data warehouse team must build this library of template applications.

For the rank and file end user, the data warehouse should consist of a library of template applications that run immediately on the user's desktop. These applications should have a limited set of user-selectable alternatives for setting new constraints and for picking new

measures. These template applications are precanned, parameterized reports.

The data warehouse team must not succumb to the temptation to give a few advanced users an ad hoc tool and then go around later to collect the applications for publishing to the rest of the user community. There are two things wrong with this scenario. First, the advanced end users are not software developers, and they will probably not build robust applications that are user friendly, documented, stable, or extensible. Second, the data warehouse manager won't know how to manage this process: When is the list of applications complete? Did we develop the most important applications first? How do we train the end users on an eclectic bunch of applications?

The data warehouse manager must create a little software shop within his or her organization whose responsibility it is to produce the precanned, parameterized reports. This software shop should be staffed with MBA types who are interested in end user issues and who have a computer science background. These people should view their job as producing a series of professional-grade software products for release to the user community. The software shop should:

- Develop an overall plan for the template applications, starting with a half dozen key templates and progressing in subsequent phases to more specialized templates.
- Build the template applications with the goal of their working immediately on the user's desktop and being changeable with *very* few button clicks and context switches.
- Build the template applications with dimension browsing capability and customized Help screen capability. An interface to the Information Dictionary should be provided in every template.
- Provide a bug reporting hotline, and responsive support that acknowledges the bug reports, suggests a workaround or provides a fix, and releases new corrected versions of the templates on a timely basis.

Comparing

A major goal of every precanned, parameterized report should be flexible and immediate comparisons. Numerical measures in a business rarely make sense unless they can be compared against something else. If XYZ Corporation's sales this quarter were 100, no one has a clue if that is good or bad. But if we are told that those sales were 50 the previous quarter, then we immediately imagine that the business is growing. Conversely if the sales were 150 last quarter, we would worry that the business is in trouble. Just thinking about this example brings forth a multitude of comparisons one would want to make along the time dimension, the customer dimension, the product dimension, the deal dimension, and combinations of those dimensions.

A comparison can either be two comparable numbers presented next to each other, or the two numbers can be combined as a single number into a calculated ratio, index, difference, percent difference, share, or some other measure. The SQL language almost always forces us to calculate these comparisons within a row of an answer set, or to put it another way, within the context of the row header. Such a rowwise comparison might look like this:

MARKET	PRODUCT	1Q96 SALES	GROWTH FROM PREVIOUS QTR
East	Apples	100	10%
East	Oranges	75	−3%
West	Apples	118	8%
West	Oranges	52	5%

The fourth column is the comparison column, and it requires both the sales from the current quarter as well as the previous quarter. SQL does not provide any way to directly make comparisons *between* rows of an answer set. There is no SQL syntax for referring to an adjacent row or a collection of rows in the answer set, thus we always think of comparisons as being calculated in the context of a single row.

Although we will wait until Chapter 16 to focus on how to build this comparison column, the point we must make here to the owners of the data warehouse is that comparisons are difficult in native SQL. The original inventors of SQL did not have comparisons as a goal. This is a shame because comparisons are at the root of most business analyses. As the owners of the data warehouse, we must therefore be especially vigilant because most query tool vendors try to avoid talking about comparisons. Good query tool vendors have addressed this issue and have a reasonable set of alternatives for performing comparisons. We can boil this down to a design principle:

It is essential for all query tools operating against a dimensional data warehouse to be able to perform comparisons flexibly and immediately. A single row of an answer set should be simultaneously able to show comparisons over multiple time periods of different grains (month, quarter, year-to-date) and comparisons over other dimensions (share of a product to a category), and compound comparisons across two or more dimensions (share change this year vs. last year). A query tool should have these comparison alternatives available in a pull down menu or its equivalent. The end user should never see the SQL that implements the comparisons.

This chapter summarizes the front room responsibilities of the data warehouse owner. What we are driving for in this section is the responsibility to make sure that comparisons can be accomplished by the front end tools. Hopefully, over the next few years, we will see vendors extending the SQL language so comparisons can be requested from query tools in a straightforward manner and the resulting query will run quickly. This will make comparisons a feature of the DBMS rather than an advanced application constructed by the IS shop.

Presenting

The second fundamental activity all end users perform with answer sets from the dimensional data warehouse is presentation. Presentation takes place on the screen and on paper, and is either textual or graphical. A few of the text presentation paradigms include:

- Page-formatted report documents with row headers, column headers, and break rows
- Transformation of numerical values into tertiles (high, medium, low), quartiles, rankings, moving averages, moving sums, and cumulative totals

- Spreadsheets with dynamic cells
- Screens with blinking and/or colored entries to show exceptions
- Screens with hot zones to allow touching and drilling down
- Screens with pivot capability to allow complicated transpositions of rows and columns.

Graphical paradigms are even more varied. They include:

- Charts of many types, including bar, pie, scatter, bubble, and hi/low/close
- Maps
- Dynamic graphs showing motion or allowing user navigation

Since there are so many creative ways to present dimensional data, it is incumbent on the owner of the data warehouse to make sure that the data can be transferred from one tool to another in a single button click. It is not acceptable for the data to be trapped in a proprietary presentation tool so that it cannot be moved downstream to a specialized presentation tool. We summarize this as a design principle:

Presentation is a separate activity from querying and comparing, and the data warehouse owner should choose tools that allow answer sets to be transferred easily by the user into multiple presentation environments for different purposes.

Asking Why

The third fundamental activity all users perform is asking why. The data warehouse owner can assist the user in asking why by providing tools that:

- Display exceptions
- Are triggered by events
- Have active agents looking for special data conditions
- Allow drilling up and down within a dimension table
- Allow drilling across to another fact table
- Allow measures to be added dynamically

All of these are techniques for responding to something on the screen with better focus or with more information. We will describe how to implement these techniques in detail in Chapter 16.

HANDING OFF THE DATA

Handing off the data is a fundamental capability that is really a combination of presentation and communication. Electronic mail is the backbone of cooperative workgroups. It is essential that all the components of query tools, including querying, comparing, presenting, and asking why, be transferable from one user to another via electronic mail. At the PC level, a user should be able to mail an instance of a query tool to another user, potentially on a remote network, and the query tool should function. It is desirable that the query tool even function in a remote network that is not physically connected to the DBMS, as long as no new queries are requested.

KEEPING THE NETWORK RUNNING FAST

The data warehouse manager has a direct responsibility for making sure that someone monitors the organization's networks to make sure that they are not slowing down the critical activities of the data warehouse, especially browsing. In those cases where even the tiniest browse queries are taking 5 to 10 seconds, it is almost always the network that is the culprit. A degradation of browsing from one second to 5 seconds is a 500 percent degradation of response time for a critical activity and users will notice it.

16

FRONT END
APPLICATIONS

Although most of this book has been about building the structural foundation of the data warehouse in a logical and physical data model, even a great foundation is only about 60 percent responsible for the success of a data warehouse. The remaining 40 percent is in the front end. In the previous chapter, we used the generic term *query tool* to describe all front ends that manage the DBMS and present answer sets to the user. In this chapter we go into depth describing the recommended architecture for a query tool, what makes an effective query tool, and what are the administrative issues surrounding a query tool.

THE INTERNAL ARCHITECTURE OF A QUERY TOOL

In Chapter 15 we showed how an ideal query tool has a bottleneck architecture, where it passes relatively small amounts of SQL down to the DBMS, and receives back relatively small answer sets. However, in most cases, a mere individual answer set does not satisfy a complete business question. A complete business question requires a *business report*. A business report simultaneously presents information in multiple ways. As we saw in the previous chapter, comparisons abound. A basic measure such as sales revenue is compared with the previous month, the previous year, the surrounding category, the entire country, and combinations of these comparisons. We must face the following design principle:

> There is a fundamental mismatch between the power and depth of an individual SQL answer set and the power and depth of a business report. In most cases, a business report must be assembled from several answer sets. Any query tool that deals with answers to business questions that can be described as business reports must deal with the issue of multiple answer sets. Conversely, a raw answer set is not a sufficient deliverable to the end user.

In addition to comparisons, there are a whole set of presentation modes that affect how a data element looks to the user. These include blinking or highlighting, allowing whole rows to be displayed or not displayed depending on values in the row, and transforming data elements into tertiles (high, medium, low), quartiles, moving sums, moving averages, rankings, cumulative totals, and break rows. Since most or all of these presentation modes are not provided in standard SQL, it is incumbent on the query tool to do a significant amount of postprocessing on the answer set.

STITCHING TOGETHER MULTIPLE ANSWER SETS

The first step in the postprocessing is dealing with multiple answer sets in order to compute comparisons. Comparisons come in an ascending hierarchy of five levels:

1. Simple comparisons
2. Multiple comparisons
3. Multidimensional comparisons
4. Mixed grain comparisons
5. Break rows

Consider the following business report:

Product	Region	Sales This Month	Growth in Sales vs. Last Month	Sales as % of Category	Change in Sales as % of Category vs. Last Month	Change in Sales as % of Category YTD vs. Last Year YTD
Framis	Central	110	** 12%	31%	3%	7%
Framis	Eastern	179	**-3%**	28%	**-1%**	3%
Framis	Western	55	5%	** 44%	1%	5%
Total Framis		344	** 6%	33%	1%	5%
Widget	Central	66	2%	18%	2%	** 10%
Widget	Eastern	102	4%	12%	5%	** 13%
Widget	Western	39	**-9%**	9%	**-1%**	8%
Total Widget		207	1%	13%	4%	** 11%
Grand Total		551	4%	20%	2%	8%

This is a typical business report, showing important relationships between products, markets, and time. There is a wealth of insight to be derived from this report. The screen shows exceptionally high values with double asterisks (**) and exceptionally low values as bold. Sales for the market-leading Framis product are up month to month but the Eastern region bears watching, especially as the company's market share is declining. This suggests some competitive pressure to look into. Sales were lackluster for the new Widget product, mostly due to a significant downturn in the Western Region, but the year-to-date category share growth is excellent. Perhaps the Western region results are a one-month anomaly due to the earthquake. Finally, overall sales for both products were moderately upward from last month and the category shares were both upward, especially compared with a year ago at this time.

The first numerical column is a simple fetch directly from the underlying database. The SQL for the six low-level product rows and this one column is easy to generate from almost any query tool:

```
select p.product—name as Product,         <== first row header
       m.region_name as Region,           <== second row header
```

sum(f.sales) as Sales_This_Month	<== *additive fact, with column label*
from sales_fact f, product p, market m, time t	<== *from clause listing all the tables*
where f.product_key = p.product_key	<== *first join constraint, fact to product*
and p.market_key = m.market_key	<== *second join constraint*
and f.time_key = t.time_key	<== *third join constraint*
and p.product_name in ('Framis', 'Widget')	<== *application constraint on product*
and t.month = 'May' and t.year = 1996	<== *application constraint on time*
group by p.product_name, m.region_name	<== *group by clause*
order by p.product_name, m.market_name	<== *order by clause*

But this only gives us the following uninteresting subset of the report:

PRODUCT	REGION	SALES THIS MONTH
Framis	Central	110
Framis	Eastern	179
Framis	Western	55
Widget	Central	66
Widget	Eastern	102
Widget	Western	39

None of the business insights we found in the overall report could have been obtained with just this subset of the report. Obviously we need fast, flexible ways to add the comparison columns and the break rows. Unfortunately, SQL does not hand us these capabilities. We have to work for them. There are four possible techniques for producing the second column, calculating the sales growth from last month:

1. Self join
2. Correlated subquery

3. Case statement
4. Separate query streams

Self Join

Self join has been a legal construct since the first version of SQL. For the comparison to last month, we in effect pretend that there is a second sales_fact table, which we denote by the label "g", and a second time table which we denote by the label "u", The new parts of the SQL that we have added to support the comparison are highlighted in boldface. The SQL is ugly:

select p.product_name as Product, m.region_name as Region, sum(f.sales) as
    Sales_This_Month,
        100 * (sum(f.sales)-sum(g.sales)) / sum(g.sales) as Growth_in_
        Sales_vs_Last_Month
from sales_fact f, product p, market m, time t,
        sales_fact g, time u
where f.product_key = p.product_key
        and f.market_key = m.market_key
        and f.time_key = t.time_key
        and g.product_key = p.product_key
        and g.market_key = m.market_key
        and g.time_key = u.time_key
        and p.product_name in ('Framis', 'Widget')
        and t.month = 'May' and t.year = 1996
        and u.month_number = t.month_number-1
        group by p.product name, m.region_name
        order by p.product_name, m.market_name

This SQL now extends the report a little:

PRODUCT	REGION	SALES THIS MONTH	GROWTH IN SALES VS. LAST MONTH
Framis	Central	110	12
Framis	Eastern	179	-3
Framis	Western	55	5
Widget	Central	66	2
Widget	Eastern	102	4
Widget	Western	39	-9

Although this SQL will run to completion on virtually every SQL compliant DBMS, it is rarely used because of a number of objections:

- Already the SQL is getting lengthy and hard to read. The specification for the comparison is not expressed directly as an intention in the SQL, and the specification is scattered awkwardly across four discontiguous parts of the SQL. It is hard to write, hard to read, and hard to debug.
- Partly for the above reasons, no commercial query tool bothers to produce this kind of SQL. You have to write it by hand.
- Our friend, the **cost-based optimizer** in the DBMS, begins to have trouble with the larger number of tables in the query. Although most DBMSs will run this SQL to completion, if several more such simple comparisons are added, the SQL rapidly freezes up, and never returns a value. Since many systems will reveal their evaluation strategy only after the DBMS returns the results, in most cases we never know what the DBMS was trying to do for 48 hours before we ABENDed the query.

Correlated Subquery

SQL-2 allowed a more flexible way to write the same query, lumping the alternate query into one place. But this method is just as ugly:

```
select p.product_name as Product, m.region_name as Region, sum(f.sales) as
Sales_This_Month,
    100 * (sum(f.sales)-(select sum(g.sales)
      from sales_fact g, product q, market n, time u
      where g.product_key = q.product_key
        and g.market_key = n.market_key
        and g.time_key = u.time_key
        and g.product_name = p.product_name
        and n.region_name = m.region_name
        and u.month_number = t.month_number-1))
    / (select sum(g.sales)
      from sales_fact g, product q, market n, time u
      where g.product_key = q.product_key
        and g.market_key = n.market_key
        and g.time_key = u.time_key
```

> **and g.product_name = p.product_name**
> **and n.region_name = m.region_name**
> **and u.month_number = t.month_number-1)**
> from sales_fact f, product p, market m, time t
> where f.product_key = p.product_key
>   and f.market_key = m.market_key
>   and f.time_key = t.time_key
>   and p.product_name in ('Framis', 'Widget')
>   and **t.month = 'May'** and t.year = 1996
> group by p.product name, m.region_name
> order by p.product_name, m.market_name

The entire bolded section of the SQL retrieves last month's sales. The bold portion of the code contains references (p, m, and t) to the main body tables. These are underlined in the bolded section. There is no way to avoid repeating the entire bolded section twice. It should be obvious that this SQL has even more problems than the self join SQL. It would be a monumental dead end for DBMS vendors to put any research or development into improving either of these techniques as a way of leveraging comparisons in dimensional data warehouses. No one is going to implement comparisons this way.

The CASE Statement

The CASE statement, introduced in SQL-92, goes a fair way toward making simple comparisons tractable. The strategy for writing our simple comparison with the CASE statement has two parts:

1. Select all the records for both this month and last month through the main query constraints.
2. Pick off this month's records and last month's records separately as the records are dropped into the answer set.

The SQL looks like this:

> select p.product_name as Product, m.region_name as Region,
>   **sum(CASE(t.month = 'May', f.sales, 0) as Sales_This_Month,**
>   **100 * (sum(CASE(t.month = 'May', f.sales, 0))**
>   **_sum(CASE(t.month= 'April', f.sales, 0)))**

/ sum(CASE(t.month = 'April', f.sales, 0))
from sales_fact f, product p, market m, time t
where f.product_key = p.product_key
   and f.market_key = m.market_key
   and f.time_key = t.time_key
   and p.product_name in ('Framis', 'Widget')
   and t.month in ('April', 'May') and t.year = 1996
group by p.product name, m.region_name
order by p.product_name, m.market_name

The t.month constraint shown in boldface near the end of the SQL lets both this month and last month through the query constraints. The first CASE statement in the bolded section tests t.month in every incoming record in the answer set to see if it is May. If the record belongs to May, then the value in that record for f.sales is added to the surrounding sum. If the value is not May, then the value of zero is added to the surrounding sum. A similar explanation holds for the other CASE statements. When all the rows have been fetched from the DBMS, the calculation for the percent difference in the SELECT list has this value:

$$100 * ((\text{May Sales})-(\text{April Sales})) / (\text{April Sales})$$

which is what it should be.

The CASE statement has the advantages that the optimizer does not get confused by the existence of false additional tables, and the SQL is relatively more compact and readable than the previous cases. However, the CASE statement is not the answer to realistic complex comparisons. It still has the following problems:

- Division by zero is not gracefully handled.
- The SQL is not compact or intentional. Few, if any, query tools will generate the CASE statement automatically behind the scenes as a way to implement comparisons.
- The CASE statement requires the main SQL query constraints be made very loose and granular. The comparison must be programmed in two places in the SQL in two ways: first in the main query constraints, where the union of all constraints in all CASE statements must be programmed. In other words, the programmer must let through everything that is going to be used

by any CASE statement, all in one place. Second, the comparison is programmed again, in each CASE statement.

- The looseness of the SQL constraints probably hampers performance in many complex queries, because in some sense a large chunk of the database must be let through to satisfy all the CASE statements. On the other hand, this big, loose query is only done once.
- The looseness of the SQL constraints and the fact that these constraints implement all the comparisons at once make it difficult to use aggregates effectively. This method works only on single fact and single dimension tables. Either aggregates would have to be ignored, or it would force the IS shop to implement aggregates using the nonrecommended LEVEL technique discussed in Chapter 13.

Separate Query Streams

All this leaves only one remaining technique, namely separate query streams. With separate query streams we fetch each component of a comparison in a separate query. The query tool then is responsible for stitching the answer sets together. Fortunately, this technique has many advantages and only a few disadvantages. The advantages of separate query streams include the following:

- Very compact, very vanilla SQL that can be issued by almost any query tool. The separate queries all look like the first SQL example in this chapter.
- Tight control on the DBMS performance because the SQL is compact and simple. The optimizer doesn't have room to get creative.
- The division-by-zero problem goes away as long as the query tool implements outer join processing on the separate answer sets. Outer join is nothing more than sort-merge on the row headers of the answer sets.
- The separate queries are amenable to the full use of aggregate navigation. Denominators of category share calculations, for instance, should surely grab the category aggregate, even when the numerator is looking for a specific low-level product.
- Dynamic edits to the overall report can often be handled by fetching only the changed column, rather than the entire report. In an interactive environment, this can be a significant difference.

- The model of postprocessing the answer set is a powerful one that can accommodate the needs for presentation processing in a query as well as the comparison processing we have been discussing.

The main disadvantage of separate query streams is:

- The query tool must manage the separate query streams. It must send a succession of queries to the DBMS, and collect and process the results. The main responsibility is to sort-merge (outer join) the various answer sets.

We summarize this long section with an important design principle:

> **Comparisons are a key element of nearly every business report.**
> **Comparisons should be implemented as separate query streams,**
> **managed by the query tool.**

ON-THE-FLY DBMS TABLES

A natural observation to make at this point is to ask why these separate answer sets cannot be held on the DBMS by populating special tables created on the fly during construction of the final report. Some of the processing, such as outer joins, can even be done on the DBMS. This approach would seem to reduce the need to manage intermediate data sets in the client query tool. Unfortunately, there are a number of practical problems in trying to make the DBMS hold the intermediate state of a report. These problems can be summarized as follows:

- Much of the final processing users need to perform on the rows of a report amounts to sequential processing, such as numbering the rows, providing ranks, cumulative totals, and break rows. Interactive report building involves not just populating these answer sets but performing complex edits on these answer sets. Relational DBMSs simply aren't good at this kind of processing.
- Really complex reports require a lot of intermediate tables. The author implemented a reporting system based on this architecture and the most complex reports needed more than 50 temporary tables on the DBMS.

- The proliferation of temporary tables on the DBMS rapidly turns into a disaster. Whenever a user report is interrupted for any reason, all the temporary tables created in progress are left on the DBMS. Although a well-written application can find and clean up orphaned temporary tables, the DBMS may accumulate hundreds of these orphans.
- The DBAs become quite uncomfortable with all of this uncontrolled table creation.
- Writing the scratch results into *shared* tables does not ease the situation although it reduces the number of scratch tables. Shared tables are now subject to contention and row locking and we have bought our way back into transaction processing.
- Finally, having a large DBMS that can hold temporary results is inviting disaster. On a PC, if the user inadvertently asks for a million-row result, quite soon the user or the PC itself will stop the process. When using a shared report scratch table, a request for a million-row result may eventually be fulfilled. We hope the result isn't spooled automatically to a printer somewhere for a 2,000 page report.

All of this can be further summarized in a design principle:

> **DBMSs constructed on the fly to hold the results of separate query streams are not recommended. The separate query streams should be sent to the client query tool for all further processing.**

USER INTERFACE RECOMMENDATIONS

In Chapter 15, we described at a high level the data warehouse owner's responsibility for providing simple user interfaces that are matched to the end user's tasks. The central idea was to provide precanned parameterized reports where, with a minimum of button clicks, the user could create a series of reports on a particular theme. We emphasized that a good user interface for a query tool presented as few distractions and interruptions to the continuity of the task as possible. Here are the basic user interface design principles:

A good user interface is based on recognizing and pointing, not remembering and typing. A good user interface minimizes the number of button clicks and context switches.

In this section we descend to the next level and talk about the desirable user interface features and styles of presentation within such an easy to use framework. We will focus on an intermediate-level query tool that presents both a view of the available data and a view of the final report. Such an intermediate tool is neither an executive report display screen nor a programming interface for an expert computer user. We choose this level of tool for discussion because this appears to be the level at which most commercial query tool products are aimed.

Visibility

In a good user interface for an intermediate-level reporting tool, important things are visible at a glance, or they can be called up with a single button click. The most basic visible things in such a query tool should be:

- The dimensions
- The constraints chosen on those dimensions
- The base-level fact table
- The current state of the report

The tool should make a significant effort to display all of these things on the screen at once. The data elements in each of these tables do not need to be displayed explicitly, but the existence of the tables is extremely important to give the user a clue as to the context of the report being built. It will not be possible or desirable to display the entire list of dimensional attributes for each dimension, but with a single click an entire dimension should be displayed. This is where a tool should *not* emphasize a snowflake physical structure. It is confusing for the user to click repeatedly while expanding or traversing a snowflake in order to select a brand name or a category name for a low-level product. It is extremely bad to present these different levels as separate windows. This would be an end user nightmare.

The current constraints in effect on the report, and on individual columns of the report, should be visible at a glance. The state of the report itself, and whether it needs to be rerun, should be visible. Not every command should invoke a rerunning of the report. The user may want to make a series of changes to a report before running it, and thus the "unrun" status of the report should be obvious. An ideal query tool should leave as much of the report on the screen as possible after every user edit, and then only query the DBMS to fill in the parts that have been invalidated by the previous edits. We state these recommendations as design principles:

> A report-writing query tool should communicate the context of the report at a glance, including especially the identities of the dimension tables and fact table, the constraints in effect on the dimensions, and the current state of the report. The report itself should be visible in a single button click.

Editing the Columns of a Report

In this section we develop two important design principles that affect user interface design. If a report can be seen on the screen, the user should be able to reach out to a column and edit it. Columns determine the contents of a report. The rows are the results returned from the DBMS. A good query tool will let the user transform a column whenever he or she can see the column. A constraint on a column should be changeable by a simple click or drag operation, where a list of available constraints is easily presented. A column should be able to be converted into a comparison just as easily. A column should be able to be converted into a sequential presentation such as a ranking, moving average, or cumulative sum with a single button click.

> If users can see something, like a column of a report, they should be able to edit it directly.

Each of these transformations on a column should invalidate only a minimal subset of the report. Converting a column from a numeric presentation to a ranking number should have no effect on the rest of the report. Recalculating and redisplaying the edited column should not requery data for any other column.

> Edits performed on report columns should leave as much of the report still valid as possible. Requerying after an edit should at most fetch the data needed to rebuild the edited column.

Once a complex report has been defined, the query tool should determine the minimum number of separate queries needed to fetch the required results. If several columns are comparing this month's sales with various other months and product groupings, then only one query will be needed to fetch this month's sales for all the columns that use that data.

Stopping a Query

It is essential that a query tool be able to immediately stop a query. The user may change his or her mind or may realize that a mistake has been made in the formulation of the query. In any case, the response to the STOP command must take place in a few seconds. With the advent of multitasking operating systems, it is essential that the query tool be able to run while the user is performing other tasks on the client machine.

> The query tool must have an immediate STOP command, and the query tool must not preempt the user's machine while it is waiting for data from the DBMS.

Executive, Analyst, and Developer Interfaces

Although this section has been aimed at the end user analyst who is both viewing reports and modifying them, it is worthwhile to contrast the differences among the executive, analyst, and developer interfaces.

The *executive interface* is mainly concerned with alerting the executive to look at something unusual in a precanned report. The executive interface must be able to automatically highlight a few key items and wait for the executive to select one of them and ask why. That screen should then be replaced with a similar screen showing a few key causal items, and again waiting for the executive to ask why. The executive interface, per se, does not need to allow the construction or modification of an individual reporting screen.

The *analyst interface* is mainly concerned with running and modifying precanned, parameterized reports. Within the boundaries defined by the pre-canned report, the analyst user should be able to change among precanned constraints on dimensions, change column presentation modes (i.e., specify comparisons, sequential operations, and formatting), and add new precanned column specifications to the report.

The *developer interface* is mainly concerned with building precanned, para-meterized reports. The developer needs to be able to see all of the fact and di-mension tables in the data warehouse, and be able to assemble clumps of them together in a precanned report template. The developer must also have full browsing capability on each dimension to build named constraints, and must be able to specify the logic of break rows in a report. The developer should be able to define computed columns, specify exception processing and alerts, and specify what happens when the executive or analyst asks for a drill down (asks *why*). The developer also needs a graphical user interface shell creation capa-bility and a programmable interface to a Help facility.

Ideally, a given query tool product can support all three of these modes of use. In some cases a user may want to employ some of the deeper capabilities. An aggressive executive may want to change a constraint on a report. An ag-gressive analyst may want to define new precanned constraints using the browser. Although this broad use can be encouraged, it is important that the user passes from one domain to the other explicitly. The executive should not see the analyst interface unless the executive specifically requests it. Similarly, the analyst should not see the developer interface unless the analyst specifi-cally requests it.

QUERY TOOL FEATURES

In this section we will describe many of the desirable features in a modern query tool. "Query tool" here will mean the environment for creating and de-livering precanned, parameterized reports.

Browsing

In Chapter 2 we described a browsing episode, where the user was looking at various attributes in the Store dimension. The central feature of the browser is the ability to display lists of distinct values for each dimension attribute and then to set constraints progressively on one or more of the attributes. Every time a constraint is set, all the lists adjust. A good browser lets users explore and understand a large dimension.

A browser not only lets users explore and understand a dimension but invites them to store a useful constraint under a name for later use. For instance, all the candy products in a store might be grouped together and given the name Candy Products. The name Candy Products is useful for identifying the constraint, and it can be used in the heading of the report. This is far better than seeing the underlying SQL. The constraint Candy Products can be thought of as a custom group. The query tool's ability to perform comparisons by placing different constraints on different columns in a report, and usually issuing different queries on each of these columns, allows a whole set of custom groups to be analyzed together. Consider the following report:

PERIOD	REGION	SALES FOR ALL PRODUCTS	SALES FOR CANDY PRODUCTS	SALES FOR MILK PRODUCTS	SALES FOR DIET PRODUCTS
1Q96	Central	110	38	55	32
1Q96	Eastern	150	47	66	52
1Q96	Western	105	29	44	39

The custom groups defined for the columns of this report should be kept in an easily accessible list so that the user can drag a group name onto a column to change its definition at any time. Notice that these groups do not have to be disjoint. Diet Products, for instance, includes some of the Milk Products and even a few of the Candy Products. This kind of disjoint grouping can only be done on the columns of a relational answer set. Rows are required by SQL in a single query to be disjoint. Later in this chapter we will discuss *pivoting*, in which the rows and columns of a report can be twisted into new configurations once the answer set has been delivered to the client query tool.

Outer Join

The ability to specify custom groups with different constraints on different columns implies immediately that some of the cells in a given column may not have a value. Suppose that our company decided to expand into Canada, and had just launched the Milk Products but not Candy or Diet Products. The report we ran in the previous example would then look like this:

Period	Region	Sales for All Products	Sales for Candy Products	Sales for Milk Products	Sales for Diet Products
1Q96	Canada	17		17	
1Q96	Central	110	38	55	32
1Q96	Eastern	150	47	66	52
1Q96	Western	105	29	44	39

The first row for Canada does not have any values for the Candy or Diet columns. The values should not necessarily be represented as zero. In this case we just didn't receive any sales data. The correct representation in the report is a blank, or perhaps the value N/A. The query tool must be able, when it is fetching the values, to supply the blanks correctly. If the column is a calculation, or a comparison, then the correct entry is also a blank, or an N/A. If each of the numerical columns in this report is a separate query, then the report is built from a simple merge-sort process on the row headers of each of the four answer sets. A relational DBMS calls this process *outer join*. This process is so basic that we give it a design principle:

> A query tool fetching multiple answer sets and combining them must always combine these answer sets using outer joins. The outer joins are almost all two-way (symmetric) outer joins.

Interface to Help

A key capability in any modern computer tool is a good interface to Help. A query tool should have four kinds of Help:

1. The printed documentation should be available on-line, with hypertext links threading the documentation to allow navigating between subjects.
2. Help for all menu commands should be accessible either by searching for the name on the command or by selecting the command and pressing the Help key or button.
3. Help for common tasks should be accessible by searching for the description of the task in the Help system.
4. Help for explaining a data element should be accessible by selecting the

data element in any view that shows a dimension table or a fact table and invoking Help. This facility is called the Information Dictionary, and is a database of explanations maintained by the DBA. The Information Dictionary contains an explanation of each data element in business terms, as well as a second, more technical explanation of how the data element was extracted into the data warehouse, and finally the name of the business expert within the company who can explain the uses of that data element.

Precanned Comparisons

A menu of comparison types should always be available. A minimal list of comparisons should include the following:

- Numerical difference
- Percent difference
- Ratio (as a decimal)
- Ratio (as a percent)
- Index (ratio as a decimal times 100) which is the same as the share
- Growth factor over N time periods

The user should be able to convert a column to a comparison by touching this menu.

Distributed Calculations: Nonadditive Measures

The sample business report shown earlier in this chapter only had one additive column, the sales this month. All the rest of the columns were comparisons expressed as percentages. A complex inventory tracking report on a database such as we developed in Chapter 3 may be filled with apparently nonadditive values such as turns, days supply, and GMROI. In a dimensional data warehouse we need to be able to fetch these kinds of measures at different grains upon request, as well as being able to insert break rows into the reports that summarize these measures at different levels. A classic shortcoming in reporting tools is the inability to present this data at different grains or correctly compute break rows.

The architecture for correctly performing these computations is very simple.

All of the underlying data in the fact tables must be additive. The query tool fetches the additive data back from the DBMS, adding the additive data as necessary to compute break row totals, and then *as the last step*, computes and displays the nonadditive quantity. In this way, nonadditive measures derived from additive base data can always be correctly presented, in every context. In a modern report writer, there is no excuse for break rows being incorrectly computed. This should be an immediate disqualifier for a candidate report writer.

 Nonadditive quantities derived from separate queries (such as ratios) can be usefully presented at differing grains and in break rows only if the additive components are fetched from the DBMS and the computation is performed in the query tool as the last step before presentation. Mathematically, we say that the computation is distributed over the sums, not the other way around.

Drilling Down

The first action an executive user usually wants to take after displaying the first report on the screen is to ask why. Asking why means "supply me with more detail." Actually it means more specifically "supply me with interesting detail relevant to this data item." Drilling down is more than descending *the* hierarchy. There is a temptation to implement a drill-down button that drops down through *the* merchandise hierarchy. Many times, however, drilling down means something different. Drilling down is really a generic term that means "give me more (or different) rows headers." In other words, take the questionable items showing on the screen and explode them out somehow.

To see that drilling down is not descending a hierarchy, consider one of our earlier example reports:

PRODUCT	REGION	SALES THIS MONTH	GROWTH SALES VS. LAST MONTH
Framis	Central	110	°° 12%
Framis	Eastern	179	**-3%**
Framis	Western	55	5%
Total Framis		344	°° 6%

This little report has several of the key elements that make up a classic dimensional data warehouse analysis. The right-hand column is a comparison, which we have identified as the most useful kind of report measure. The comparison is expressed as a nonadditive growth percentage. The column is also marked to draw the user's attention to *exceptions*. The exceptions are growth numbers that fall above or below specified thresholds. Exception handling is directly related to drilling down. Although obviously the user might want to drill down on some other number or numbers in the report, the report designer has tried to guess which numbers will be significant. Perhaps the executive has told the report developer what the thresholds should be.

Suppose that the executive points at the −3 percent result for Framis sales growth, and asks Why. What should we do? We could certainly drill down through the product hierarchy by adding the Size attribute to the row header list. That might be interesting:

PRODUCT	REGION	SIZE	SALES THIS MONTH	GROWTH SALES VS. LAST MONTH
Framis	Central	2 oz	34	** 10%
Framis	Central	4 oz	36	** 13%
Framis	Central	10 oz	40	** 11%
Framis	*Total Cental*		110	** 12%
Framis	Eastern	2 oz	63	**-2.8%**
Framis	Eastern	4 oz	60	**-3.1%**
Framis	Eastern	10 oz	56	**-2.9%**
Framis	*Total Eastern*		179	-3%
Framis	Western	2 oz	19	5%
Framis	Western	4 oz	17	4%
Framis	Western	10 oz	19	6%
Framis	*Total Western*		55	5%
Total Framis			344**	6%

To our disappointment, after studying this data we don't see a revealing pattern when we drill down on the size in the product hierarchy. It seems that all of our sizes are uniformly affected. Even if there was another level of product to descend to, it is unlikely that it would be very useful. If our query tool implements only a single drill-down philosophy, we have run out of interesting options.

Fortunately, it is easy to make drill down much more powerful. The first realization is that any attribute added from any of the dimension tables is a legitimate way to drill down. Adding another attribute in general always forces more detail to be presented.

Instead of the Size attribute being automatically selected, we should just opportunistically drag in whichever attribute would seem to make the most sense. Maybe we suspect that our sales force is inconsistent. Let us add Sales Team to the first report instead of Size:

PRODUCT	REGION	SALES TEAM	SALES THIS MONTH	GROWTH SALES VS. LAST MONTH
Framis	Central	Chicago	52	** 21%
Framis	Central	St. Louis	28	5%
Framis	Central	Dallas	30	6%
Framis	*Total Central*		110	** 12%
Framis	Eastern	New York	93	4%
Framis	Eastern	Boston	75	5%
Framis	Eastern	Wash DC	11	**-15%**
Framis	*Total Eastern*		179	**-3%**
Framis	Western	Los Angeles	18	5%
Framis	Western	San Fran	16	4%
Framis	Western	Seattle	21	6%
Framis	*Total Western*		55	5%
Total Framis			344	** 6%

Now the answer jumps out of the data. We have a marked inconsistency in our sales teams. The big positive outcome in the Central region was due to just one of the sales teams in Chicago. Similarly, the big negative slide in the Eastern region was due to the poor performance of the Washington DC sales team. We have now drilled down in a promising direction. We can summarize this story with a design principle:

Drilling down does not mean descending a predetermined hierarchy. It means being able to quickly ask for additional row headers from any of the dimensions joined to the fact table. It also means being able to remove row headers and drill down in a different direction.

Advanced Exception Handling

The simple example of exception handling in the above example is just one way to draw the user's attention to unusual data. The goal is to provide better and better ways to find the unusual data elements. For individual data elements, a simple list of exception handling techniques should include at least the following:

- Red/green or flashing indicators for exceptional items
- Limiting the displayed report only to exceptional items or throwing out the exceptional items
- Limiting the displayed report to rows with null values or throwing out the null values
- Marking as exceptional if in top or bottom N of report
- Marking as exceptional if in top or bottom $N\%$ of report
- Marking as exceptional if in top or bottom $N\%$ of contribution to the column total
- Marking as exceptional if above or below specific numeric thresholds

An advanced capability would include:

- *Agents* that perform a complex calculation, possibly on data not showing in the report, that mark the data as exceptional if it falls outside a trend or forecast range
- *Triggers* that mark the data as exceptional if an event occurs somewhere in the data warehouse environment, such as a threshold being exceeded, or a date occurring, or a specific set of transactions being processed

Agents and triggers are an exciting new area for data warehouse vendors to exploit for exception handling applications. There are no established categories of these kinds of capabilities yet. The prospective owner of a data warehouse should ask the vendor to describe how agents and triggers work and how well integrated into the overall data warehouse framework these capabilities are. For example, can more than one kind of query tool benefit from agents and triggers?

Context-Specific Drill-Down Targets

A different kind of advanced drill-down capability is the context-specific drill down to a different report. For example, if the executive in our sales report example had selected the original -3% number that was so worrisome, a context-specific drill-down request might have taken the executive to an entirely different kind of report, which we might call a Sales Growth Drill Down Report. This is a report with special different columns that was purpose-built to analyze why there was an alarming trend in month-to-month sales growth.

In this case, when we drop into the new report context, we must inherit the constraints from the higher-level report along each supported dimension. We can further provide control for the user by interpreting his or her selection as we jump to the lower-level report. In other words:

- If the user has selected the entire column (Sales Growth) then we drop into the lower-level report constraining the report to the row headers that have exceptional (marked) entries in the selected column.

But,

- If the user has instead selected just a span of cells in the Sales Growth column then we drop into the lower-level report to those row headers corresponding to the selected cells, ignoring the exceptional highlighting.

Interaction with Aggregates

The need for an aggregate navigator should be obvious from the above drill-down scenarios. As we add and subtract row headers, we lose and gain the ability to use prestored aggregates. An aggregate navigator takes away the complex responsibility of correctly jumping to the right aggregate each time we make a change.

Drilling Across

In the previous section we discussed drilling down and we pointed out how drilling down is nothing more than changing the row headers of the report. Drilling across, however, is a very different concept. If we have a value chain, or at least if we have two or more fact tables that share dimensions, we can combine them in a single report by drilling across. Suppose we have manufacturer's shipments to a set of stores, and further down the value chain we have store sales. The manufacturer's shipments fact table might have the following dimensions:

Shipments: Time

              Product

              Store

              Manufacturer's Deal

              Carrier

The store sales fact table might have the following dimensions:

Sales: Time

              Product

              Store

              Consumer Promotion

              Consumer

As we pointed out in Chapter 5, we can use these two fact tables together if the common dimensions are *exactly* the same. In other words, the three shared dimensions of time, product, and store need to be literally the same dimension tables.

It is easy to visualize how a drill-across report works if we first imagine two separate reports using the same row headers from the two fact tables. This is possible only if we choose the row headers from the common dimensions. For instance, a report from manufacturing shipments might look like this:

PRODUCT	WEEK OF	QUANTITY SHIPPED
Framis	Jan 10, 1996	66
Framis	Jan 17, 1996	76
Framis	Jan 24, 1996	59

And a report from store sales might look like this:

PRODUCT	WEEK OF	QUANTITY SOLD
Framis	Jan 10, 1996	62
Framis	Jan 17, 1996	63
Framis	Jan 24, 1996	74

It should be intuitively obvious that we can combine these two reports into a drill-across report by using our familiar technique of outer joining on the row headers. This yields the combined drill-across report:

PRODUCT	WEEK OF	QUANTITY SHIPPED	QUANTITY SOLD
Framis	Jan 10, 1996	66	62
Framis	Jan 17, 1996	76	63
Framis	Jan 24, 1996	59	74

We could create interesting comparison columns between the quantity shipped and quantity sold, like the running excess inventory. Notice that such a comparison column is a strong argument for the query tool performing the calculation locally, because in theory the shipments and sales databases and their respective dimension tables could be in different physical databases, or even on separate machines.

The drill-across logic works as long as the row headers chosen for a particular report have exactly the same meaning in both fact tables and their respective dimensions. If the two product dimension tables differ at all, either the report will be misleading or a runtime error will result. The same thing would happen if the user attempts to use a row header from a nonshared dimension. For example, if the user dragged the carrier name from the carrier dimension into the report, the report could not run, because the second query on sales would not be able to perform the join of the carrier dimension to the sales fact table.

A more subtle issue is how to handle the case where the report is constructed with common row headers, but the user has placed a constraint on a noncommon dimension, like carrier. In this case, the report can be constructed and run to completion, but it would seem prudent to warn the user or supply a note on the final report that there is a constraint on a nonshared dimension.

We summarize this section with a design principle:

> Drilling across two or more fact tables is well defined as long as the
> row headers chosen for the particular report have exactly the same
> meaning in all the fact and dimension tables involved. Constraints
> may be applied to nonshared dimensions in one or more fact tables,
> but it would be advisable to warn the user of this condition either at
> runtime or on the report itself.

Extending SQL's Aggregation Operations

In Chapters 3 and 7 we pointed out several times that anything that acts like
an account balance, such as an inventory level or actual account balance, is
semiadditive because it cannot be added across the time dimension. We also
pointed out that a time sequence of inventories or balances could be usefully
summarized by averaging across the time dimension. Unfortunately, we found
that this is not the same as using SQL's AVG function. We are left with an awkward two-step application in which we test for the cardinality of the time constraint, and then use this answer to divide out the SUM of the inventories or
account balances (not the AVG).

As data warehouse owners, we have to provide users a way to do this. In the
short term, before the DBMS vendors extend SQL to handle this case, we
must build query tools so that these two steps are performed as if they were
one step. Conceptually, we extend the list of SQL aggregate functions from
SUM, MIN, MAX, AVG, and COUNT to include PERIODAVG and PERI-
ODCOUNT. PERIODAVG gives the correct period average of a measure by
dividing by the cardinality of the time constraint taken by itself. PERIOD-
COUNT actually returns this cardinality. If the query tool can be programmed
to include this function then this should be done. If the query tool cannot be
programmed this way, then the end user will have to manually divide any such
measure by the correct time cardinality with no support from the query tool.
Obviously the best solution is for the DBMS vendors to extend their versions
of SQL to handle this case.

Notice that the PERIODAVG function is useful for fully additive time series facts as well. For example, to see if sales for this quarter are running ahead
of sales averaged across the whole year, one could build a straight comparison

between PERIODAVG(sales) for the quarter and PERIODAVG(sales) for the year. The two numbers would be comparable because they would both be expressed at the grain of the time measurement, whether it is daily, weekly, or monthly.

An interesting generalization of PERIODAVG and PERIODCOUNT would be something like DIMENSIONAVG and DIMENSIONCOUNT. In this case the function would have to specify the dimension as well as the fact to be summarized over. DIMENSIONAVG(sales, STORE) would give the average sales for all the stores implied by the constraint on the STORE dimension. This solves the same problem that PERIODAVG does, because the application cannot use the SQL AVG function to divide correctly by the number of stores.

Break Rows

Break rows are a very common way to present report data. We used break rows in the example we developed earlier in this chapter:

Product	Region	Sales This Month	Growth in Sales vs. Last Month	Sales as % of Category	Change in Sales as % of Category vs. Last Month	Change in Sales as % of Category YTD vs. Last Year YTD
Framis	Central	110	** 12%	31%	3%	7%
Framis	Eastern	179	**-3%**	28%	**-1%**	3%
Framis	Western	55	5%	** 44%	1%	5%
Total Framis		344	** 6%	33%	1%	5%
Widget	Central	66	2%	18%	2%	** 10%
Widget	Eastern	102	4%	12%	5%	** 13%
Widget	Western	39	**-9%**	9%	**-1%**	8%
Total Widget		207	1%	13%	4%	** 11%
Grand Total		551	4%	20%	2%	8%

The Total Widget, Total Framis, and Grand Total rows are break rows. Break rows are certainly not a new concept, but they are not provided explicitly in SQL. SAS programmers who are used to the simple BREAK BY command will page madly through the SQL manual looking for BREAK BY. It should be right after GROUP BY and ORDER BY, but it isn't. The DBMS vendors are just starting to add this command to their extended SQL syntaxes. This is good, because correctly performing BREAK BY in a query tool is messy. As we discussed earlier, the challenge is to correctly present the nonadditive entries. Except for the first sales column, all the break row entries in the above report are distributed computations where the ratios are computed after the underlying additive items are separately added up. The query tool must hold these underlying additive entries in a separate location because they usually cannot be derived from the report at break row calculation time.

Behavioral Constraints

An interesting and difficult application is the tracking of behavior. This can take many forms but a basic example would be defining a group of customers (in a retail setting) who all spent more than $100 in your stores last month. This group is defined solely by their purchase behavior. There is no attribute in the customer dimension that we can constrain on. Yet we would like to name this group and repeatedly use it in queries. How did my Big February Purchasers do in March? How long have my Big February Purchasers been customers and what is their monthly average purchase level? How many of the Big February Purchasers also responded to a recent mailing? This last question might be the intersection of two behaviorally defined groups of customers.

We may be able to isolate the group of customers we want only by running a very complex report. After running the report, we have the names of these customers as row headers (perhaps) but how do we then capture this group and use it over and over?

The lack of any usable attribute for clumping together the behavioral group suggests that we may have to enumerate them in a long list. It is impractical to enumerate them in a constraint because the list may be thousands long. A practical technique, however, is to build a special table consisting only of the customer keys (using the example), and giving it the name Big_February_Purchasers. This table can be built when the original behavior defining report is first run. If, in addition to the customer name, the customer key is displayed, then a simple command can use the customer key column on the report to build the special table.

There are several ways the Big_February_Purchasers table can be added into a typical star join query, but the one that universally seems to perform most efficiently on a range of DBMSs is to build the typical query and simply add on a phrase in the WHERE clause constraining the fact table's customer key to the list of customer keys in Big_February_Purchasers. This is shown in bold below in the following:

```
select p.product_name, sum(f.sales_dollars)
from sales_fact f, product p, store s, time t
where f.product_key = p.product_key
    and f.store_key = s.store_key
    and f.time_key = t.time_key
    and f.customer_key=big_February_purchasers.customer_key
    and <product constraints>
    and <store constraints>
    and <time constraints>
group by p.product_name
order by p.product_name
```

Again, it is up to the data warehouse owner either to add this capability in the developer version of the query tool, or to insist that the vendor provide it as a standard function.

If the keys stored in the Big_February_Purchasers table are stored in sorted order, it makes it particularly easy to perform set manipulations on behavioral groups. For example, we might want to find the intersection, the union, or the set difference between Big_February_Purchasers and Big_March_Purchasers. If the keys are stored in sorted order, then a very simple application can generate any of these set manipulations in a single pass through the two files.

Pivoting

Pivoting is a useful function for rearranging the rows and columns of a report after it is fetched from the DBMS. As we have explained in this book, SQL delivers the data in a very characteristic and definite way. The answer set comes back as a set of rows where everything in a given column has the same definition, and the underlying data is aggregated up by the unique row header combinations.

Pivoting tools allow the row headers and column headers to be scrambled in arbitrary combinations. This has the effect of rearranging the main body data. Consider a simple report like this:

PRODUCT	REGION	THIS MONTH	LAST MONTH
Framis	Central	110	12
Framis	Eastern	179	-3
Framis	Western	55	5
Widget	Central	66	2
Widget	Eastern	102	4
Widget	Western	39	-9

This can be rearranged by pivoting into the equivalent report:

PRODUCT	REGION	CENTRAL	EASTERN	WESTERN
This Month	Framis	110	179	55
This Month	Widget	66	102	39
Last Month	Framis	12	-3	5
Last Month	Widget	2	4	-9

It is characteristic of a pivot operation, that the unique values in at least one of the columns, in this case Region, become the headers of separate columns themselves, in this case Central, Eastern, and Western. It is easier to experience this than it is to explain it in words. (It is a minor historical footnote that the author (RK) himself coined the term *pivoting* in trying to describe the effects of this operation in various tools at Metaphor Computer Systems in the early 1980s.)

Handing Off the Answer Set

All query tools need to do a good job of handing off the answer set to adjacent tools. There will always be tools that will be better than the query tool itself in presenting data in the form of graphics, analyzing data, pivoting data, or remotely mailing data. Although we all dream of automatic data movement from tool to tool, this remains confusing to end users and difficult to keep working on the typically chaotic user's desktop. Although it is very simple, the most useful command is a user-initiated copy. The user should be able to grab the entire report with one button click and take it for pasting into another tool.

Although new operating systems may remove the 32 K limit on the Windows clipboard, another useful simple command that allows very large reports to be copied is creating a file that can be read by another program. Such a command needs to distinguish between Excel and Lotus file formats because, absurdly, they are completely incompatible.

We hope that the simple act of copying a report to another tool will give the user the option of registering the copy as a hot link that will be maintained by the origin and destination tools. So far, the practical use of such a capability remains more of a dream than a reality.

Printing

Printing is another form of handing off the answer set. In this case it is to paper. Paper is a very useful medium but its size means that we have to do special things to make a report understandable when it crosses more than one sheet of paper. A good query tool must paginate a large report both horizontally and vertically by repeating row headers and column headers on separate pages. A good query tool should also have a "scrunch" mode where it forces the report to fit on a page no matter what.

Batch Operation

Batch operation is useful for a number of purposes. A report can be scheduled to run at a certain time or when an event triggers it. Batch operation can also be used for stress testing. A number of workstations can be set up to run a series of reports. The resultant multiple user load can be a good simulation of a real user environment. Special features that assist in this stress testing include the capabilities to:

- Endlessly cycle a set of reports
- Randomly stagger the arrival times of queries to more accurately simulate user behavior
- Automatically log query IDs, runtimes, and delay times in a central database to allow analysis of the stress test

ADMINISTRATIVE RESPONSIBILITIES

In this final section we summarize the primary administrative responsibilities that the owner of a dimensional data warehouse has when supporting one or more major query tools. Once again we remind ourselves that the term *query tool* in this book refers generically to all applications that maintain a session with the DBMS, send relatively small amounts of SQL to the DBMS, and receive back relatively small answer sets.

Tool Training and Data Training

We have made the point in this book that the centerline of successful data warehouse applications is the precanned, parameterized report. Most users of query tools with precanned, parameterized reports range from occasional managers to serious analytic users. A small group of executives use only the presentation and drilling down facilities of the query tool, and a small group of professional developers use the query tools to produce precanned, parameterized reports for others.

The bulk of the training requirements will be for the large middle group of analyst users who are running and modifying precanned, parameterized reports. For most of these users, a full day's training course is a lot. Even if they will attend a full-day session, half the session needs to be devoted to the content of the data in the warehouse, and at most the remaining half devoted to the mechanics of running the tool.

Prejoins and Query Tool Metadata

A basic administrative responsibility for supporting a query tool is maintaining a dictionary of joins between the various fact and dimension tables so that users never have to be concerned with joins. All query tools should be fully preconfigured so that users do not see this step.

Query tools increasingly rely on additional **metadata** to smooth the way for users. The query tool may know which fact table fields are additive, which are semiadditive, and which cannot be added. It would be helpful if the query tool knew which numeric fields were balances or inventory levels and automatically used PERIODAVG instead of AVG for these fields. It would be helpful if every numeric field in the fact table had a default formatting specification. All of these helpful additions must be maintained somewhere. Typically, each tool from each vendor privately maintains this metadata. The professional application developers in the IS shop need to maintain this metadata.

Information Dictionary

The information dictionary is a small database containing descriptions of all tables and fields in the data warehouse. This database should be accessible at all times from within the query tool so that a user can review the definition of a table or a data element, understand how the data is derived, and be able to call a live resource within the organization of whom more detailed questions can be asked. The maintenance of this information resource is an important step in making users feel comfortable with the data warehouse.

Browsing Support

The owner of a data warehouse must make sure that users are easily able to construct queries. One of the hardest steps is entering valid constraints on dimensional attributes. If the query tool does not have a first-rate browser, the data warehouse owner must provide one. A sure sign that the user community needs a browser is if the users are *writing down* valid values for product names, brands, or categories (for instance) on cheat sheets at their desks so that they can remember what to type in. A standalone browser can be built in Visual Basic or Power Builder in a few days by a competent developer. There is no excuse for a modern data warehouse to lack a good browser tool.

Public and Private Constraint Groups

Since a browser is used mostly to set up constraints on dimension tables, the data warehouse needs a systematic way to store and manage these constraints. It is not acceptable to force the user to construct complex constraints from scratch each time a report is changed. Constraints need to be named so that the users can identify them and so that the names can be used in report headings to explain the report. Ideally, these named constraints should be either private or public. Private constraints are ones seen only by a particular user. The individual user must be able to create and delete such constraints at will. Public constraints are ones seen by the entire user community. Public constraints should be created or deleted only by a user with special privileges. Care must be taken with private constraints so that when a user mails an active query tool instance (a report) to another user, the ability to use any private constraints goes with the query tool instance.

Public and Private Behavioral Groups

Behavioral groups have the same characteristics as constraint groups, although they are stored differently on the DBMS. Recall that behavioral groups are precisely those groups that cannot conveniently be described by constraints on any dimensional attributes. Large behavioral groups may have thousands of members. Behavioral groups will normally be stored as special separate tables containing only a sorted list of the keys of a particular dimension.

Again, behavioral groups probably need to have private and public flavors, with the same rules for creating and deleting as constraint groups. Behavioral groups named in an active query tool instance that is passed from one user to another must remain valid.

Aggregation Navigation Metatables and Statistics

The data warehouse owner must plan on storing and maintaining metatables to support the aggregate navigation activities. These tables will be vendor specific, but some of the implementations are quite complex, with as many as 100 tables. Although these tables are not large in a data warehouse sense, they represent a noticeable administrative complexity. The best thing that can be said about these vendor-specific tables is that if the aggregate navigator is a separate layer serving all networked query tools and all underlying DBMSs, the aggregate navigator and all of its metadata could probably be replaced by another aggregate navigator from another vendor without jeopardizing the investment made in the end user applications or the physical database design of the aggregates.

Extract Tool Metatables

In Chapter 14 we discussed the eleven steps of a dimensional data warehouse extract system. Several of these steps will require metadata to assist in finding changed records, administering the dimensional keys, completing attributes, and running quality assurance checks on the loaded data. In a complex data warehouse environment there will probably be a variety of tools used to implement this process, both from third-party extract tool vendors and in the form of home-grown applications written by IS.

Because the administrative procedures and use of metadata can grow insidiously, it is incumbent on the data warehouse owner to systematically record all the procedures and uses of metadata that may be scattered across multiple systems. At this point in its development, the data warehousing industry lacks a standard for these procedures and for the categories of metadata.

17

THE FUTURE

The data warehousing market is moving quickly as all the major DBMS and tools vendors are trying to respond to the need for data access expressed by IS shops. Although it is risky to speculate about the future in such a dynamic environment, it is still useful to identify important categories. The industry has been far too technology driven and has not been enough IS and end user driven. The IS and end user community must more clearly make its needs known to the vendors.

SOFTWARE IS THE KEY

Although there are a number of exciting and worthwhile advances being made in hardware, mostly in the area of parallel processing, the future of data warehousing belongs to software. Over the next several years there will be larger gains made in performance and value delivered to end users through software advances than through hardware advances. This is not so much a general advertisement for software as it is a commentary on the relatively primitive software we are dealing with today. The areas of today's DBMS software that will be improved significantly in the next few years include the following:

- Optimization of the execution strategy for star join queries
- Indexing of dimension tables for browsing and constraining, especially multi-million-row dimension tables

- Accessing (and hence indexing) of the composite key of large fact tables
- Completing SQL so that it can process business questions
- Support of low-level data compression
- Support of parallel processing
- Dimensional database design tools
- Dimensional database extract, administration, and QA tools
- End user query tools

It is worth noting that there are probably several $100-million-dollar businesses in the above list.

OPTIMIZING THE EXECUTION STRATEGY FOR STAR JOIN QUERIES

The current generation of relational DBMSs is far too unstable when processing star join queries. The optimizer should virtually never process some of the dimensions, then the fact table, and then the remaining dimensions. This usually means that the DBMS is writing a scratch subset of the fact table to the disk and then is testing this scratch subset against the remaining dimensions one record at a time. The result is a query that runs 10 to 100 times as long as it should. This will often happen because the optimizer has decided that the constraints on some of the dimensions are too weak or too complicated. The DBA is forced to fight with the optimizer to make it process all the dimensions first. The DBA's tools are usually frustratingly indirect. The DBA can declare individual dimension attributes to be high or low cardinality, hoping that the optimizer will lower its objections to constraints on those attributes. The DBA can directly overwrite the system statistics to fool the optimizer into thinking that a particular kind of query is more okay. All of this is nonsense. Relational DBMSs need to recognize the star join as a specific case at table declaration time, and invoke an entirely different optimizer to handle these schemata.

There are interesting optimization issues for star joins, but they are much narrower than the general case of "Coddian" relational processing. The optimization strategies will be profoundly influenced by the development of multi-access composite indexes for the fact tables. In general, although each star join query has very much the same template SQL (see Chapter 1), the significance of the constraints on the various dimensions will vary wildly. The nature of the optimization game will be to see which of many possible sets of dimensional keys can be used to most efficiently access the fact table.

There are two interesting sets of dimension keys in a star join query. One is the set of key combinations presented by the dimensions under the user's constraints. A crude view of this set is that it is the Cartesian product of all the keys separately generated by the dimension constraints. A more refined view might try to exploit correlations among the dimensions to reduce the candidate key set before it is presented to the fact table. The second set of dimension keys is the set defined by the fact table itself. Of course, the place to look for these keys is in the master fact table index(es). The simplest evaluation strategy is to take the first set of dimensionally defined composite keys and look them up one at a time in the fact table index. A more complex strategy is to decide at some point that the list of dimension candidates is actually larger than the list of keys in the fact table itself, and that doing the lookup in the reverse direction would be more efficient. An even more elaborate approach would be to dynamically switch between these two strategies as the matches between the dimension tables and the fact table are being processed.

Of course, if a given set of user constraints results in an astronomical list of candidate dimension keys, it may be the case that a judiciously computed aggregate would be a more effective way to improve performance than any optimization strategy. Earlier in the book we stated that the two most effective ways for the DBA to control dimensional data warehouse performance were to (1) keep the optimizer performing correctly, and (2) build useful aggregates. If either of these approaches has not been fully exploited, then an IS shop is wasting time and money pursuing hardware solutions.

Another way to think about indexes and optimization is that the whole approach needs to be far more deterministic. The old romantic relational notion that the DBMS would discover the relationship between two tables that were presented in a query and then decide how to process them together needs to be replaced with the view that there are only a very small number of tables in a star join schema, and that these tables have predetermined relationships to each other that don't need to be discovered thousands of times per day. Especially since these tables are static during the day in between table loads, we can afford to build very expensive static indexes that aid in querying. B-Tree indexes are pretty good at data access, but they are also pretty good at data update. We don't need the update benefit. We can afford to build much more complex inverted indexes that don't need to be updated during transaction processing. B-Tree indexes are 25 years old. Surely the research in indexing techniques at the major universities over the last 25 years holds promise of improved performance for large multidimensional data structures like our fact tables.

INDEXING OF DIMENSION TABLES

The indexing of dimension tables serves quite different goals than the indexing of fact tables. While with fact tables we are interested in attacking the fact table through its composite key to get large answer sets, with dimension tables there are three important query modes:

1. SELECT DISTINCT queries on single dimension attributes
2. SELECT DISTINCT queries on one attribute with constraints on another attribute
3. WHERE clause constraints on one or more attributes in a multitable join query

The first two query modes support the end user in browsing. As we remarked earlier, ideally both of these query modes should be satisfied through the use of indexes without needing to fetch individual dimension records and accumulate and sort their values. The use of bit vector indexes should also make the second query mode much faster than one normally sees in conventional DBMSs today. Recall that it probably is important to not snowflake the dimension table. We want to preserve the ability to co-browse combinations of attributes in a single denormalized dimension table with very high performance. It is very important that support for these browsing queries be extended up to very large dimension tables, especially customer lists that are many millions of records.

The resolution of WHERE clause constraints in multitable join queries may be able to rely on mechanisms fundamentally different from the servicing of browsing queries. The resolution of WHERE clause constraints is part of the architecture of a multitable join, and could involve the production of a *stream* of sorted dimension keys to the fact table. This is not the same as producing the set of distinct values of an attribute. It is possible that this third query mode is actually implemented as a stream that is presented, a key at a time, to the fact table lookup process.

FAST SUBSTRING SEARCH

Although substring searching in text fields is a relatively minor theme in data warehousing, the use of the LIKE statement with wild cards in the WHERE clause has often been treated as if it were a bad idea because most optimizers force a relation scan on the dimension table in this case. This is another case where fast indexing technology has been available that could make this kind of search extremely fast. PATRICIA trees were explained clearly by Knuth in volume 3 of his *Art of Computer Programming* (Addison Wesley). These structures allow every possible substring of text to be an entry point in an index lookup. In other words, every substring, whether it is a leading substring or an embedded substring, is equally fast when looked up.

GEOGRAPHIC INDEXES

Although again not a dominant theme in data warehousing, there have been some very powerful indexing techniques developed specifically for geographic data. These indexes allow queries that ask for all the geographic entities near a central geographic point to be retrieved. Although some vendors have touted these geographic lookup capabilities as multidimensional, this is not the kind of multidimensional database we have been concerned about in this book.

DATA COMPRESSION

An interesting side effect of many of the more powerful indexing schemes is that it is possible to use the information in the index to compress the original data. This has not been a high priority for OLTP, because the compressing and decompressing of the data slows down transaction processing. However, in the dimensional data warehouse our priorities are completely different. We may well be willing to invest a significant amount of computation to create a static data structure that is dramatically compressed. Even a factor of two would be economically significant. Another side effect of compression often is that performance of retrievals improves because in a general sense, a given disk block holds several times as much data. This is one of those features that is likely to sweep the data warehouse market like a brush fire because once one of the vendors offers a very significant data compression capability, that vendor will have a noticeable sales advantage that is easy for customers to understand and easy for salespeople to sell.

The deployment of powerful composite indexing schemes for fact tables may possibly offer a means to compress the data in another way. If all the accesses to the actual data were to come through the index, then the storage of the key values in the data itself is redundant. It might be possible to take the keys out of the actual data altogether. For some of the skinny fact tables with four keys and four additive facts, this might harvest a 50 percent reduction in the database size without any other form of compression.

PARALLEL PROCESSING

Parallel processing has been advertised by hardware and software vendors as solving data warehouse performance problems. Although parallel processing holds some real promise for improving query performance for end users, it is still only the #3 technique for attacking performance issues, well behind (1) getting the optimizer to correctly approach the query, and (2) building aggregates.

Parallel processing has already made for significant improvements in data loading and indexing. These back room activities are much more predictable and controllable than querying. A data load can often be sorted into clumps of keys each of which can be processed as a separate job. These jobs can then run in parallel. Data loading and indexing are very CPU intensive, and even if the parallelism is not fully carried out all the way through the I/O subsystems, the difference in loading and indexing between a uniprocessor and an 8- or 12-way SMP or MPP machine is very significant.

Parallel processing for large queries is a more slippery subject. Most of what has been parallelized to date has been full table scans where no indexes are in use. Some vendors have even tried to argue that this style of lookup is the future of data warehousing because theoretically all queries can be reduced to a full fact table scan. This is nonsense. A properly tuned data warehouse with powerful indexing technology and a reasonable set of aggregates will beat the full table scan approach every time.

A few vendors are beginning to attack the parallelization of highly indexed multitable joins. This should certainly be possible, because at the core of the fact table lookup the DBMS is simply trying to match the dimension key set from the constrained dimension tables with the dimension key set represented by the fact table index. Since both of these sets will almost certainly be available in sorted order, it is easy to imagine partitioning this job by ranges of keys and parceling the job out to multiple parallel processors. The trick is to load balance the separate jobs intelligently so that they all finish in about the same time. This load balancing requires a sophisticated understanding of the sparseness of the two key sets.

However, in a busy end user environment, where hundreds of users may be competing for the resources of 10 or 20 CPUs, it is less than clear how much benefit parallelization of the queries will bring. The ideal case is an expensive single-user query on an empty machine. This query will obviously benefit from parallelization. But in a busy end user environment, it may not be desirable to invoke the overhead of splitting a single-user process into many subprocesses, each of which is managed as a separate job by a different CPU. Instead of 100 user requests competing for 10 CPUs, we might have 1,000 user requests because each one has been parallelized 10 times. To be fair to the designers of parallel operating systems and parallel DBMSs, this lesson has certainly long since been learned, and they are working hard to reduce the extra process overhead associated with splitting a single-user job into parallel processes, and have sophisticated techniques for only partially splitting a job across a big machine. However, a word of caution is in order in this area, because the end user benefit is less clear in this case than for loading and indexing. This may be a case of a technology benefit as opposed to a user benefit.

SMARTER CACHING

It might also be possible to improve the performance of queries if the DBMS had more of a notion of the user's session. Although we have argued that the user eventually ranges widely over the whole database, it may be the case that a strong correlation exists from query to query in a user session that could be exploited. This would argue for disk caching at a user session level rather than at a database or operating system level.

SYNTAX EXTENSIONS FOR SQL

Much grief could be saved by making SQL more intentional. One way to look at the difficulty of writing end user applications in SQL is that the application design can't tell the DBMS what the user is doing. Comparisons are the worst example because of the business significance of comparisons. As we saw in the previous chapter, we have to go to great contortions to request a comparison. We need something like a simple alternate function that takes a measure from the fact table and a fragment of the where clause and interprets the fragment as replacing only the constraints in the main query that apply to the dimension mentioned in the alternate function. Then the percent growth calculation would look like this:

100*sum(f.sales) / sum(alternate(f.sales where t.month = 'April'))

Some additional thinking needs to be done to handle the self-referential case where we want a constant offset of one month. Perhaps we could write something like this:

100*sum(f.sales) / sum(alternate(f.sales where t.monthnum = t.monthnum_1))

Sequential processing is not supported in standard SQL at all. The Red Brick DBMS has a series of sequential operators to handle most of the important cases like Rank, N-Tile, Cumulative, MovingAvg, MovingSum, and RatioToReport. Red Brick also supports Break By and Break By Distributed for break row processing. These functions can be used in both the SELECT list as well as the WHERE clause. For example, the phrase WHERE RANK(f.sales) <= 10 restricts the answer set to the top 10 sales values.

Finally, as suggested in the previous chapter, SQL could be extended to handle semiadditive balances and inventory levels with PERIODAVG, PERIOD-COUNT, as well as DIMENSIONAVG, and DIMENSIONCOUNT.

EVENT TRACKING

Certain SQL applications that are trying to pick out patterns from time series data could be made much simpler with the ability to identify events in time and then align them to a common virtual starting point. For instance, if a set of customers were identified that all had made some pattern of purchases, we would like to track this cohort group in succeeding months. The problem is that all the customers had different months in which the purchase pattern was observed. Perhaps this could be a generalization of the behavior study group discussed in the previous chapter where we simply stored away the set of customer keys that defined the set of customers that exhibited interesting behavior. To generalize the concept, we want to store not only the customer key but the defining moment in time where the interesting behavior occurred. This defining point in time becomes the time=0 starting point for each customer. Now we need special syntax for this artificial relative time rather than the real time so that we can treat the artificial time as if it is a normal time key even though we have defined it on the fly.

ADMINISTRATIVE TOOLS

In Chapters 13 and 14 we discussed a number of administrative processes that have to be managed in an ad hoc way by the IS staff. These included:

- The eleven steps of extracting, key administration, loading, indexing, and quality assurance
- The building of aggregates

In Chapter 12 we discussed the fundamental act of doing the logical design from an understanding of the end user requirements and the available data. In all of these cases, the data warehouse designer needs coordinated suites of tools to assist in this process. At this point in time there are no tools that directly target the needs of dimensional data warehouse design. A good CASE tool that not only designed the logical schemas but put in place the administrative metadata for administering keys, building aggregates, loading, indexing, and quality assurance would have a major impact on the industry.

DESIGN PRINCIPLES FOR A DIMENSIONAL DATA WAREHOUSE

This appendix collects together, in order, all of the design principles developed in this book.

Chapter 2: The Grocery Store

> The first step in the design is to decide what business process(es) to model, by combining an understanding of the business with an understanding of what data is available.

> The second step in the design is to decide on the grain of the fact table in each business process.

> A data warehouse almost always demands data expressed at the lowest possible grain of each dimension, not because queries want to see individual low-level records, but because queries need to cut through the database in very precise ways.

> The number of base sales transaction line items in a business can be estimated by dividing the gross revenue of the business by the average price of a sales item.

➤ The fact table in a dimensional schema is naturally highly normalized.

➤ Efforts to normalize any of the tables in a dimensional database solely in order to save disk space are a waste of time.

➤ The dimension tables must not be normalized but should remain as flat tables. Normalized dimension tables destroy the ability to browse, and the disk space savings gained by normalizing the dimension tables are typically less than 1 percent of the total disk space needed for the overall schema.

➤ Most data warehouses need an explicit time dimension table even though the primary time key may be an SQL date-valued object. The explicit time dimension is needed to describe fiscal periods, seasons, holidays, weekends, and other calendar calculations that are difficult to get from the SQL date machinery.

➤ Drilling down in a data warehouse is nothing more than adding row headers from the dimension tables. Drilling up is subtracting row headers. An explicit hierarchy is not needed to support drilling down.

➤ The product dimension is one of the two or three primary dimensions in nearly every data warehouse. Great care should be taken to fill this dimension with as many descriptive attributes as possible. Retail product dimension tables should have at least 50 attributes.

➤ A nonadditive calculation, such as a ratio like gross margin, can be calculated for any slice of the fact table by remembering to calculate the *ratio of the sums*, not the sum of the ratios. In other words, the computation must be distributed over the sums, not the other way around.

➤ Customer counts are usually semiadditive when they occur in time snapshot fact tables because they double count activity across products during the customer event. In these cases they can be correctly used in user applications only by restricting the keys in the nonadditive dimensions to single values.

Chapter 3: The Warehouse

All measures that record a static level, such as inventory levels, financial account balances, and measures of intensity such as room temperatures, are inherently nonadditive across time. However, in these cases the measure may be usefully aggregated across time by *averaging over the number of time periods*.

Document control numbers such as order numbers, invoice numbers, and bill of lading numbers usually are represented as degenerate dimensions (i.e., dimension keys with no corresponding dimension table) in fact tables where the grain of the table is the document itself or is a line item in the document.

Exceptions to absolute additivity in the fact table can be made where the additive measures are more conveniently delivered in a view. Examples include computed time spans from a large number of date fields, as well as extended monetary amounts derived from unit costs and prices. In such a case it is important to have all users access the view instead of the underlying table.

Transaction-level fact tables have a characteristic structure, with as much surrounding context as possible expressed in conventional dimensions. Frequently a degenerate dimension such as a purchase order number is present. The list of facts is almost always a single amount field.

A transaction-level fact table must in most cases be accompanied by some form of snapshot table to give a practical view of a process.

Chapter 4: Shipments: The Most Powerful Database

For any company that ships products to customers, or performs a similar function, the best place to start a data warehouse is with shipments.

Any dimension whose records automatically define a point in space is capable of supporting multiple-nested geographic hierarchies.

It is natural and common, especially for customer-oriented dimensions, for a dimension to simultaneously support multiple independent hierarchies. Drilling up and drilling down within each of these hierarchies must be supported in a data warehouse.

Two loosely correlated attributes that have a many-to-many relationship can be modeled either as a single compound dimension, such as the ship-to-bill-to example, or they can be modeled as separate dimensions, at the designer's discretion.

A significant effort should be made to allocate allowances, discounts, and activity-related components of cost down to the line item (i.e., product) level in businesses that ship products to their customers.

Chapter 5: The Value Chain

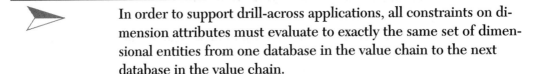

In order to support drill-across applications, all constraints on dimension attributes must evaluate to exactly the same set of dimensional entities from one database in the value chain to the next database in the value chain.

Chapter 6: The Big Dimensions

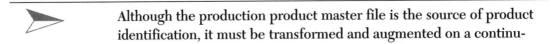

Although the production product master file is the source of product identification, it must be transformed and augmented on a continuing basis in order to serve as the product dimension in the data warehouse. The primary steps needed are the generalization and/or replacement of the primary product key, and the completion and quality assurance of the descriptive attributes.

A typical dimension contains one or more natural hierarchies, together with other attributes that do not have a hierarchical relationship to any of the attributes in the dimension. Any of the attributes, whether or not they belong to a hierarchy, can freely be used in drilling down and drilling up.

Do not snowflake your dimensions, even if they are large. If you do snowflake your dimensions, be prepared to live with poor browsing performance.

The best approach for tracking changes in really huge dimensions is to break off one or more minidimensions from the dimension table, each consisting of small clumps of attributes that have been administered to have a limited number of values.

The use of the Type Two slowly changing dimension requires that the dimension key be generalized. It may be sufficient to take the underlying production key and add two or three version digits to the end of the key to simplify the key generation process.

The creation of generalized keys is usually the responsibility of the data warehouse team, and always requires metadata to keep track of the generalized keys that have been used already.

The Type Two slowly changing dimension automatically partitions history and an application must not be required to place any time constraints on effective dates in the dimension.

Chapter 7: Financial Services, Especially Banks

Average period balances in financial data warehouses and in inventory data warehouses can be calculated by generalizing the SQL AVG function to instead compute Average Period Sum. Until the DBMS vendors provide the functionality, Average Period Sum must be computed in the end user's application.

In data warehouses where a dimension must describe a large number of heterogeneous items, the recommended technique is to create a core fact table and a core dimension table in order to allow queries to cross the disparate types, and to create a custom fact table and a custom dimension table for querying each individual type in depth.

The primary core facts should be duplicated in the custom fact tables. This virtually eliminates the need to access two fact tables in a single query in a heterogeneous product schema.

Chapter 8: Subscription Businesses

Pay-in-advance business scenarios typically require the combination of a transaction-grained fact table as well as a monthly snapshot-grained fact table in order to answer questions of transaction frequency and timing, as well as questions of earned income in a given month.

Chapter 9: Insurance

An appropriate design for a property and casualty insurance data warehouse is a short value chain consisting of Policy Creation and Claims Processing, where these two major processes are represented both by transaction fact tables and monthly snapshot fact tables. This data warehouse will almost certainly need to represent a number of heterogeneous products (coverage types) with appropriate combinations of core and custom dimension tables and fact tables. Finally, the large insured party and covered item dimensions will need to be decomposed into one or more minidimensions in order to provide reasonable browsing performance and in order to accurately track these slowly changing dimensions.

Chapter 10: Factless Fact Tables

 Events are often modeled by a fact table containing a number of keys, each representing a participating dimension in the event. Such event tables often have no obvious numerical facts associated with them, and hence are called factless fact tables.

 Coverage tables are often tables of events that didn't happen. Coverage tables are usually factless in the same way as event-tracking tables.

Chapter 11: Voyage Businesses

 The primary characteristic of a voyage schema is the need to place origin and destination dimensions in the fact table for both the leg and the overall trip.

Chapter 12: Building a Dimensional Data Warehouse

 The nine decision points of a complete database design for a dimensional data warehouse consist of deciding on:

- The processes, and hence the identity of the fact tables
- The grain of each fact table
- The dimensions of each fact table
- The facts, including precalculated facts
- The dimension attributes with complete descriptions and proper terminology

- How to track slowly changing dimensions
- Physical storage decisions, including aggregations, heterogeneous dimensions, minidimensions, and query modes
- The historical duration of the database
- The urgency with which the data is extracted and loaded into the data warehouse.

Chapter 13: Aggregates

The use of prestored summaries (aggregates) is the single most effective tool the data warehouse designer has to control performance.

The creation of aggregate fact tables records always requires the creation of artificial keys in each of the dimensions being aggregated.

If aggregates are represented in the original dimension and fact tables by means of the Level field construct, then every query ever presented to that schema must constrain the Level field to a single value or double counting will occur.

Each type (grain) of aggregate should occupy its own fact table, and should be supported by the proper set of dimension tables containing only those dimensional attributes that are defined for that grain of aggregate.

The single most effective way to control an aggregation explosion, but still benefit from the value of aggregates, is to make sure that each aggregate summarizes at least 10 and preferably 20 or more lower-level items.

A loose constraint, or no constraint, in a base-level fact table is actually a tight constraint in an aggregate fact table.

Only one sort order on the master composite index on the fact table needs to be built, since other sort orders based on missing dimensional constraints should be handled by separate aggregate tables instead.

An aggregate navigator is an essential component of a data warehouse because it insulates the end user applications from the changing portfolio of aggregations, and allows the DBA to dynamically adjust the aggregations without having to roll over the applications base.

Chapter 14: The Back Room

The eleven steps in the daily production extract are:

1. Primary extraction (read the legacy format)
2. Identifying the changed records
3. Generalizing keys for changing dimensions
4. Transforming into load record images
5. Migration from the legacy system to DDW system
6. Sorting and building aggregates
7. Generalizing keys for aggregates
8. Loading
9. Processing exceptions
10. Quality assurance
11. Publishing

Chapter 15: The Front Room

In the tradeoff between power and ease of use, ease of use must always come first. End users will not use a tool that seems too complicated. If the tool is perceived as complicated, either IS will have to use the tool on the end user's behalf, or the tool will not be used.

Simplicity is mostly a function of whether the user can get to the desired result in "one button click," where that button click is obvious from the user interface. If the user believes that the query tool is simple by this definition, then the query tool will probably be spontaneously and repeatedly used.

For the rank-and-file end user, the data warehouse should consist of a library of template applications that run immediately on the user's desktop. These applications should have a limited set of user-selectable alternatives for setting new constraints and for picking new measures. These template applications are precanned, parameterized reports.

It is essential for all query tools operating against a dimensional data warehouse to be able to perform comparisons flexibly and immediately. A single row of an answer set should be simultaneously able to show comparisons over multiple time periods of different grains (month, quarter, year-to-date), comparisons over other dimensions (share of a product to a category), and compound comparisons across two or more dimensions (share change this year vs. last year). A query tool should have these comparison alternatives available in a pull down menu or its equivalent. The end user should never see the SQL that implements the comparisons.

Presentation is a separate activity from querying and comparing, and the data warehouse owner should choose tools that allow answer sets to be easily transferred by the user into multiple presentation environments for different purposes.

Chapter 16: Front End Applications

There is a fundamental mismatch between the power and depth of an individual SQL answer set and the power and depth of a business report. In most cases, a business report must be assembled from several answer sets. Any query tool that deals with answers to business questions that can be described as business reports must deal with the issue of multiple answer sets. Conversely, a raw answer set is not a sufficient deliverable to the end user.

➤ Comparisons are a key element of nearly every business report. Comparisons must be implemented as separate query streams, managed by the query tool.

➤ On-the-fly tables on the DBMS to hold the results of the separate query streams are not recommended. The separate query streams must be sent to the client query tool for all further processing.

➤ A good user interface is based on recognizing and pointing, not remembering and typing. A good user interface minimizes the number of button clicks and context switches.

➤ A report-writing query tool should communicate the context of the report at a glance, including especially the identities of the dimension tables and the fact table, the constraints in effect on the dimensions, and the current state of the report. The report itself should be visible in a single button click.

➤ If users can see something, like a column of a report, they should be able to edit it directly.

➤ Edits performed on report columns should leave as much of the report still valid as possible. Requerying after an edit should at most fetch the data needed to rebuild the edited column.

➤ The query tool must have an immediate STOP command, and the query tool must not preempt the user's machine while it is waiting for data from the DBMS.

➤ A query tool fetching multiple answer sets and combining them must always combine these answer sets using outer joins. The outer joins are almost all two-way (symmetric) outer joins.

➤ Nonadditive quantities derived from separate queries (such as ratios) can be usefully presented at differing grains and in break rows only if the additive components are fetched from the DBMS and the computation is performed in the query tool as the last step before presentation. Mathematically, we say that the computation is distributed over the sums, not the other way around.

 Drilling down does not mean descending a predetermined hierarchy. It means being able to quickly ask for additional row headers from any of the dimensions owned by the fact table. It also means being able to remove row headers and drill down in a different direction.

 Drilling across between two or more fact tables is well defined as long as the row headers chosen for the particular report have exactly the same meaning in all the fact tables and dimension tables involved. Constraints may be applied to nonshared dimensions in one or more of the fact tables, but it would be advisable to warn the user of this condition either at runtime or on the report itself.

A SYSTEM CHECKLIST FOR A PERFECT DIMENSIONAL DATA WAREHOUSE

This appendix lists recommended steps in building a perfect dimensional data warehouse. The steps listed here pertain mostly to the technical and architectural issues in building a data warehouse. This list does not attempt to define all of the internal presentations, justifications, budgeting, and commitment creation steps that need to go on when building an enterprise data warehouse.

- ☐ Preliminary complete list of affected user groups prior to interviews.
- ☐ Preliminary complete list of legacy data sources prior to interviews.
- ☐ Data warehouse implementation team identified.
    - ☐ Data warehouse manager identified.
    - ☐ Interview leader identified.
    - ☐ Extract programming manager identified.
    - ☐ Database architect identified.

- ☐ End user groups to be interviewed identified.
- ☐ Data warehouse kickoff meeting with all affected end user groups.
- ☐ End user interviews.
    - ☐ Marketing interviews.
    - ☐ Finance interviews.
    - ☐ Logistics interviews.
    - ☐ Field management interviews.
    - ☐ Senior management interviews.
    - ☐ Six-inch stack of existing management reports representing all interviewed groups.
- ☐ Legacy system DBA interviews.
    - ☐ Copy books obtained for candidate legacy systems.
    - ☐ Data dictionary explaining meaning of each candidate table and field.
    - ☐ High-level description of which tables and fields are populated with quality data.
- ☐ Interview findings report distributed.
    - ☐ Prioritized information needs as expressed by end user community.
    - ☐ Data audit performed showing what data is available to support information needs.
- ☐ Data warehouse design meeting.
    - ☐ Major processes identified and fact tables laid out.
    - ☐ Grain for each fact table chosen.
        - ☐ Choice of transaction grain vs. time period accumulating snapshot grain.
    - ☐ Dimensions for each fact table identified.
    - ☐ Facts for each fact table with legacy source fields identified.
    - ☐ Dimension attributes with legacy source fields identified.
    - ☐ Core and custom heterogeneous product tables identified.
    - ☐ Type two slowly changing dimension attributes identified.

- ☐ Demographic minidimensions identified.
- ☐ Initial aggregated dimensions identified.
- ☐ Duration of each fact table (need to extract old data up front) identified.
- ☐ Urgency of each fact table (e.g., need to extract on daily basis) identified.
- ☐ Implementation staging (first process to be implemented . . .).
- ☐ Block diagram for production data extract (as each major process is implemented).
  - ☐ Subsystem for reading legacy data.
  - ☐ Subsystem for identifying changed records.
  - ☐ Subsystem for handling slowly changing dimensions.
  - ☐ Subsystem for preparing load record images.
  - ☐ Migration system (mainframe to DBMS server machine).
  - ☐ Subsystem for creating aggregates.
  - ☐ Subsystem for loading data, handling exceptions, guaranteeing referential integrity.
  - ☐ Subsystem for data quality assurance check.
  - ☐ Subsystem for data snapshot backup and recovery.
  - ☐ Subsystem for publishing, notifying users of daily data status.
- ☐ DBMS server hardware.
  - ☐ Vendor sales and support team qualified.
  - ☐ Vendor reference sites contacted and qualified as to relevance.
  - ☐ Vendor on-site test (if no qualified, relevant references available).
    - ☐ Vendor demonstrates ability to support system startup, backup, debugging.
  - ☐ Open systems and parallel scalability goals met.
  - ☐ Contractual terms approved.
- ☐ DBMS software.

☐ Vendor sales and support team qualified.

    ☐ Vendor team has implemented a similar data warehouse.

    ☐ Vendor team agrees with dimensional approach.

    ☐ Vendor team demonstrates competence in prototype test.

☐ Ability to load, index, and quality assure data volume demonstrated.

☐ Ability to browse large dimension tables demonstrated.

☐ Ability to query family of fact tables from 20 PCs under load demonstrated.

☐ Superior performance and optimizer stability demonstrated for star join queries.

☐ Superior large dimension table browsing demonstrated.

☐ Extended SQL syntax for special data warehouse functions.

☐ Ability to immediately and gracefully stop a query from end user PC.

☐ Extract tools.

    ☐ Specific need for features of extract tool identified from extract system block diagram.

    ☐ Alternative of writing home-grown extract system rejected.

    ☐ Reference sites supplied by vendor qualified for relevance.

☐ Aggregate navigator.

    ☐ Open system approach of navigator verified (serves all SQL network clients).

    ☐ Metadata table administration understood and compared with other navigators.

    ☐ User query statistics, aggregate recommendations, link to aggregate creation tool.

    ☐ Subsecond browsing performance with the navigator demonstrated for tiny browses.

☐ Front end tool for delivering parameterized reports.

    ☐ Saved reports that can be mailed from user to user and run.

☐ Saved constraint definitions that can be reused (public and private).

☐ Saved behavioral group definitions that can be reused (public and private).

☐ Dimension table browser with cross-attribute subsetting.

☐ Existing report can be opened and run with one button click.

☐ Multiple answer sets can be automatically assembled in tool with outer join.

☐ Direct support for single-dimension and multiple-dimension comparisons.

☐ Direct support for multiple comparisons with different aggregations.

☐ Direct support for average time period calculations (e.g., average daily balance).

☐ STOP QUERY command.

☐ Extensible interface to HELP allowing warehouse data tables to be described to user.

☐ Simple drill-down command supporting multiple hierarchies and nonhierarchies.

☐ Drill across that allows multiple fact tables to appear in same report.

☐ Correctly calculated break rows.

☐ Red-Green exception highlighting with interface to drill down.

☐ Ability to use network aggregate navigator with every atomic query issued by tool.

☐ Sequential operations on the answer set such as numbering, top N, and rolling.

☐ Ability to extend query syntax for DBMS special functions.

☐ Ability to define very large behavioral groups of customers or products.

☐ Ability to graph data or hand off data to third-party graphics package.

☐ Ability to pivot data or to hand off data to third-party pivot package.

☐ Ability to support OLE hot links with other OLE aware applications.

- ☐ Ability to place answer set in clipboard or TXT file in Lotus and Excel formats.
- ☐ Ability to print horizontal and vertical tiled report.
- ☐ Batch operation.
- ☐ Graphical user interface development facilities.
    - ☐ Ability to build a startup screen for the end user.
    - ☐ Ability to define pull down menu items.
    - ☐ Ability to define buttons for running reports and invoking the browser.
- ☐ Consultants.
    - ☐ Consultant team qualified.
        - ☐ Consultant team has implemented a similar data warehouse.
        - ☐ Consultant team agrees with dimensional approach.
        - ☐ Consultant team demonstrates competence in prototype test.

A GLOSSARY FOR A DIMENSIONAL DATA WAREHOUSE

A.C. NIELSEN   supplier of syndicated summaries of grocery and drug store scanner data, principally to manufacturers and retailers.

ACID PROPERTIES   *a*tomicity, *c*onsistency, *i*solation, and *d*urability. The requirements for a serious OLTP system defined by the Transaction Processing Performance Council.

ACTIVITY-BASED COSTS   costs that are reported on the basis of the true incremental activity required, rather than on an unchanging standard value.

ADDITIVE (FACTS)   measurements in a fact table that are able to be added across all of the dimensions.

AGGREGATED FACTS (SQL)   the items in an SQL SELECT list that are one of: SUM, COUNT, MIN, MAX, or AVG.

AGGREGATES   precalculated and prestored summaries that are stored in the data warehouse to improve query performance.

ALIAS (SQL)   a short identifier in an SQL expression that stands for a physical table name.

ALLOCATED INVENTORY   inventory that has been assigned for shipment to a particular customer before it has actually been shipped.

ALLOWANCE   an amount subtracted from the list price of a product, typically as a result of a promotion or a deal. Usually shown on the invoice, but called an "off invoice" allowance.

ANSWER SET   the set of rows returned to the end user as a result of an SQL expression presented to a relational DBMS.

ANY   a logical expression type in SQL.

APPLICATION CONSTRAINT (SQL)   a portion of the WHERE clause in SQL that defines a constraint on values usually within a dimension table. To be contrasted with a join constraint.

ASSET   an item that appears on the balance sheet of a company that represents something owned by the company or something owed to the company by someone else. Bank loans are assets from the bank's point of view because they are owed to the bank.

ATTRIBUTE   a field in a dimension table.

AVERAGE ORDER BACKLOG   the average length of time that orders have been waiting.

BACK END TOOL   a software application, typically resident on both the client and the server, that assists in the production data extract process. Compare with *front end tools*.

BASELINE SALES (OF A PROMOTION)   the level of sales that would have occurred if there had been only regular sales.

BDI   brand development index. The ratio of the percentage of households purchasing a brand in a local market to the percentage of households purchasing the brand in a larger market, such as Total United States.

BEHAVIOR SCORE   figure of merit that is assigned to a customer based on purchase patterns or credit patterns.

BEHAVIORAL GROUP   a large group of customers or products that is used in an end user analysis or report, but which cannot be defined by constraining on dimensional attributes, and is too large to be defined by an SQL IN clause. The behavioral group is often defined from an original analysis that isolates interesting purchase behavior or credit behavior.

BOTTOM-UP VIEW   the perspective of a company based on summarizing a large amount of detailed data.

BRAND DEVELOPMENT INDEX   see *BDI*.

BROWSE QUERY   a SELECT DISTINCT query on a single dimension table to enumerate the values of an attribute.

BULGE OF PRODUCT   the visible movement of product down the value chain as expressed in a drill-across report.

BUSINESS REENGINEERING   an organizational restructuring based on a fundamental reexamination of why an organization exists.

CANNIBALIZATION   the growth of sales of one product causing the slowing of sales of another product. Usually referring to two products made by the same manufacturer.

CATEGORY DEVELOPMENT INDEX   see *CDI*.

CAUSAL   something that is thought to be the cause of something else. Causal factors in sales usually refer to ads, displays, coupons, and price reductions.

CDI   category development index. The ratio of the percentage of households purchasing a category in a local market to the percentage of households purchasing the category in a larger market, such as Total United States.

COMPOSITE KEY   a key in a database table made up of several fields. Same as *concatenated key*.

CONCATENATED KEY   see *composite key*.

CONFORMING DIMENSIONS   dimensions that have exactly the same set of primary keys and same number of records. Two conformed dimensions can be combined into a single dimension by creating the union of the attributes.

CONSTRAINT   a phrase in the SQL WHERE clause. A constraint is either a join constraint or is an application constraint.

CONTINUOUSLY VALUED (FACTS)   a numeric measurement that is usually different every time it is measured. Continuously valued measurements should be facts in the fact table.

CONTRIBUTION (P&L)   the profit in a business measured by subtracting the allowances, discounts, costs of manufacturing, and costs of sales from the list price.

COPY BOOK   the traditional COBOL header file that describes all the fields in the file.

CORE TABLE   the fact table or the dimension table in a heterogeneous product situation that is meant to span all of the products at once. Compare with *custom table(s)*.

COST-BASED OPTIMIZER   the software in a relational database that tries to determine how to process the query by assigning estimated "costs" to various table lookup alternatives.

COVERAGE (TABLE FOR A PROMOTION)   a fact table, typically factless, that records all of the products that are on a promotion in a given store, regardless of whether or not they sold.

CUBE   a name for a dimensional database, usually referring to the simple case of product, market, and time.

CUSTOM TABLE   the fact table or the dimension table in a heterogeneous product situation that contains facts or attributes specific to one set of products, where those facts or attributes are incompatible with the other sets of products. See *core table*.

CUSTOMER MASTER FILE   a company's master list of customers, usually maintained by the order processing legacy application.

CUSTOMER TRACKING (FINANCIAL SERVICES)   the effort to identify an individual human customer across multiple financial accounts, by social security number, address, or some other indicator.

DAILY ITEM MOVEMENT   the total of sales of each item in each store at the end of each day.

DATA CUBE   see *cube*.

DATA DEPENDENCIES MODEL   the bottom-up data design methodology that enumerates every logical relationship among all the possible data elements.

DATA EXTRACT   the process of copying data from a legacy system in order to load it into a data warehouse.

DATA QUALITY ASSURANCE   the step during the production data extract process where the data is tested for consistency, completeness, and fitness to publish to the user community.

DATA WAREHOUSE   a copy of transaction data specifically structured for query and analysis.

DAYS SUPPLY (INVENTORY)   the number of days the current inventory level would last at the current rate of sales.

DB2   the IBM relational database system, first developed on the MVS operating system.

DBA   database administrator.

DDW   dimensional data warehouse.

DECISION SUPPORT   the activity of using data to make decisions in an organization.

DEGENERATE DIMENSION   a dimension key, such as an invoice number, a ticket number, or a bill of lading number, that has no attributes, and hence has no actual dimension table.

DEMAND SIDE   the flow of processes in a business starting with finished goods inventory and progressing through to customer sales. Compare with *supply side*.

DEMOGRAPHIC MINIDIMENSIONS   subsets of the customer (or store) dimension that are made into a separate artificial little dimension to facilitate rapid browsing and the handling of slowly changing dimensions.

DENORMALIZE to allow redundancy in a table so that table can remain flat, rather than snowflaked or normalized.

DEPLETIONS same as shipments. Usually refers to a warehouse drawing down inventory in response to customer orders.

DESCRIPTIVE MODEL a model of an organization that is based as much as possible on what actually takes place rather than what should take place. Compare with *normative model*.

DIMENSION an independent entity in the model of an organization that serves as an entry point, or as a mechanism for slicing the additive measures of the organization.

DIMENSION TABLE a table in a star join schema with a single part primary key.

DIMENSIONAL DATA WAREHOUSE a set of databases for decision support designed as star joined schemas.

DIMENSIONAL MODEL the top-down design methodology that for each business process enumerates relevant dimensions and facts.

DIRTY CUSTOMER DIMENSION a customer dimension in which the same person can appear multiple times, possibly with slightly different name spellings and other attributes.

DISCRETE (DIMENSION ATTRIBUTES) data, usually textual, that takes on a fixed set of values, like the flavor of a product.

DRILL ACROSS the act of requesting data from two or more fact tables in a value chain in a single report.

DRILL DOWN the act of adding a row header or replacing a row header in a report to break down the rows of the answer set in greater detail.

DRILL UP the act of removing a row header or replacing a row header in a report to break down the rows of the answer set in less detail.

EARNED INCOME the income that a company is allowed to report in a given time period based on providing a service during that time period. Money paid in advance cannot be reported as income until it is earned.

END-AISLE DISPLAYS a form of promotion in grocery and drug stores. The display racks are often provided by the product manufacturers.

ENTITY RELATION MODEL a model of an organization's data in which the objective has been to remove all repeated values by creating more tables.

EQUAL ACCESS the original promise of relational databases: the ability to retrieve data based on any criteria present in the data.

EVENT TRACKING TABLE a fact table, frequently factless, where the dimensions of the table define a description of an event, such as an insurance description of an automobile accident.

EXISTS   a logical expression type in SQL.

EXTENDED COST   the unit cost multiplied by a quantity to give an additive value.

FACT   a measurement, typically numeric and additive, that is stored in a fact table.

FACT TABLE   the central table in a star join schema, characterized by a composite key, each of whose elements is a foreign key drawn from a dimension table.

FACTLESS FACT TABLE   a fact table that happens to have no facts.

FILTER (ON FACT RECORDS)   a type of application constraint that constrains on the numeric values of one or more facts.

FLASH TOTAL   a summary total reported from an operational system, such as orders or shipments, usually reported on a daily basis, that can be used to check the integrity of the current data warehouse data load.

FLAT FILE DATABASE   an application, usually implemented on a mainframe computer, that relies on nonrelational flat files, such as IBM VSAM files.

FOREIGN KEY   a field in a relational database table whose values are drawn from the values of a primary key in another table. In a star join schema the components of a composite fact table key are foreign keys with respect to each of the dimension tables.

FROM CLAUSE (SQL)   the SQL clause that lists the tables required by the query.

FRONT END TOOL   a client tool that fetches or manipulates data stored on a relational database. Compare with *back end tool*.

GENERALIZED KEY   a dimension table primary key that has been created by generalizing an original production key such as a product number or a customer. Generalized keys are required to handle slowly changing dimensions as well as aggregates.

GIGABYTE   one billion bytes.

GLOSSARY   a brief explanation of terms used in the book.

GMROI   gross margin return on inventory, equal to the number of turns of inventory multiplied by the gross margin percent. A measure of the return on each dollar invested in inventory.

GRAIN   the meaning of a single record in a fact table. The determination of the grain of a fact table is the second of four key steps in the design of a star join schema.

GROSS MARGIN the gross profit expressed as a percentage of gross revenue.

GROSS PROFIT the gross revenue less the cost of the goods.

GROSS REVENUE the total revenue paid to a company by its customers.

GROUP BY CLAUSE (SQL) the SQL clause that lists the unaggregated facts in the SELECT list, that is, everything that is not a SUM, COUNT, MIN, MAX, or AVG.

GROWING THE MARKET (IN A PROMOTION) a desirable outcome of a promotion that causes overall sales of a product category to grow, instead of causing cannibalization.

GUI graphical user interface. A style of computer interface characterized by windows, icons, the use of graphics, and the use of a mouse pointing device.

HETEROSKEDASTIC FORWARD PIPELINING a fantasy product feature, used by vendors to distinguish themselves from their competition.

HETEROGENEOUS PRODUCTS a set of products with some incompatible attributes and facts. A characteristic design challenge in financial service environments.

HIERARCHICAL DATABASE an older style of database, typified by IBM's IMS database, that does not allow equal access.

HOUSEHOLDING (FINANCIAL SERVICES) the effort to assign an account or an individual to a household of accounts or individuals for marketing purposes.

IMS (1) the IBM hierarchical database used by many companies for legacy systems. Criticized for not providing equal access for decision support; (2) a leading supplier of syndicated pharmaceutical data.

IRI Information Resources, Incorporated. One of the two leading suppliers, along with A.C. Nielsen, of syndicated scanner data from grocery stores and drug stores.

JOIN CONSTRAINT (SQL) the portion of the SQL WHERE clause that bookkeeps the join relationships between the fact table and the dimension tables.

JOIN QUERIES queries involving the fact table and one or more dimension tables.

JULIAN DAY NUMBER a representation of a calendar date as the simple count of days from the beginning of an epoch, such as Jan 1, 1900. True Julian dates are numbered in the millions and are not often used as the literal basis of date values.

LEGACY SYSTEM an operational system for entering data about the company's operations. May not be a transaction system or a relational system. Usually resides on a mainframe computer.

LIABILITY   an item that appears on the balance sheet of a company that represents money the company owes to someone else. Bank deposits are liabilities from a bank's point of view because they must be paid back.

LIFT (OF A PROMOTION)   the increase of sales over the baseline value that can be attributed to the effects of the promotion.

LINE ITEM   an individual line of a control document such as an invoice, usually identifying a single product within the invoice. Most often used as the grain of the associated fact table.

LOGICAL DESIGN   the phase of a database design concerned with identifying the relationships among the data elements. Compare with *physical design*.

LOSS PARTY (INSURANCE)   any individual or entity associated with a claim (a loss), including injured parties, witnesses, lawyers, and other service providers.

MANY-TO-MANY RELATIONSHIP   a logical data relationship in which the value of one data element can exist in combination with many values of another data element, and vice versa.

MARKET BASKET ANALYSIS   a kind of analysis in retail environments that seeks to understand all the products purchased by a customer in a single shopping event.

MBA   master of business administration. A graduate college or university degree requiring extensive understanding of how commercial businesses are organized and managed.

MERCHANDISE HIERARCHY   a set of attributes in the product dimension that define an ascending many-to-one relationship. Common to all manufacturing and retail environments.

METADATA   any data maintained to support the operations or use of a data warehouse. Nearly all back end tools and front end tools require some private metadata in the form of specifications or status. Often the metadata is outside the relational database. There are no coherent standards for metadata. Distinguished from the primary data in the dimension tables and the fact tables.

MIGRATE   the step of moving data from one computer to another.

MIRRORED DATABASE   a physical organization of data where the entire database is duplicated on separate disk drives. Mirrored databases offer a number of performance and administrative advantages.

MIS JOIN   the join between a fact table and a dimension table in a data warehouse. Reflects the emphasis within IS on careful administration of the primary relationships between dimension tables such as customer and fact tables such as product sales.

MPP   massively parallel processing. A parallel hardware organization that deemphasizes the sharing of memory resources. Compare with *SMP*.

MULTITABLE JOIN QUERY   one of the two characteristic types of queries in a data warehouse environment. Involves the joining of one or more dimension tables to a single fact table. Contrasted to browse queries.

NONADDITIVE (FACTS)   a fact that cannot logically be added between records. May be numeric and therefore must usually be combined in a computation with other facts before being added across records. If nonnumeric, can be used only in constraints, or counts, or groupings.

NORMALIZE   the process of removing redundancy in data by separating the data into multiple tables.

NORMATIVE MODEL   a model of an organization that describes how an organization is supposed to function. Compare with *descriptive model*.

ODS   operational data store. An archive of original operational data, perhaps untransformed from its original legacy format. Not intended for direct data warehouse querying, either because it is not in the final, quality assured format, or because it is too voluminous to be kept in an on-line relational database.

OFF-INVOICE ALLOWANCES   typically deal- or promotion-related subtractions from the list price shown on the invoice. Part of deriving the net invoice amount, which is what the customer is supposed to pay on this line item.

OFF-INVOICE DISCOUNTS   typically financial terms related subtractions from the list price shown on the invoice. Part of deriving the net invoice amount, which is what the customer is supposed to pay on this line item.

OLAP   on line analytic processing. A term meant to contrast with OLTP. OLAP is a loosely defined set of principles that provide a dimensional framework for decision support. The term OLAP also is used to define a confederation of vendors who offer nonrelational, proprietary products aimed at decision support.

OLTP   on line transaction processing. The original description for all the activities and systems associated with entering data reliably into a database. Most frequently used with reference to relational databases, although

OLTP can be used generically to describe any transaction processing environment.

ONE-TO-MANY RELATIONSHIP   a logical data relationship in which the value of one data element can exist in combination with many values of another data element, but not vice versa.

OPERATIONAL DATA STORE   see *ODS*.

ORDER BY CLAUSE (SQL)   the SQL clause that determines the ordering of rows in the answer set.

OUTER JOIN   the merging of two answer sets of data by making the row headers be the union of all values in the two sets of data.

OUTRIGGER TABLE   a secondary dimension table attached a dimension table. An outrigger table is a physical design interpretation of a single logical dimension table. Occurs when a dimension table is snowflaked.

P&L   profit and loss. Also known as an income statement. The P&L is the classic logical ordering of revenues and costs to represent a progression from gross revenues down to a bottom line that represents net profit.

PARENT-CHILD DATABASE   a hierarchical organization of data typically involving a header and a set of line items. The star join approach strips all the information out of the header (parent) and leaves it as a degenerate dimension.

PARTITIONING OF HISTORY   the natural correspondence between dimension table entries and fact table records when a Type 2 slowly changing dimension has been implemented. See the discussion in the main text.

PHYSICAL DESIGN   the phase of a database design following the logical design that identifies the actual database tables and index structures used to implement the logical design.

PIVOTING   changing the arrangement of the rows and columns in a tabular report, where frequently the row or column headings are derived from distinct values in the data itself.

POINT OF SALE SYSTEM   the cash registers and the associated in-store computers in a retail environment.

POS   see *point of sale system*.

PRICE POINT ANALYSIS   the breakdown of product sales by each discrete transaction price. Requires a fact table with fine enough grain to represent each price point separately.

PRIMARY KEY   a field in a database table that is uniquely different for each record in the table.

PROCESSES   the primary operational processes in an organization. The identification of the candidate business processes is the first step in a data warehouse design. A business process, in order to be used in a data warehouse, must be supported by one or more production data sources.

PRODUCT MASTER FILE   a company's master list of products, usually maintained by a manufacturing or purchase order legacy application.

PRODUCTION DATA EXTRACT   a snapshot taken of production data.

PRODUCTION DATA LOAD   the entire process of extracting production data from a legacy application, transforming it, loading and indexing it, quality assuring it, and publishing it.

PROMOTION   an event, usually planned by marketing, that features one or more causal items such as ads, displays, or price reductions. Also thought of as a deal or sometimes as a contract.

PSEUDOTRANSACTION   a step needed in some production data extract systems, where a nontransactional legacy system is analyzed to see what changed from the previous extract. These changes are then made into artificial (pseudo) transactions in order to be loaded into the data warehouse.

PUBLISHING USED DATA   the most succinct way to describe the overall responsibility of the data warehouse. The data is used because it is almost always copied from a legacy system.

PULL DOWN LIST   a user interface effect in a front end tool that displays a list of options for the user. The most interesting pull down lists in a data warehouse come from browse queries on a dimension attribute.

QUERY   an SQL SELECT statement passed from the front end application (typically on the end user's client machine) to the relational DBMS.

QUERY TOOL   as used in this book, any client application that maintains a session with the DBMS, sending relatively small amounts of SQL, and receiving back relatively small answer sets.

REASON CODE   a field used in conjunction with a transaction dimension to describe why the transaction took place. Reason codes are valuable for returns and cancellations.

REFERENTIAL INTEGRITY   a mandatory condition in a data warehouse where all the keys in the fact tables are legitimate foreign keys relative to the dimension tables. In other words, all the fact key components are subsets of the primary keys found in the dimension tables at all times.

RELATIONAL DATABASE   a database system that supports the full range of standard SQL.

REPOSITORY   a repository in the data warehouse sense usually is the same as an ODS. See *ODS*.

ROW HEADER   the nonaggregated components of the SQL select list. Will always be listed in the SQL group by clause.

SABRE   American Airlines' reservation system, one of the world's busiest and most successful transaction processing systems.

SALES INVOICE   the control document that describes a sale. Usually contains multiple line items that each represent a separate product sold.

SELECT DISTINCT (SQL)   an SQL statement that suppresses duplicate rows in the answer set.

SELECT LIST (SQL)   the list of column specifications that follows SELECT and comes before FROM in an SQL query. Each item in the select list generates a column in the answer set.

SEMIADDITIVE (FACT)   a numeric fact that can be added along some dimensions in a fact table but not others. Transaction counts in daily or monthly snapshots typically cannot be added along the product dimension if the definition of transaction is an entire market basket purchase. Inventory levels and balances cannot be added along the time dimension, but can be usefully averaged over the time dimension.

SHELF DISPLAYS   tags, racks, or other promotional mechanisms used in a retail environment.

SKU   stock keeping unit. A standard term in manufacturing and retail environments to describe an individual product.

SLICE AND DICE   the standard description of the ability to access a data warehouse through any of its dimensions equally.

SLOWLY CHANGING DIMENSIONS   the tendency of dimension records, especially in the product and customer dimensions, to change gradually or occasionally over time. Slowly changing dimensions may be handled with three different techniques, which are described in the text.

SMP   symmetric multiprocessing. A parallel hardware organization that emphasizes the sharing of memory resources.

SNAPSHOT   a kind of fact table that represents the status of accounts at the end of each time period. Daily snapshots and monthly snapshots are common. Snapshots are required in a number of businesses such as insurance where the transaction history is too complicated to be used as the basis for computing snapshots on the fly.

SNOWFLAKE   a normalized dimension where a flat single table dimension is decomposed into a tree structure with potentially many nesting levels. Snowflaking generally compromises user understandability and browsing performance.

SPARSE   a fact table that has relatively few of all the possible combinations of key values. A grocery store item movement database is not considered sparse because 5 percent to 10 percent of all the key combinations for SKU, store, and day will be present. An airlines frequent flyer database is extremely sparse because very few of the customer, flight number, day combinations actually appear in the database.

SQL   the standard language for accessing relational databases.

STAR JOIN SCHEMA   a specific organization of a database in which a fact table with a composite key is joined to a number of single-level dimension tables, each with a single primary key. Successful data warehouses usually are based on star join schemas.

STATIC SNAPSHOT   a snapshot taken at a particular moment of rapidly changing transaction data, which is then saved in the data warehouse.

STOCK KEEPING UNIT   see *SKU*.

SUBROGATION (INSURANCE)   the act of an insurance company selling the rights remaining in a claim, such as the right to sue someone for damages.

SUPPLY SIDE   the part of the value chain in a manufacturing company that starts with purchase orders for ingredients and parts and ends with finished goods inventory. Physically the supply side is the manufacturing operation. Compare with *demand side*.

SYNDICATED DATA SUPPLIERS   companies that collect data, clean it, package it, and resell it. A.C. Nielsen and IRI are the principal syndicated data suppliers for grocery and drug store scanner data, and IMS and Walsh America are the principal syndicated data suppliers for pharmaceutical data.

SYNONYM (SQL)   an SQL statement that creates logical copies of a table that can be used separately in a SELECT statement.

TAKEAWAY   consumer purchases.

TEMPORAL INCONSISTENCY   the tendency of an OLTP database to change its primary data relationships from moment to moment as transactions are processed. This inconsistency impacts end users in two primary ways: (1) The database is constantly changing as they query it, and (2) old history is not necessarily preserved.

TEMPORARY PRICE REDUCTION   a promotional technique in retail environments.

TERABYTE   one trillion bytes.

TEXTUAL (DIMENSION ATTRIBUTES)   dimension attributes that are actually text or behave like text.

TIME SHIFTING (OF A PROMOTION)   the tendency of some promotions to cause the customer to defer purchases until the promotion is on, and then not make purchases after the promotion for a prolonged period. In the most serious cases, the promotion accomplishes nothing except to allow the customer to buy products cheaply.

TOP-DOWN VIEW   the perspective of a company based on starting with most global description of the company and its mission and preceding to subdivide this perspective until the objectives of the analysis have been accomplished. The top down view rarely touches the lowest level of detail in a company. Data warehouse design techniques begin with a top-down view.

TPR   temporary price reduction, a form of promotion.

TRANSSHIPMENTS   shipments of product that occur between the warehouses belonging to the manufacturer or belonging to the retailer.

TRANSACTION   an indivisible unit of work. A transaction processing system either performs an entire transaction or it doesn't perform any part of the transaction.

TURNS (INVENTORY)   the number of times in a given period (usually a year) that the inventory must be completely replenished in order to keep up with the observed rate of sales.

TWINKLING DATABASE   the tendency of a transaction processing database to be constantly changing the data the user is attempting to query.

UNIVERSAL PRODUCT CODE   the standard bar-coded value found on most grocery and drugstore merchandise.

UPC   see *Universal Product Code*.

VALUE CHAIN   the sequence of processes that describe the movement of products or services through a pipeline from original creation to final sales.

VIRGIN TERRITORY   the portion of disk storage that is unoccupied prior to a data load. In a static database experiencing no in-place updates or inserts, and with a primary sort order with time as the leading term in the sort, all data loading takes place in virgin territory.

WALSH AMERICA   a leading supplier of syndicated pharmaceutical data.

USER'S GUIDE FOR STAR TRACKER™

OVERVIEW

Star Tracker™ has been developed as a tool for answering real business questions in terms that businesses find most useful. While most database reporting and query tools can do an adequate job of formulating simple queries and reports, they often fall short in their ability to produce the meaningful and sophisticated business metrics and ratios that can be extracted from large, complex databases. The key features that make Star Tracker unique include the following:

- Explicit support for the *dimensional model* of a business through SQL
- Automatic *multiquery strategy* for assembling complex reports involving comparisons, multiple time grains, multiple product groupings, and multiple sale and geography groupings
- Creation of the optimum *minimal query set* for a multiquery report
- *Outer join* support for merging separate answer sets
- *Interfield browsing* within a dimension
- *Protected fields* in the browser to inhibit the inadvertent fetching of very long lists
- User-defined private and public *constraint groups*
- A library of *comparison functions* between constraint groups

- A library of *sequential functions* impossible to program in SQL, including rank, tertile, quartile, moving average, and moving sum
- Special extensions to the SQL aggregation operators for *period average sums and counts* that support average period balance and inventory calculations as well as comparisons of additive measures across dissimilar time intervals
- *Break rows* with correct handling of all simple and compound measures
- *User-defined calculations* among fact table columns that are *correctly additive* across all aggregations and break rows
- Red-Green highlighting of *exceptional values* in report columns using five criteria
- *Drill-down* capability that assigns a separate drill-down target to every report column
- Full column and selected cell *drill-down modes*
- *Drill-across* capability to query two or more fact tables in the same report
- Creation of *study groups* that are records of behavioral outcomes otherwise impractical to express in terms of attribute constraints, such as the Big Sellers in 1Q93
- Creation of *derivative study groups* via union, intersection, and set difference
- Full report and selected cell *report copying* through the clipboard to other applications
- Multifont *printing* with horizontal and vertical pagination
- *Saving and retrieving of reports* with long filenames
- Automated *debugging facilities* for reporting bugs to Star Tracker support

ABOUT THE USER'S GUIDE

This *User's Guide for the Star Tracker* is intended for the end user who will be running reports from a desktop PC as well as for the business analyst who is responsible for formulating the ratios, metrics, and reports that provide information for running a business. A companion appendix, *Star Tracker System Administrator's Guide*, covers Star Tracker's installation, data dictionary, and database interfaces, as well as database schema considerations.

This *User's Guide* contains the following sections:

- *Star Tracker Basics* covers the actions necessary to run an already formulated report, including connecting to the database, selecting an existing report, running the report, and printing it.

- *Star Tracker Main Window* section describes the elements in the main report window, and explains their significance. It also covers the use of enhanced features such as drill downs and exceptions, which, if implemented in a report, can be used to refine data analysis.
- *Browsing and Defining Groups* tells you how to preview your database contents and how to use browsing to build constraint groups that greatly simplify reporting in very large databases.
- *Building a New Report* provides a step-by-step guide to producing a report using the demonstration Order/Account database available via the author's web page at http://www.rkimball.com.
- *Other Features* describes less-used Star Tracker features, such as SQL capture.

STAR TRACKER BASICS

This section describes actions needed to start up Star Tracker, connect to a database, select and run a predefined report, and print out the report.

Starting up Star Tracker

To start up Star Tracker, double-click the STARTRAK.EXE file. You can also locate and double-click Star Tracker icon in a program group. Star Tracker only runs in Windows environments. It shows a picture of the Big Dipper.

Selecting a Database

After Star Tracker completes its opening sequence the Database Finder dialog box seen in Figure D.1 will appear.

This dialog is used to select the database that you want to use. Single-click a database name to select it. For example, click the database name *ACCESS: ORDERS.MDB: Orders*. In this example, ACCESS represents the name of the database server being used. The master database name is ORDERS.MDB. The System Administrator has selected tables that relate to orders, and given

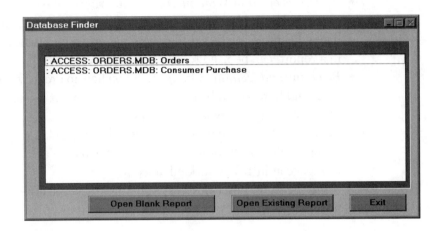

FIGURE D.1

Database Finder dialog.

it a working database name of "Orders." The System Administrator could have created other working databases in this master database, for example, "Consumer Purchase."

Once the database has been selected by clicking it you can choose to either run an existing, previously defined report, or define a new report from scratch. To run a previously defined existing report for this database, click the **Open Existing Report** button.

To create a new report from scratch, either double-click the report's name, or click the **Open Blank Report** button after selecting the database.

Logging onto the Database

If you are connecting to a remote database via an ODBC connection, you will be asked to log into the database after you first select a database. If you are connecting to an ACCESS database on your local PC, you will not see the login dialog.

When the login dialog appears, enter your password, and if requested, your database user ID. When you type into the password field you will not see the actual letters you type for security reasons.

After you have entered your user name and password, click the **OK** button.

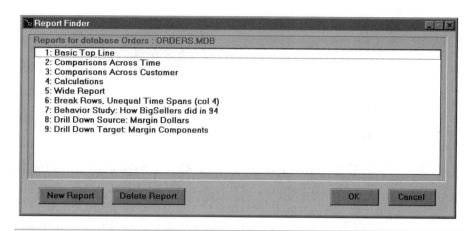

FIGURE D.2

Report Finder dialog.

Opening an Existing Report

When you ask Star Tracker to open a previously defined existing report you will see the dialog box shown in Figure D.2.

To open a particular report select the name of the report by clicking on it, then click the **OK** button. You may also open a report directly by double-clicking its name. If you are running the demonstration database, double click *1: Basic Top Line*.

Running the Report

After the report is selected, the application's main Star Tracker window will open. This window, described in the following section of this *User's Guide*, contains two main parts: The Report Definition section occupies the top half of the window. The spreadsheet in the bottom half of the window contains the report results. To run a report, click the **Run Report** button. This produces a report by accessing the database for current information. The speed of running any report is a function of the report's complexity and the intrinsic speed of your database server.

FIGURE D.3

Run Report button.

If you are running the demonstration database, click the **Run Report** button shown Figure D.3 to run the Basic Top Line report. This will take a few seconds to run, depending on the speed of your PC.

*HINT: Press your PC's **Esc** key to enlarge the report spreadsheet so it occupies the entire window. Press it again to toggle back to the original two-part depiction. If you scroll to a remote location on the spreadsheet, press CTRL-H to return Home, and CTRL-E to jump to the End of the report.*

Printing a Report

To make a hard copy of your report, select **Print** from the **File** menu on Star Tracker window's menu bar. For more information on printing, see the Other Features section.

STAR TRACKER MAIN WINDOW

Most of the features and controls for Star Tracker are found in the main window, shown in Figure D.4. The main window is divided into two sections. The top half depicts the report definition while the bottom half contains the report results. We will begin by examining the report definition section of this window. Your screen may differ in some small details from the illustration because Star Tracker is constantly being upgraded.

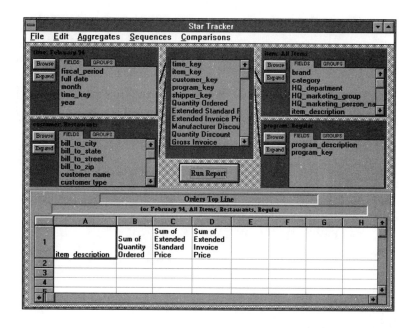

FIGURE D.4

Main window.

About Tables

The data in your database is stored in tables, which can be thought of as very large spreadsheets. In database tables, a column is often called a field, while a row is sometimes called a record. We will refer to a table's fields and records throughout this document. Each of the rectangles in the report definition area represents a table in your database.

In a Star Tracker report definition, the central table in a database is the fact table. In our example Basic Top Line report, the fact table is named Orders. The tables which surround the fact table on the left and right are called dimension tables. In our example these are labeled Time, Customer, Item, and Program.

FIGURE D.5

Fact table depiction.

The Orders Fact Table

The first several fields in Figure D.5, such as time_key, item_key, customer_key, and program_key, are pointers to the dimension tables. Key fields may be of little interest because they contain pointer numbers that are not related to business measurements. The remainder of the fields in this fact table, such as Quantity Ordered and Extended Standard Price, are fact fields.

When you define a report you can add fact columns to the report result by dragging their names from the fact table down to the report spreadsheet column in which you want them to appear. Defining reports is covered in a later section of this *Guide*.

Additive and Nonadditive Facts

Facts that can meaningfully be summed are called additive facts. In our example, Quantity Ordered is an additive fact because it is meaningful if it summed over several time periods, several items, or several customers.

Because your system administrator has identified additive versus nonadditive facts in the Data Dictionary, Star Tracker will not let you inadvertently attempt to sum nonadditive facts.

Calculated Facts

Certain very useful measurements may not be in the fact table, but can be calculated on the basis of existing facts. Your fact table may contain such computed facts that have been defined by the system administrator. Calculated fact names are marked by an asterisk (*). In our example Orders table, Average Standard Price and Average Standard Cost are calculated facts. They are always composed of additive facts so that they will be valid regardless of the choice of groups.

Dimension Tables

Dimension Tables contain information that lets you access specific subsets of facts in your database. Dimensions are the keys to facts. For example, if your fact database contained invoice line-item detail it might have time, product, and customer dimensions. Each dimension, such as customer or item (see Figure D.6) has its own dimension table.

Our sample Orders database has dimensions of time, customer, item, and program.

In a database with many dimensions you may want to zoom in on a particular dimension table to see more of its field or group names at once. To do this, click the **Expand** button. This produces an enlarged view of the dimension table and of its associated fact table. To zoom back out again, click the **Reduce** button.

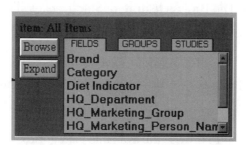

FIGURE D.6

Item dimension table showing fields.

Dimension Attributes

Each dimension may have a number of attribute fields that categorize the dimension in a number for different ways that can be used for identifying facts. For example, consider the following three dimensions with some of their possible attribute fields:

- Item—accessible by attribute fields like brand, category, and diet indicator
- Customer—accessible by attribute fields like customer name, and various bill-to and ship-to attributes
- Time—accessible by attribute fields like fiscal period, month, and year

In an item table there will be a record of each different item that our database tracks.

When you define a report you can add dimension attribute columns to the report by dragging their field names from a dimension table down to the report spreadsheet column in which you want them to appear. Defining reports is covered in a later section of this *Guide*.

To view a dimension's attribute fields, click the **FIELDS** tab in the dimension's depiction area. If you look at the attribute fields in our example database's Item dimension, you will find attributes such as item_key, item_description, category, brand, etc.

Simple Attribute Browsing

The Browse feature of Star Tracker allows you to see what different values of an attribute your database contains. Browsing has many more purposes, covered in the following section on Groups, but we will describe a simple use here.

In the example Orders database, suppose you want to view the various Category attributes available in the Item dimension. To do this, first click the Browse button in the Item dimension's depiction area. This switches you to Star Tracker's Browse window, shown in Figure D.7.

To browse the available Categories, double click on the word "Category". In a few moments a list appears (see Figure D.8), which shows each unique value of category that has been included in the database's Dimension table. From this list you can see that our sample database may contain information on five categories: Candy, Cleaning Supplies, Frozen Foods, Salty Snacks, and Soft Drinks. To browse the available brands, double click on that field.

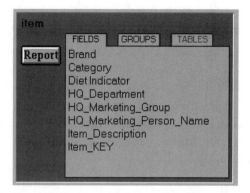

FIGURE D.7

Browse header control for Item dimension.

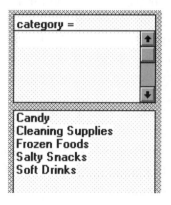

FIGURE D.8

Browse result list for Item: Category.

To return to Star Tracker's main window, select **Exit** from the Browser's **File** menu, or click the **Report** button in the Browser's depiction panel.

Groups

Dimension Groups are sets of one or more dimension attribute *values*, used to define a specific subset of facts you want to use in your report. For example, instead of a report column being Quantity Ordered, you could qualify the column to be Quantity Ordered of *Salty Snacks*.

Star Tracker provides an intuitive point-and-click browsing method for defining groups. This simple process gives you enormous power to tailor a report for specific business needs. In most cases, your System Administrator will already have defined many groups that you can use in your reports. You may add additional groups using the point-and-click browser.

To view the groups that have been already defined for a dimension, click the **GROUPS** tab in that dimension's depiction area. Our example database's Item dimension shown below includes groups like Candy, Cleaning Supplies, and Soft Drinks.

Base Groups

In order to run a Star Tracker report, each dimension must be constrained. The primary constraint used for a given dimension is called the base group, and the group name appears immediately after the dimension name in the dimension's depiction area. In the Item dimension example in Figure D.9, "all items" has been selected as the base group. This means that the report will show each item in the database.

Base groups set the range and default scale for the entire report. For example, if you select a time dimension base group of 1Q94, your report cannot contain dates that fall outside of the first quarter of 1994, and all comparison will use this time range as a basis. You can request, however, that within the base range, dates be broken down into a finer *scale* within a base range. The technique for doing this is described in the section Adding Dimension Columns. The example in Figure D.10, also selected from the Order Top Line example, shows the Time dimension, which has the group "February 94" selected as its base.

FIGURE D.9

Item dimension table showing groups.

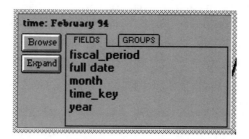

FIGURE D.10

Time dimension table with "February 94" as base group.

The use of group definitions allows you to correctly run a report even if the actual contents of a group varies over time.

Comparison Groups

Many business metrics involve percents, ratios, or differences that compare one set of measurements against another. Comparison groups can be used to form a variety of ratios, percentages, and other metrics as shown in the following examples:

Item Dimension

- Sales ratio of Candy vs. Salty Snacks
- Sales percent of Cleaning Supplies vs. Total Products

Customer Dimension

- Quantity shipped to Convenience Stores vs. Delicatessens

Time Dimension

- April sales this year vs. last year
- YTD sales this year vs. YTD sales last year

Each of these examples requires a comparison, and the sets being compared are defined by dimension groups. The base group must constitute one of the pairs for each comparison. For example, if I was reporting on this month's sales then the base group of the report's time dimension would likely be something like "This Month," or "July 1994," depending on the group definitions available.

Report Results

The spreadsheet-like portion of Star Tracker main window shown in Figure D.11 contains the report results.

*HINT: Press your PC's **Esc** key to enlarge the Report Spreadsheet so it occupies the entire window as shown above. Press it again to toggle back to the original two-part depiction.*

File	Edit	Aggregates	Sequences	Comparisons

Orders Top Line

for February, 1994, All Items, Customer Type: Restaurant, Regular Program

	A	B	C	D	E	F	G	H
1	item_description	Sum of Quantity Ordered	Sum of Extended Standard Price	Sum of Extended Invoice Price				
2	Athletic Drink	76	$22,134.37	$21,478.30				
3	Beef Stew	94	$12,322.64	$12,072.37				
4	Buffalo Jerky	67	$6,101.48	$5,947.16				
5	Chicken Dinner	93	$54,954.42	$53,487.06				
6	Clear Refresher	88	$24,419.60	$23,795.68				
7	Dried Grits	87	$20,095.14	$19,660.69				
8	Dry Tissues	92	$3,359.97	$3,298.04				
9	Extra Nougat	79	$87,799.82	$85,384.20				
10	Fizzy Classic	87	$28,780.78	$28,169.26				
11	Fizzy Light	93	$57,232.86	$56,030.88				
12	Lasagna	98	$31,605.86	$31,035.52				
13	Lots of Nuts	73	$22,308.63	$22,064.25				
14	Onion Slices	101	$17,443.08	$16,978.85				
15	Paper Towels	94	$5,674.22	$5,490.68				
16	Power Chips	96	$9,938.07	$9,661.82				
17	Salty Corn	86	$17,079.70	$16,554.44				
18	Strong Cola	105	$11,942.10	$11,754.04				
19	Sweet Tooth	96	$28,362.03	$27,570.27				
20	Turkey Dinner	93	$4,951.00	$4,670.36				

FIGURE D.11

Report results for Orders Top Line.

Row 1 of the Report Spreadsheet contains the report's column titles. Note: Because many of Star Tracker's intermediate calculations are done in this spreadsheet the spreadsheet can scroll backward to reveal cells prior to Row 1 or Column A. Similarly, you might find unlabeled columns of data somewhat to the right of the data you requested. These are also intermediate results. *Your* report data begins at cell location A1, and all of the meaningful data columns are labeled. Rows and columns used by Star Tracker for intermediate results won't show when you print your report or copy and paste it to another document or spreadsheet.

Formatting Reports

You can alter the format of report data just as in a spreadsheet. First highlight the column you want to format by clicking the column's header label (A, B, C, . . .). Then choose **Format Column** from the **File** menu. the Format Finder dialog will open as shown in Figure D.12.

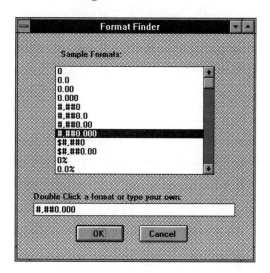

FIGURE D.12

Format Finder dialog.

You can choose one of formats from the Sample Format list by double-clicking to select it. Format characters have the following meanings:

0   Significant digit (will be shown as least or most significant digit even if zero).

Placeholder digit (blank if zero in least or most significant digit position).

.   Indicates position of the decimal point.

,   Will create comma at that position.

$ Dollar sign will be placed before the number.

%   Percent sign will be placed after the number (value remains the same).

Date formats may also be altered using the standard spreadsheet m-d-y conventions. The Sample Format list contains several date formats that automatically convert to the m-d-y convention when they are double-clicked. Also in the Sample Format list are two integer date formats that can be useful for sorting date values.

Sorting Reports

You can sort reports by invoking the sort commands in the Edit menu. To initiate a sort, first highlight the column you want to sort by clicking its alphabetic header letter. Then activate the sort by choosing either **Sort Ascending** or **Sort Descending** commands from the **Edit** menu. You can sort just one column in the result spreadsheet. To undo the sort, select **Remove Sort.**

Hiding a Column

If a report contains a column you don't want to show in a printed version of the report you can hide it. First highlight the column by clicking its alphabetic header letter, then choose **Hide Column** from the **Edit** menu. The word "[hidden]" will be added to the column label. When you print the report, the column will be calculated but not shown. To unhide a column, highlight then choose **Hide Column** again to reverse the original hiding process.

Deleting a Column

If you want to permanently delete a column from a report, first highlight the column by clicking its alphabetic header letter then choose **Delete Column** from the **Edit** menu. Or, simply press the Delete key.

Editing a Column Heading

Star Tracker automatically assigns each report column a heading based on the calculation that was used to produce the heading, such as "Ratio of Sum of Quantity Ordered for 1Q94 vs. 1Q93." To make a report easier for others to read or understand you might want to change that to another title like "Unit Ratio This Year vs. Last." Changing a column heading doesn't alter the underlying results calculation.

First, highlight the column whose heading you want to change by clicking its alphabetic header letter. Then select **Edit Heading** from the **File** menu. The Column Header Editor dialog will open. Enter your new heading and click **OK**. If you want to use your new heading each time you run the report, be sure to save the report before closing it.

To restore the system-supplied heading completely delete your custom heading in the Column Header Editor dialog shown in Figure D.13.

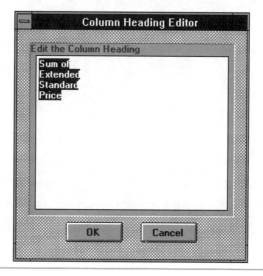

FIGURE D.13

Column Heading Editor dialog.

Exception Reporting

You may want to produce a report that emphasizes exception or out-of-bounds conditions. Star Tracker provides a powerful tool for identifying and reporting exceptions, for example:

- Show only the top 10 salespeople
- Show only the bottom 20 customers
- Highlight the products which have more than 25 percent market share
- Highlight the customers which have had a negative sales growth

To activate exception reporting for a column, first highlight the column by clicking its alphabetic header letter. Then select **Define Exceptions** from the **Edit** menu. This opens the Exception Conditions dialog shown in Figure D.14.

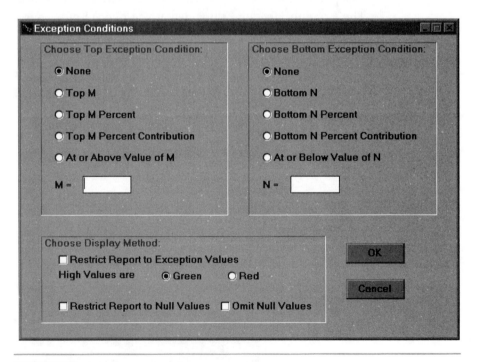

FIGURE D.14

Exception Conditions dialog.

You can set exception conditions for upper bounds, lower bounds, or both using the Choose Top and Choose Bottom panels in the dialog. The letter M represents the upper bound breakpoint and the letter N represents the lower bound breakpoint.

The following selection options are available:

- Top M: The top (or bottom) M values will be selected.
- Top M percent: The top (or bottom) M percent of values will be selected.
- Top M percent contribution: The top (or bottom) M percent total column sum will be selected.
- At or above/below: Values above (or below) M will be selected.

Items that are selected can be highlighted in two ways: First, the report can be restricted to show *only* the rows that contain exceptions. Second, the exceptions can be highlighted in color.

To restrict the report to only the exception rows, check **Restrict Report to Exception Values** box. To restrict the report to only null values, check **Restrict Report to Null Values.** To omit the rows with null values check **Omit Null Values**.

To color-highlight exception values, click either the **green** or **red** checkbox. If red is selected for high values then green will be used for low, and vice versa.

Drilling Down in a Report

Sometimes while reading a report you might want to examine the source of a number or ratio in greater detail. This process, sometimes called "drill down," is supported by Star Tracker through its drill-down feature. In order to drill down, you or the report designer needs to have previously created a drill-down target report for a particular column in your first report. To define a drill-down target, select a column in your report and invoke the Define Drill Down command in the Edit menu. You will be presented with the standard report finder window. When you double click on one of the reports, that report will become the drill-down target for the original column. Using this approach, you can define separate drill-down targets for each column in a report.

Run the Item Top Line Report to produce the result shown in the Report Results section. Suppose in this report, you want to discover which customers are ordering a particular product. We have predefined a drill-down report for the example named Item Margin Drill Down. When you select in the Sum of Margin Dollars column, you can invoke the Drill Down command in the File menu. The Item Top Line Report will be replaced by the Item Margin Drill Down report.

The Item Margin Drill Down report will inherit all of the constraints of the previous report. In addition, it will further restrict itself to the exceptional values specified in the selected column of the first report.

The exceptional values are determined by how you made your selection in the Sum of Margin Dollars column in the first report. If you selected the column header cell (i.e., the whole column) then the second report will be restricted to all the green and red cells found in that column. If instead you selected one or more individual cells in that column, the second report will be restricted to all the selected cells, regardless of their green and red highlighting.

After running the second report, you may remove the restriction to the specific rows described in the previous paragraph by invoking the Remove Drill Down Constraints command in the Edit menu. Now the second report will be constrained only by the inherited groups of the first report. These inherited groups, of course, may be changed at any time simply by double clicking on a group name or dragging a group name to a comparison column in the usual way.

The Item Margin Drill Down report may itself have defined drill-down targets in any of its columns. In this way, a drill-down path may be followed to an arbitrary depth. (See Figure D.15.)

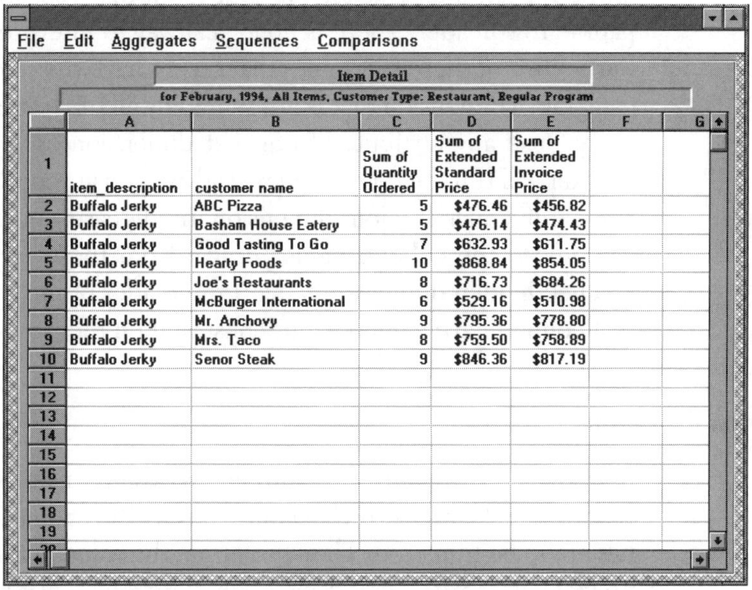

	A	B	C	D	E	F	G
1	item_description	customer name	Sum of Quantity Ordered	Sum of Extended Standard Price	Sum of Extended Invoice Price		
2	Buffalo Jerky	ABC Pizza	5	$476.46	$456.82		
3	Buffalo Jerky	Basham House Eatery	5	$476.14	$474.43		
4	Buffalo Jerky	Good Tasting To Go	7	$632.93	$611.75		
5	Buffalo Jerky	Hearty Foods	10	$868.84	$854.05		
6	Buffalo Jerky	Joe's Restaurants	8	$716.73	$684.26		
7	Buffalo Jerky	McBurger International	6	$529.16	$510.98		
8	Buffalo Jerky	Mr. Anchovy	9	$795.36	$778.80		
9	Buffalo Jerky	Mrs. Taco	8	$759.50	$758.89		
10	Buffalo Jerky	Senor Steak	9	$846.36	$817.19		
11							
12							
13							
14							
15							
16							
17							
18							
19							

FIGURE D.15

Drill-Down example.

Drilling Across in a Report

Star Tracker allows reports to be built that rely on multiple fact tables. After building a report in the usual way, you may invoke the Drill Across command in the File menu. You are then allowed to pick any other database that Star Tracker can access. Only those databases that share dimensions can be usefully linked with the Drill Across command, however.

After invoking the Drill Across command and selecting the next database, you will able to add columns from the new database to the existing report. You may continue the process of drilling across to as many databases as you wish, subject to the restrictions discussed below. Drilling across is ideal for assembling reports that examine an entire value chain of fact tables, such as inventory, orders, shipments, and customer take away.

Two restrictions apply to Drill Across. First, if you insert a row header (a dimension attribute) from a dimension that is not shared by all of the fact tables in the report, Star Tracker will notify you that you must remove the incompatible row header. There is no logical way to interpret such a row header in the context of those fact tables that do not have the dimension. Second, if you constrain a dimension that is not shared by all the fact tables in the report (but do not use any attributes from that dimension as row headers), then Star Tracker will run the report, but will advise you at report runtime that you have a constraint on a "hidden" dimension. In this case you may want to apply a special edit to the column names drawn from those fact tables with the constrained hidden dimension to alert the reader of the report that the values in that column have a nonobvious constraint on them.

Inserting Break Rows

Star Tracker's Break Row feature allows you to insert subtotal rows into your report. To set a break row you must specify the column on which the break totals are to be triggered. Then each time the value in this column changes, the previous rows are summed and a summary total row is inserted into the report.

To see how break rows work, open and run the Monthly Order Top Line report. This is similar to the Orders Top Line used in previous examples, but includes totals for each month for 1Q94.

After the report has been run, select the first column (Item Description) by clicking the **A** button on the spreadsheet. Then select **Set Break Rows** in Star Tracker's **File** menu. A dialog box will open in which you can set the caption for the subtotal rows. The default caption, "Total*" is used in the example. In the dialog, the asterisk (*) character is used to represent the break value text. Thus, for the first subtotal caption in the report, "Total*" becomes "Total Athletic Drink."

The illustration in Figure D.16 shows the Monthly Orders Top Line report with added subtotals. A subtotal row has been added for each product.

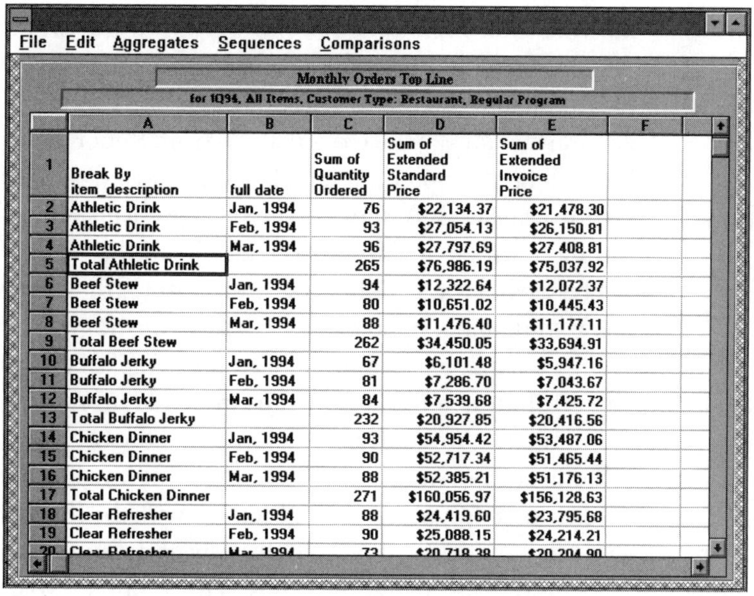

File Edit Aggregates Sequences Comparisons

Monthly Orders Top Line

for 1Q94, All Items, Customer Type: Restaurant, Regular Program

	A	B	C	D	E	F
1	Break By item_description	full date	Sum of Quantity Ordered	Sum of Extended Standard Price	Sum of Extended Invoice Price	
2	Athletic Drink	Jan, 1994	76	$22,134.37	$21,478.30	
3	Athletic Drink	Feb, 1994	93	$27,054.13	$26,150.81	
4	Athletic Drink	Mar, 1994	96	$27,797.69	$27,408.81	
5	Total Athletic Drink		265	$76,986.19	$75,037.92	
6	Beef Stew	Jan, 1994	94	$12,322.64	$12,072.37	
7	Beef Stew	Feb, 1994	80	$10,651.02	$10,445.43	
8	Beef Stew	Mar, 1994	88	$11,476.40	$11,177.11	
9	Total Beef Stew		262	$34,450.05	$33,694.91	
10	Buffalo Jerky	Jan, 1994	67	$6,101.48	$5,947.16	
11	Buffalo Jerky	Feb, 1994	81	$7,286.70	$7,043.67	
12	Buffalo Jerky	Mar, 1994	84	$7,539.68	$7,425.72	
13	Total Buffalo Jerky		232	$20,927.85	$20,416.56	
14	Chicken Dinner	Jan, 1994	93	$54,954.42	$53,487.06	
15	Chicken Dinner	Feb, 1994	90	$52,717.34	$51,465.44	
16	Chicken Dinner	Mar, 1994	88	$52,385.21	$51,176.13	
17	Total Chicken Dinner		271	$160,056.97	$156,128.63	
18	Clear Refresher	Jan, 1994	88	$24,419.60	$23,795.68	
19	Clear Refresher	Feb, 1994	90	$25,088.15	$24,214.21	
20	Clear Refresher	Mar, 1994	73	$20,718.38	$20,204.90	

FIGURE D.16

Report with break rows.

Using Studies in a Report

Star Tracker allows you to define a constraint on a dimension that is a "behavioral outcome" defined from a previous report, rather than a constraint based on attribute vales in that dimension. For example, suppose that you ran a report identifying the products that were Big Sellers in 1Q93. You can define these Big Sellers to be a "study" and then use that study in any subsequent report, such as a follow up report that tracked these Big Sellers during 1994. This facility is especially useful for large dimensions such as Product or Customer where the ability to enumerate individual items in a Star Tracker group definition is awkward.

A study may be defined in three different ways. Physically, a study is a separate table in the database consisting of a single column containing the distinct values of the dimension key that define the contents of the particular study. The first and most powerful way to define a study is to prepare a report (such as Big Sellers in 1Q93), and to include the key attribute from the dimension on which you want to define the study. For the products included in the Big Sellers you would drag the product key (actually the item key in the sample database) into the report and run the report. You then select the product key column and invoke the Create Study from Report command in the Edit menu. You will be prompted for a table name and a description. The file name must be a legitimate SQL table name (i.e., no blanks or punctuation) and the description can be any text string that fits in the blank provided on the screen.

The second way to define a study is to enter the browser facility as if you were going to define a regular Star Tracker constraint group. After specifying the group constraints in the usual way, instead of making a group, you invoke the Create Study command from the Group menu. You will prompted for the table name and the description as described in the previous paragraph. In and of itself, this second study mechanism does not provide any advantages over defining a regular group, but in combination with the third way to define studies, described in the next paragraph, this way of defining studies can be quite useful.

The third way to define a study is to combine two or more previous studies using Union, Intersection, or Set Difference. To access these set operations, click on the STUDIES tab in the desired dimension and then click on the EX-PAND command. Below the list of studies are two blank fields and various command buttons. To create a new study based on the intersection of two previous studies, drag the desired study names from the study list into the two boxes and select the Intersection command. When these operations have been done, click on the Create Study command. The familiar dialog box will appear, asking for the table name and description of the new study.

To delete a study, drag its name from the study list into the first blank box and click on the Delete Study command.

To use a study in a report, set the report up in the usual way. Click on the STUDIES tab in the desired dimension and double click the desired study. The report description just above the spreadsheet area will append "in STUDY-NAME" to the description of the constraints on the affected dimension where STUDYNAME is the name of your selected study. The constraint implied by the use of the study will be AND'ed into the constraints on that dimension. Thus, you may use either the default constraint group (such as All Items) or a specific constraint group (such as Category: Candy) in addition to using a study. The result will be the logical AND (i.e., intersection) of these two kinds of constraints.

To remove the use of a study from a report, make a selection within the appropriate dimension table, and then invoke the Remove Study from Report command in the Edit menu. You must select within the desired dimension table first so that Star Tracker can figure out which study you are trying to remove from the report. Note that removing the use of a study from a report is not the same thing as permanently deleting a study from the system. Deleting a study is described in a previous paragraph.

BROWSING AND DEFINING GROUPS

Star Tracker requires that a base group be selected for every dimension before a report can be run. Groups can be created at any time using the Browser. This section describes how to use the Browser to examine your database contents and to define groups.

Opening the Browser

To open the browser, click the **Browse** button in the depiction panel of the dimension you want to browse.

Example: Use the Database Finder and Report Finder to return to the "Order Top Line" report in the "ORDERS.MDB: Orders" database (see Star Tracker Basics section). Then click the **Browse** button in the Customer dimension depiction area. The browser will open to the depiction of the Customer dimension table. See Figure D.17.

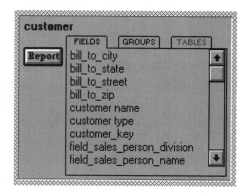

FIGURE D.17

Browser—Customer table in Fields mode.

Viewing Existing Groups

To view the names of groups already defined for the customer dimension, click the **GROUPS** tab at the top of the panel. Note that a number groups are already defined, as shown in Figure D.18. Return to the field list by clicking the **FIELDS** tab at the top of the panel.

Viewing a Group Definition

To view the definition of an existing group, double-click the group name in the group display. As an example, you may view the definition of the group "Customer Type: Deli" by double-clicking its name in Figure D.18.

Defining New Groups

New groups are defined by browsing the field or fields you want to use to create the group. This method allows you to preview the contents of the group while you are defining it.

Browsing a Single Field

To browse a single field, double-click the desired field name in the table's field list. This opens a frame with three parts:

- At the top of the frame there is a label field that, in the example below, says "bill_to_city =". This is a *constraint label*.

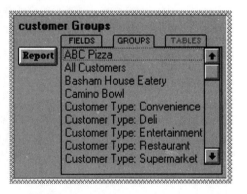

FIGURE D.18

Browser—Customer table in Groups mode.

- Immediately below the constraint label is a field that contains any *constraint tokens* that you might select.
- The bottom field of the frame lists *browse tokens*: unique values found while browsing this field. By *unique*, we mean that even if there were multiple records with the same value, the token would occur only once in the table. When a token is selected, it selects all records containing this value.

Example: Double-clicking the "bill_to_city" field name in the customer table browser window above produces the browse frame shown above. In Figure D.19, there are just two tokens: "Los Angeles" and "San Francisco". There are no constraints in the example shown.

Browsing Multiple Fields

To add an additional browse frame, simply click on another field name in the table's field list. This places an additional browse frame to the right of the existing one(s).

Example: Double-click the "customer_name" field name at the top of the browse windows to add a second browse frame for this field, as shown in Figure D.20.

FIGURE D.19

Browser—bill_to_city frame, unconstrained.

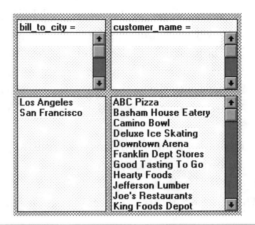

FIGURE D.20

Browser_bill_to_city and customer_name frames, unconstrained.

Adding a Simple Constraint

When you define a group you usually want to limit it to encompassing just a subset of all possible dimension values. For example, you might want to create a product group constrained to just your own products, or a time group constrained to 3rd Quarter 1995. You define the subsets you want by constraining one or more fields to just the token values you want. The simplest way to do this is to double-click a token value. This selects the value and places it in the top part of the browser frame where it becomes part of the group's constraints.

Example: In the Figure D.20 depiction, which shows two browse frames, double-click "Los Angeles" in the bill-to-city frame. This enters the token "Los Angeles" into constraint portion of the frame, resulting in a constraint that reads "bill_to_city = 'Los Angeles' ". (The single quotes around the 'Los Angeles' token are needed for proper formation of the database query). Because you double-clicked, the action also initiated a refresh of the entire browse. See Figure D.21. Single-clicking the token would have added it to the constraint list but not initiated the refresh.

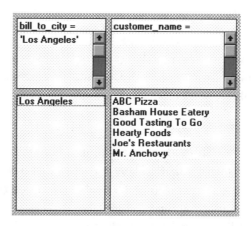

FIGURE D.21

Browser with bill_to_city constrained to Los Angeles.

Note: On adding this constraint, it was immediately applied to all of the browse panels. The number of tokens in the customer_name frame has been reduced from its original number (20) to *just those six customers whose bill_to_address is Los Angeles.* You can immediately see the effects of a change in the constraint definition.

Removing a Constraint

You can remove a constraint by simply erasing it. Click anywhere in the constraint token list in the upper middle of the frame. This highlights all of the tokens in the frame. Then press the **Delete** key. The constraint will be erased, and the browse will be updated to reflect the change.

Removing a Browse Frame

You can remove a field frame by clicking in constraint label field at the top of the frame. This highlights the label. Then press the **Delete** key. The frame will disappear. You can restore the frame by double-clicking the field name in the dimension depiction panel.

Multiple Constraints

Star Tracker's ability to use multiple constraints in a single dimension group is a very powerful aid to defining groups for large dimensions. Consider, for example, the problem of defining a customer group in a retail-store product table. Such a table might contain 100,000 products, but you are interested only in a few.

Since each such entry is probably unique and you have 100,000 tokens to choose from for your constraint, neither you nor your PC will be able to handle such a task. It's likely, however, that besides UPC and description fields the product dimension table will also contain other attributes that will assist you in subsetting the product table. In a retail database these might include such attributes as department, manufacturer, brand, size, and color.

Using this technique you can successively "home in" on the product set you want without browsing an entire very large dimension table.

Example: From the example shown in Adding a Simple Constraint single-click the first three customer name tokens to add them to the constraint token list. The resulting Browse window is shown in Figure D.22.

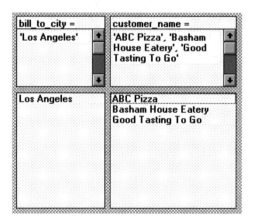

FIGURE D.22

Browser_bill_to_city and customer_name both constrained.

Logical Connections in Constraints

In a constraint such as the one illustrated in Multiple Constraints the tokens selected within a field are connected by implied logical ORs, while the constraints across multiple fields are connected with implied logical ANDs. Thus, the compound constraint defined in the example above would be interpreted as:

WHERE (bill_to_city = 'Los Angeles') **AND** (customer_name = 'ABC Pizza' **OR** 'Basham House Eatery' **OR** 'Good Tasting to Go')

Advanced Constraints

Constraints based on other operators, such as less than, greater than, not equals, between, and like, may be entered to a limited extent into the constraint box in the browser. The syntax of the constraint is passed directly through to the underlying DBMS, and hence there may be some syntactical differences from DBMS to DBMS. In Access, the following entries are valid:

Entry	*Meaning*
<100	Any numerical value less than 100
<"M"	Any text value that sorts before M. Note the double quotes.
between 100 and 200	Numeric values between 100 and 200.
between "C" and "DZZ"	Text values starting with C and D.
<>"Lasagna"	Any text value not equal to Lasagna.
like "Diet*"	Any text value starting with Diet. Note the asterisk as wild card.

Oracle, Sybase, and Red Brick may use single quotes as delimiters, and will probably use % as a wild card. While it is possible to use this facility for complex Boolean expressions, the user interface was not designed to support such use.

Creating Groups

After you have defined a constraint for a dimension using one of the techniques in the preceding section, you can convert the constraint into a group definition.

In Figure D.23 shows the browser with bill_to_city constrained to 'Los Angeles'. This constraint could be used to define a group. Now, suppose we added a new customer with a Los Angeles bill_to_city.

The makeup changes when we added the new customer. Since the customer has a 'Los Angeles' bill_to_city it would be added to the group and the Los Angeles group would contain seven rather than six customer names.

Creating a Simple Group

To create a group, first set up the constraints for the group using the Browser. Then select **Create Group** from the Browser's **Group** menu. You will be prompted for the group name. Enter the name and click **OK**. The group will be created. A group name can't be a duplicate of another group name.

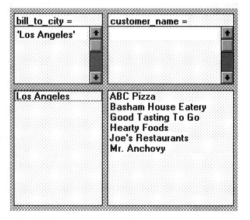

FIGURE D.23

Browser with bill_to_city constrained to Los Angeles.

Creating a Group Cluster

Frequently you will want to create a set of similar groups with one group for each unique instance of a token. In the example in Figure D.24, suppose you wanted to create a group for each bill_to_city. You could do this by creating simple groups for each city, or much more easily by requesting Star Tracker to create a cluster of groups--one for each unique value of bill_to_city.

As an example, first open the browser, double-click on the bill_to_city field, then select the title "bill_to_city =" at the top of the bill_to_city panel.

Next select **Create Group Cluster** from the Browser's Group menu. You will be prompted for the name template, which will be common for each group in the cluster. Enter "Bill-to City:*" in the template field as shown in Figure D.25. The asterisk will be replaced in each group name by the unique value of the group.

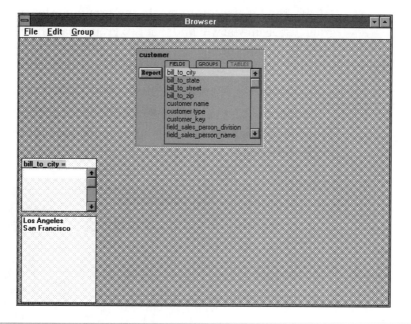

FIGURE D.24

Selecting a Field for a group cluster.

FIGURE D.25

Entering a group cluster name template.

Click the OK button to create the group cluster. When you examine the group list again you will find that two groups have been added, corresponding to the two values of bill_to_address, as shown in Figure D.26.

Deleting a Group

To delete a group select the group name in the browser group list and press the **Delete** key.

FIGURE D.26

Group example with bill-to city cluster.

Deleting a Group Cluster

To delete a set of groups, select the command Delete Group Cluster in the Group menu. You may be advised to display the group list (and make a selection in it). You will then be asked to supply enough leading characters to specify the group names you wish to delete. For instance, in the above figure, if you supply "Cust", you will delete all groups beginning with these characters.

Generalized Browsing: Tables Tab

When you click the **Tables** tab in the Browser's list panel you will see a list of all of the tables that are associated with your current database. These include the dimension and fact tables already discussed, as well as several other auxiliary tables, such as the tables used to store group definitions. You can browse the contents of these auxiliary tables in the same way that you browse the dimension and fact tables. In the Tables mode, group creation is disabled.

BUILDING A NEW REPORT

This section describes how to build a new report or modify an existing one. In general, the following steps may be required:

1. Select a database and click New Report.
2. Set the report's scale by dragging dimension field names to your report.
3. Set the base groups for each dimension.
4. Select primary facts by dragging fact field names to your report.
5. Apply alternative aggregates or ranks to the fact fields in your report, if desired.
6. Build comparison groups, if desired.
7. Run the report.

The following sections describe each step of this process and provide examples using the sample database shipped with Star Tracker.

Selecting a Database

In Star Tracker main window, select **Change Database** in the **File** menu. Choose the database you want in the Database Finder dialog, then click the **Open Blank Report** button.

Example: In the Database Finder open a blank report for the database labeled "ACCESS: ORDERS.MDB: Orders"

Adding Dimension Columns

To add a dimension column to your report, drag the attribute field name from the dimension depiction area to the report spreadsheet. If you drop it to the right of existing attribute columns it will be positioned immediately right of existing columns. If you drop it over an existing column it will be positioned to the left of that column.

Example: The beginning of this section showed you how to open a blank report for the labeled "ACCESS: ORDERS.MDB: Orders" database. In blank report, click the customer_name attribute in the customer dimension table and hold down the left mouse button. While the button is held down, drag the attribute name down to column A of the report spreadsheet, and release the mouse button. This drag-and-drop action will put the attribute name, customer_name, into the spreadsheet as the header (row 1) of column A.

The main window will now look like the one shown in Figure D.27.

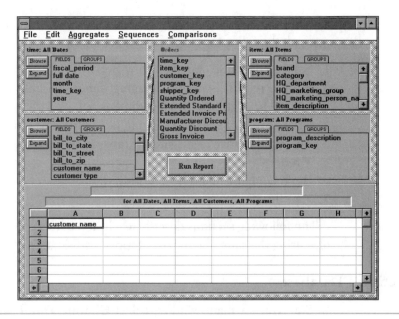

FIGURE D.27

Main window with first report column: Customer Name.

Deleting Attribute Columns

To delete an attribute column from a report, first highlight the column by clicking its alphabetic header letter then choose **Delete Column** from the **Edit** menu.

Choosing Base Groups

When you first open a new report, the base group for each dimension is set to a default value selected by your System Administrator. In the example above the default base groups are set to All Items, All Customers, etc.

Before running a report, you will need to choose the base you want to use for reporting. To choose a base group, first click the **GROUPS** tab in the dimensions depiction panel. Group names will be shown in blue. To choose the base group, double-click on the group name.

Example: In the sample report that you are building select, by double-clicking, the following base group:

time:	**4Q94**
customer:	**Customer Type: Restaurants**
item:	**Category: Soft Drinks**
program:	**Regular Program**

This sets the basis of the report. See Figure D.28. Taken together, this set of groups tells you (except for comparisons) what the basis of the facts will be. You also know, from the dimension columns you have chosen, which of these will be enumerated. Your report will list each individual customer within the group of Restaurants, and will list totals for Soft Drinks for each restaurant.

In order to run this report you must still add one or more fact columns.

Adding Fact Columns

Fact columns are added to a report in much the same way as adding attribute columns, except that their names are dragged from the fact table instead of from a dimension table. They will automatically be placed to the right of the attribute columns.

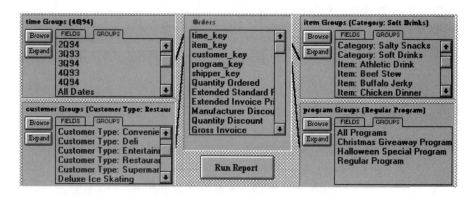

FIGURE D.28

Table depiction with base groups selected.

In a report, fact columns are always additive. By default, they represent the sum of the values of the fact over one or more dimensions.

Nonadditive facts are treated as attributes and will be placed in the left-hand columns with other attributes.

Aggregate Types

When you initially drag a fact name to the report Star Tracker will label it "Sum of <fact name>". Star Tracker is aware that it will sum over one or more dimensions, and labels the column accordingly. It assumes that what you want is a sum of the individual records. If you want an alternative aggregation such as Maximum, Minimum, or Average, first highlight the new column by clicking its alphabetic header letter. Then select the new type of aggregate you want from the main window's **Aggregates** menu. This changes the fact column's aggregation method.

The First Fact Column

To add a fact column to the report, drag-and-drop the fact column name from the fact table to the report spreadsheet. The first fact column you add will be placed immediately to the right of report's dimension columns. Subsequent facts will be placed where you put them as long as they are to the right of the attributes.

	Sample Report 1					
	for 4Q94, Category: Soft Drinks, Customer Type: Restaurant, Regular Program					
	A	B	C	D	E	F
1	customer name	Sum of Quantity Ordered				
2	ABC Pizza	41				
3	Basham House Eatery	44				
4	Good Tasting To Go	41				
5	Hearty Foods	50				

FIGURE D.29

Simple report.

Example: Add a fact to the report that you are making. Drag the fact name **Quantity Ordered** from the fact table depiction to the second column of the report. You now have defined a dimension column, base groups, and one fact column. You are now ready to run this report. Click the **Run Report** button to run the report in Figure D.29.

There are nine report lines, one for each of the distinct values of restaurant name that comprise the customer dimension's Restaurants group. Note that the Quantity Ordered column has automatically been renamed "*Sum of Quantity Ordered*". Star Tracker recognizes that this is an aggregate and names it accordingly.

Adding Additional Fact Columns

If you are adding subsequent facts and want to place the new column to the right of existing columns, drag the name to the right of the right-most column already in the report. If you want the new column to be placed within the existing facts, drag the name to an existing fact column, and the new fact will be added immediately to the left of the target column.

Example: Add a second identical fact column to your report by dragging the fact name **Quantity Ordered** from the fact table depiction to the third column of the report, and run the report in Figure D.30.

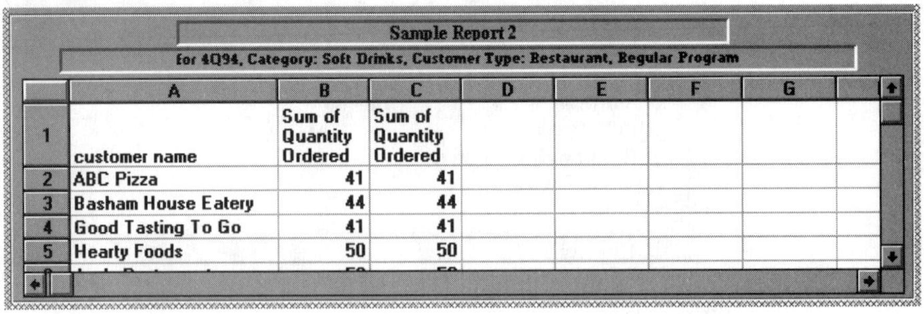

FIGURE D.30

Example report with two Quantity Ordered columns.

Comparisons

Business analysis frequently revolves around comparisons: This year vs. last year, my products vs. your products, our products vs. the entire marketplace. Star Tracker provides an extraordinarily powerful and easy way of generating such comparisons through the use of comparison groups.

Complex multidimensional comparisons is not simple to generate, so Star Tracker provides several aids to ensure that comparisons are meaningful at any level of scale.

Adding a Comparison Group

The first step in making a comparison is to select the group on which we want to base the comparison. Recall that in our example, we selected a base time period of 1Q94. Suppose we want to compare this (our current quarter) with results for last year: 1Q93.

Example: In the main window (shown in Figure D.31, click the **GROUPS** tab in **time** dimension depiction. This opens the list of groups available to you. Drag and drop the group 4Q93 from the time groups into column C of the report. The report changes to the picture shown below. Note that column C is now qualified, reading Sum of Quantity ordered for 4Q93, reflecting the change we just made. Note also that the time dimension's base group remains

	A	B	C	D	E	F	G	
1	customer name	Sum of Quantity Ordered for 4Q94	Ratio of Sum of Quantity Ordered for 4Q94 vs. 4Q93					
2	ABC Pizza	41	0.84					
3	Basham House Eatery	44	0.96					
4	Good Tasting To Go	41	0.76					
5	Hearty Foods	50	1.39					
6	Joe's Restaurants	52	0.91					
7	McBurger International	44	1.00					

Sample Report 4
for 4Q94, Category: Soft Drinks, Customer Type: Restaurant, Regular Program

FIGURE D.31
Sample report with comparison group: 4Q93.

4Q94, as originally set, and that the label for column 2 now is labeled with the base group, to distinguish it from the alternative group we just added. Column 2 will contain the same values as before; only its label has been changed for clarity.

Run the sample report at this time, to see the difference in quantities order for 4Q93 (the comparison group) and 4Q94 (the base group).

Computing a Comparison

Once you have introduced alternative groups for a dimension into your report you can calculate a comparison between the facts for the base group and the comparison group. To do this, first select a column that is qualified by an alternative group. Then apply the comparison you want to use from the **Comparison** menu.

Example: Highlight column C of the report by clicking its header letter then choose Ratio from the **Comparison** menu. The heading of column C will change as shown in Figure D.32. Run the report to see the ratio of orders for 4Q93 to 4Q94.

FIGURE D.32

Example report—with column C expressed as a ratio.

Reversing a Comparison

The inverse of a comparison can be easily calculated by selecting Reverse Comparison from the selection menu.

Example: Suppose instead of the ratio of 4Q94 to 4Q93, we wanted the report to contain the ratio of 4Q93 to 4Q94. We can accomplish this simply by highlighting column C of the report by clicking its header letter then choosing **Reverse Comparison** from the **Comparison** menu. The report in Figure D.33 would result.

FIGURE D.33

Example report with ratio reversed.

Independent Comparisons

A fully set up comparison, such as the one developed in the last three figures, can be made independent of the main base group of the report by dragging a group name from a group list with the shift key held down. This would allow, for example, a column to be defined in the previous report that was the ratio of all of 1993 to all of 1994, even though the base group of the report remained 1Q94. This command can only be applied to a fully set up comparison column.

Sequence Columns

Often, business measurements are expressed as sequence metrics rather than as values. A sequence might expressed as a simple rank (1, 2, 3, . . . n), as a range (high, medium, low), or a more complex measure such as a moving sum. Star Tracker provides several methods of including sequences in a report.

Building a Sequence Column

To build a sequence column, first build a fact column. This column may contain simple facts, facts for alternative groups, or comparisons. The select the type of sequence you want from the main window's **Sequences** menu.

Example: In the sample report, highlight column C of the report (the ratio) by clicking its header letter. Then choosing **Rank** from the **Sequences** menu. Rerun the report, and instead of ratios the column will contain the *rank* of each ratio relative to all of the ratio values. See Figure D.34.

	A	B	C	D	E	F	G
	Sample Report 6						
	for 4Q94, Category: Soft Drinks, Customer Type: Restaurant, Regular Program						
1	customer name	Sum of Quantity Ordered for 4Q94	Rank of Ratio of Sum of Quantity Ordered for 4Q93 vs. 4Q94				
2	ABC Pizza	41	3				
3	Basham House Eatery	44	5				
4	Good Tasting To Go	41	1				
5	Hearty Foods	50	8				
6	Joe's Restaurants	52	4				
7	McBurger International	44	6				

FIGURE D.34

Example report with column C expressed as a rank.

Types of Ranks

Star Tracker provides the following types of Sequences:

rank   The ordinal of the fact value beginning with 1, in
                      ascending order

cume   The cumulative sum of the fact value

moving average   The mean of the previous 3 values of the fact
                      (inclusive)

moving sum   The sum of the previous 3 values of the fact
                      (inclusive)

tertile   The third into which the value falls relative to all
                      other values: Low, Medium, or High

quartile   The quadrant into which the value falls relative to
                      all other values: 1st, 2nd, 3rd, or 4th

value   Exits the ranking operation and returns the
                      column to its values

Average Period Calculations

Star Tracker provides two measurements that are specific to the time dimension: AveragePeriodSum and AveragePeriodCount. Suppose that you have a
nonadditive fact such as bank balance. It makes no sense to sum bank balance
over a time period. However, bank balance can be summed over other dimensions: The sum of an individual's various bank balances or the sum of bank
balances for a customer group both have meaning.

Average period sum computes an average by summing the fact values over
all dimensions including time, then dividing the resulting values by the number of time periods in the time dimension group.

OTHER FEATURES

This section describes miscellaneous features of Star Tracker such as report printing.

Printing a Report

Reports can be easily formatted and printed. To print a report, simply select **Print** from the **File** menu. This will produce a formatted report. The report's header will contain the report title and base group selections. This will be followed by the report values with columns labeled as shown on your screen. Hidden columns will be omitted. The report footer contains the date and page number. Reports may span multiple pages both horizontally and vertically.

Report formats may be altered by selecting **Print Setup** from the **File** menu. This opens the dialog shown in Figure D.35. Various report printing settings may be changed in this dialog.

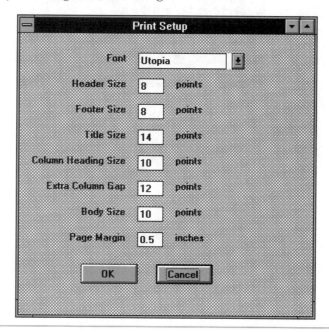

FIGURE D.35

Print Setup dialog.

Showing SQL

System analysts can examine the SQL (structured query language) being sent by Star Tracker to the database server by selecting Show SQL from the File menu. This opens the dialog box in Figure D.36, which contains recently executed queries.

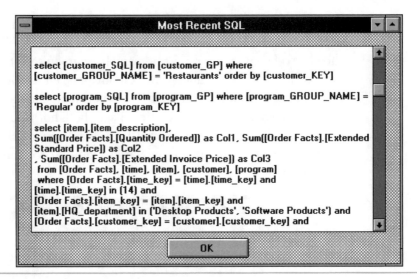

FIGURE D.36

SQL dialog.

System Administrator's Guide for Star Tracker™

Overview

Star Tracker has been developed as a tool for answering real business questions in the terms that businesses find most useful. While most database reporting and query tools can do an adequate job of formulating simple queries and reports, they often fall short in their ability to produce the meaningful and sophisticated business metrics and ratios that can be extracted from large, complex databases.

The enormous quantities of transaction-level data from point-of-sale and banking systems, combined with low-cost high-capacity relational database servers introduces a new source of business information calling for new, highly sophisticated analytical techniques. Star Tracker supplies these techniques, and is specifically designed to be used for analyzing extremely large databases.

About the System Administrator's Guide

This *System Administrator's Guide for Star Tracker* is intended for the DBA or system administrator who will be setting up the environment in which Star

Tracker is used, as well as for the business analyst who wants to explore in detail the inner workings of Star Tracker. A companion document, the *User's Guide for Star Tracker*, covers Star Tracker's windows, menus, and controls, and contains examples of use.

This *System Administrator's Guide* contains the following sections:

Star Tracker Architecture covers the Star Tracker's client/server relationships and the components that comprise the system.

Star Tracker Installation covers installation of the Star Tracker software on a client PC, and how to configure the serving database to support the system. A sample STARTRAK.INI file is presented in its entirety.

STAR TRACKER ARCHITECTURE

This section describes Star Tracker's architecture in a client/server relationship.

System Overview

Star Tracker is a PC tool that runs in conjunction with a relational database management system (DBMS). The tool is designed to run in a PC client under Windows 3.1 or later, and Windows 95. The DBMS may reside on a network server, or be colocated in the PC with the Star Tracker client application. The illustration in Figure E.1 shows the important components of Star Tracker in a typical client/server configuration.

Connectivity between the client application and server database is typically provided via a LAN using Microsoft's Open Database Connectivity (ODBC) software on the client side, and the DBMS vendor's ODBC-compliant gateway on the server side. ODBC server software is available for most major relational database servers and Star Tracker explicitly supports Red Brick, Oracle, Sybase, and Informix. As an alternative, a PC-compatible serving database, such as MS Access, may be colocated in the PC with the client application.

As shown in the illustration in Figure E.1, the following components are required for the operation of Star Tracker.

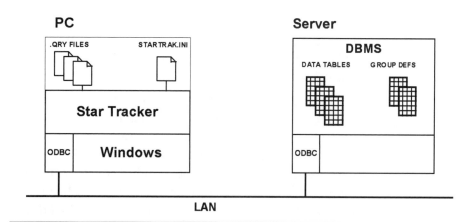

FIGURE E.1

Star Tracker client/server components.

Client Components

Star Tracker client software: This software is installed as a typical Windows application in the client PC.

ODBC Client Software: Microsoft ODBC software must be installed in the client PC for client/server installations. ODBC is not required if Microsoft Access is being used as the database in a non-networked PC.

STARTRAK.INI file: The STARTRAK.INI file contains parameters needed by ODBC, and also contains database table and field definitions. This file is added to the client PC at installation time by the System Administrator. It is located in the client's STARTRAK directory.

Saved Query files: Saved Query files (.QRY files) contain predefined report definitions that Star Tracker can run from the client machine. Saved Queries are automatically created when a user saves a modified or newly created report, and they can also be independently loaded by the System Administrator to allow the end user to run reports without having originally created them. Saved Query files are located in the client's STARTRAK directory.

Server Components

Database Management System (DBMS): This is an ANSI SQL–compatible relational database management system, such as Red Brick, Oracle, Sybase, or Informix.

ODBC Server Software: ODBC server software is required. In some cases this will be colocated with the DBMS, and in some cases this may be located in the PC as gateway compatibility software.

Data Tables: These are the DBMS tables to be queried by Star Tracker. They are classified by their contents as either *dimension* tables or *fact* tables, and must be capable of being joined in a star join schema.

Group Definitions Tables: These tables reside in the DBMS and contain definitions of Star Tracker *groups* that can be shared by multiple Star Tracker users. There must be a group definition table associated with each dimension table in the star join schema(s).

STAR TRACKER INSTALLATION

This section describes the installation of Star Tracker on the client system. It also describes in detail the STARTRAK.INI file and the contents of the Group Tables in the DBMS.

Client Software Installation

All of the Star Tracker components required for the PC client are contained on Star Tracker installation disks or on the Star Tracker CD-ROM. Upgrades to Star Tracker software are available on the author's home page: http://www.rkimball.com.

Running Setup

To install Star Tracker, place the CD-ROM included with this book into your CD-ROM drive. From the Windows Program Manager, select **Run** from the **File** menu. Assuming that your CD-ROM drive is drive D, enter the command line:

D:\SETUP

Then click the OK button. This will launch the SETUP program.

Unless you specify otherwise, the setup program will create a directory called STARTRAK on your hard disk in which the application and its supporting files will be installed.

Star Tracker is a Visual Basic program. If you do not already have Visual Basic 3.0 installed on your computer, the Setup Program will install several .DLL files and .VBX files in your STARTRAK directory required for running Visual Basic programs. To uninstall Star Tracker, simply delete the STARTRAK directory and all its contents.

The setup program will also install a STARTRAK.INI file in your WINDOWS directory. This file contains database descriptions. Consequently, it must be customized to describe specific databases you will be accessing with Star Tracker. This customization process is discussed in a later section of this guide. The STARTRAK.INI file supplied with the system contains descriptions needed for accessing all the databases described in this book.

TUTORIAL DATABASE

Star Tracker installation disks contain a small tutorial database (ORDERS.MDB), which is referenced in *the User's Guide* (Appendix D). This database uses a runtime version of Microsoft Access, also included on the installation disks. You do not need to install ODBC in order to use this tutorial database. The CD-ROM version of Star Tracker supplied with this book contains all of the databases described in the book. These databases, as well as the ORDERS database, reside on the CD-ROM. A local Access database will be created automatically by Star Tracker to house the auxiliary files that Star Tracker needs.

Customizing the STARTRAK.INI File

The STARTRAK.INI file contains parameters Star Tracker needs to find and interpret database contents. This section describes each section of the STARTRAK.INI file. The final section of this *System Administrator's Guide* contains a complete STARTRAK.INI file illustrating all parameter uses.

It is a text file located in the STARTRAK directory. The STARTRAK.INI file contains a header section followed by one or more database sections. Each database section can contain one or more database family sections. A database family must define a star join schema containing one fact table and one or more dimension tables:

[header section]
[database section]
    [family section]
        family name
        fact table name
        fact table field definition(s)

          . . .

        dimension table definition(s)

          . . .

        time dimension table name
    [family section]

          . . .

[database section]

Each line in the STARTRAK.INI file follows the same syntax of label-colon-space-parameter, for example:

Fact Table Caption: Detergents Facts

Any line in the file may be commented out by preceding the label with the keyword "Comment".

Header Section

The Header Section appears first in STARTRAK.INI, and contains the following parameters:

Date: *yymmdd*
Time: *hhmm*
Query Path: *pathname*
Default Font: *fontname*
Private Group User Name: *username*
ODBC database: *database_name*
ODBCSRV: *server_name*

ODBCDSN: *ODBC DSN*
ODBCDBQ: *default_database_name*
ODBCUID: *user_id*
ODBCPWD: *password*

yymmdd: The date on which the .INI file was last modified. (not automatic)

hhmm: The time at which the .INI file was modified. (not automatic)

pathname: The directory path to the directory containing Star Tracker's. .QRY saved query files.

fontname: The name of the default font used to print Star Tracker reports.

secret: The enabling password supplied to your organization to allow Star Tracker to access ODBC databases. Of course, it is not literally "secret."

username: The user name for this workstation that will be used by Star Tracker to identify and view private constraint definitions. The user name Public is used to make public accessible constraint definitions.

database_name: Default value of ODBC database name for the Login dialog.

server_name: Default value for ODBC server name for the Login dialog.

ODBC DSN: Default value for the ODBC DSN parameter for the Login dialog.

default_database_name: Default value for ODBC database for the Login dialog.

user_id: Default value for ODBC User ID for the Login dialog.

password: Default database logon password, normally omitted. User will be prompted if this is omitted.

Database Section

The .INI file may contain one or more database sections. Each database section starts with the following three parameters, which may be followed by multiple family sections:

Database Type: *type_name*
Database Path: *path_name*
Database Name: *database_name*
Allow Drill Across: Yes / No
Single Dimension Display: *Yes / No*
Auto Pretty Print Field Names: Yes, **Abbreviations:** SKU, ID, PO, HQ, KEY

type_name: Database brand name: **ORACLE, ACCESS, REDBRICK, SYBASE, INFORMIX**

path_name: DOS pathname of the database if local; otherwise **null**.

database_name: Database file name if local, database name if server.

Allow Drill Across enables the ability to drill across between fact tables. The fact tables must be on the same DBMS. Single Dimension Display affects the formatting of the depiction area. Schemas with more than six dimensions will use the single-dimension display mode regardless of this setting. Auto Pretty Print Field Names affects the capitalization of names on the screen. Every word token will start with an initial capital letter. Words can be made all capitals by declaring them as abbreviations, as in the example above.

Family Section

Syntax Notes: In the following section:

. . . means multiple instances allowed.

[ ] means optional parameter.

Each database section may contain one or more family sections. Each family describes a group of tables that comprise a star join schema—one fact table, and one or more dimension tables. The same table may appear in multiple families. For example, a PRODUCTS table might appear in a family used for retail sales reporting and for manufacturing.

To minimize end user confusion, each family is listed as a separate database in Star Tracker's Database Finder dialog. Each family section contains the following parameters:

Family: *family_name*
Fact Table Name: *fact_table_name*
Fact Table Caption: *fact_table_caption*
Fact Table Additive Field: *additive_ field_name*, **format** = *fac_ format_ template*
   [. . .]
[Calculation: {*calculation_name*} = {*expression*}, **format** = *calculation_ format_template*]
   [. . .]
Dimension Table Name: *dim_table_name*, **Dimension Key:** *dim_key*, **Fact Key:** *fact_key*, [**Level Field**: *level_ field_name*],

> **Group Table:** *group_table_name,* [**protect**: *protected_field_ name* [, . . .]]
>
> [. . .]
>
> **Date Field:** *date_field_name,* **table name** = *table_name,* **type** = *field_ type,*
>
> > **format** = *date_format_template*
>
> **Time Dimension Table Name:** *time_table_name*

Note: The third, fourth, and fifth parameters (Fact Table Additive Field, Calculation, and Dimension Table Name) can be repeated as many times as necessary. The Dimension Table Name parameter must be present. The other two are optional, although the database will not be very useful without some additive facts.

family_name: Name for the family, used in the Database Finder dialog.

fact_table_name: SQL name of the family's fact table.

fact_table_caption: Caption to be used for the fact table in the Reporter main window.

additive_field_name: SQL field name of *additive* fact table field.

fact_format_template: Visual Basic format template for displaying data from this field in the Reporter's results spreadsheet.

database_name: Database file name if local, database name if server.

calculation_name: Name for "calculated column" in results table.

expression: Numeric expression definition consisting of result column names and arithmetic operators.

calculation_format_template: Visual Basic format template for displaying data from this calculated field in the Reporter's results spreadsheet.

dim_table_name: SQL name of dimension table.

dim_key: SQL field name of dimension table key used for joining this dimension table to the fact table.

fact_key: SQL field name of fact table key used for joining the fact table to this dimension table.

level_field_name: SQL field name of fact table field used to identify levels for aggregations.

group_table_name:: SQL table name of table containing group definitions (i.e., TIME_GP).

protected_field_name: SQL field name(s) of fields that have browse protection.

date_field_name: SQL name of field to be date-type translated.

table_name: SQL name of table containing field to be date-type translated.

date_format_template: Visual Basic date format template of translation result.

time_table_name: SQL name of time dimension table.

Group Tables

Each dimension table in the database must have a corresponding group table into which Star Tracker will place group values created for report definitions. The name of group tables must be the same as the name of the dimension table, postfixed by the string "_GP". Thus, if you have a dimension table named TIME, Star Tracker will automatically create a table named TIME_GP and will place an entry for the default empty group with the name "All Times".

Dummy Table

A table called DUMMY is required in order to support certain SQL constructs. This table will be created automatically by Star Tracker if it is not present in the database.

Studies Table

A table called STUDY_DICT is required in order to support Star Tracker's use of behavioral studies. This table will be created automatically by Star Tracker if it is not present in the database. It is initially empty. Entries are made in this table when the user defines studies. The studies themselves are additional tables named by the user when the studies are created.

Aggregate Map Table

A table called AGGREGATE_MAP is required in order to support Star Tracker's automatic aggregate navigation. This table will be created automatically by Star Tracker if it is not present in the database. It is initially empty. The administrator interested in using this facility should look at the Aggregate Map table supplied with the ORDERS database to see how it is filled in. This is a new facility just added to Star Tracker. Current documentation for aggregates will be maintained on the web at http://www.rkimball.com.

EXAMPLE STARTRAK.INI FILE

The following example shows the contents of a typical STARTRAK.INI file.

Date: 940509
Time: 0813
Query Path: C:\STARJOIN\
Default Font: Utopia
Default ODBC database: testdb
Default ODBCSRV: dsqueryip
Default ODBCDSN: RB
Default ODBCDBQ: testdb
Default ODBCUID: system
Comment ODBCPWD: secret
Comment Autostart: stj0025.qry

Database Type: REDBRICK
Database Path: null
Database Name: SUDS
Allow Drill Across: No

Family: Suds
Fact Table Name: FACT
Fact Table Caption: Detergents Facts
Fact Table Additive Field: PSS, format = 0
Fact Table Additive Field: PUNITS, format = 0
Fact Table Additive Field: UNITS, format = 0
Fact Table Additive Field: UNITSQ, format = 0
Fact Table Additive Field: SPMU, format = 0
Fact Table Additive Field: SPMEQ, format = 0
Fact Table Additive Field: DOL, format = $#,##0
Fact Table Additive Field: SPMDOL, format = $#,##0
Fact Table Additive Field: DIS, format = 0
Fact Table Additive Field: CAD, format = 0
Fact Table Additive Field: MAD, format = 0
Fact Table Additive Field: LAD, format = 0
Fact Table Additive Field: ADISAD, format = 0
Fact Table Additive Field: APPU, format = 0
Fact Table Additive Field: ANPU, format = 0

Dimension Table Name: MARKET, Dimension Key: MKTKEY; Fact Key: MKTKEY, Group Table: Market

Dimension Table Name: PRODUCT, Dimension Key: PRODKEY; Fact Key: PRODKEY, Group Table: Product, protect: PRODDESC, protect: PRODKEY

Dimension Table Name: PERIOD, Dimension Key: PERKEY, Fact Key: PERKEY, Group Table: Period

Time Dimension Table Name: PERIOD

Database Type: ACCESS

Database Path: C:\ACCESS\

Database Name: ORD-ACCT.MDB

Allow Drill Across: Yes

Family: Orders

Fact Table Name: Order Facts

Fact Table Caption: Orders

Fact Table Additive Field: Quantity Ordered, format = #,##0

Fact Table Additive Field: Extended Standard Price, format = $#,##0.00

Fact Table Additive Field: Extended Invoice Price, format = $#,##0.00

Fact Table Additive Field: Manufacturer Discount, format = $#,##0.00

Fact Table Additive Field: Quantity Discount, format = $#,##0.00

Fact Table Additive Field: Gross Invoice, format = $#,##0.00

Fact Table Additive Field: Shipping Charge, format = $#,##0.00

Fact Table Additive Field: Invoice Adjustments, format = $#,##0.00

Fact Table Additive Field: Net Invoice, format = $#,##0.00

Fact Table Additive Field: Extended Standard Cost, format = $#,##0.00

Fact Table Additive Field: Margin Dollars, format = $#,##0.00

Fact Table Additive Field: Tax Dollars, format = $#,##0.00

Calculation: {Average Standard Price} = {Extended Standard Price}/{Quantity Ordered}, format = $#,##0.00

Calculation: {Average Invoice Price} = {Extended Invoice Price}/{Quantity Ordered}, format = $#,##0.00

Calculation: {Average Standard Cost} = {Extended Standard Cost}/{Quantity Ordered}, format = $#,##0.00

Calculation: {Margin Percent} = 100*({Margin Dollars}/{Extended Standard Price}), format = 0.0%

Calculation: {Discounts} = {Manufacturer Discount}$SH{Quantity Discount}, format = $#,##0.00

Calculation: {Discount Percent} = 100*(({Manufacturer Discount}+{Quantity Discount})/{Extended Standard Price}), format = 0.00%

Calculation: {Adjustment Percent} = 100*({Invoice Adjustments}/{Extended Standard Price}), format = 0.00%

Calculation: {Average Tax Rate} = 100*({Tax Dollars}/{Net Invoice}), format = 0.000%

Dimension Table Name: time, Dimension Key: time_key, Fact Key: time_key, Group Table: time

Dimension Table Name: item, Dimension Key: item_key, Fact Key: item_key, Group Table: item, protect: item_key

Dimension Table Name: customer, Dimension Key: customer_key, Fact Key: customer_key, Group Table: customer

Dimension Table Name: program, Dimension Key: program_key, Fact Key: program_key, Group Table: program

Date Field: full date, table name = time, type = Text Date, format = mmm, yyyy

Time Dimension Table Name: time

Family: Consumer Purchase

Fact Table Name: Consumer Purchase

Fact Table Caption: Consumer Purchase

Fact Table Additive Field: Purchase Qty, format = #,##0

Fact Table Additive Field: Purchase Dollars, format = $#,##0.00

Calculation: {Average Retail Price} = {Purchase Dollars}/{Purchase Qty}, format = $#,##0.00

Dimension Table Name: time, Dimension Key: time_key, Fact Key: time_key, Group Table: time

Dimension Table Name: item, Dimension Key: item_key, Fact Key: item_key, Group Table: item, protect: item_key

Dimension Table Name: customer, Dimension Key: customer_key, Fact Key: customer_key, Group Table: customer

Date Field: full date, table name = time, type = Text Date, format = mmm, yyyy

Time Dimension Table Name: time

Index